COLLINS

C000092912

GLASGOW
STREETFINDER
COLOUR ATLAS

Contents

HarperCollins*Publishers*

Published by Collins
An Imprint of HarperCollins*Publishers*
77-85 Fulham Palace Road, Hammersmith, London W6 8JB

Copyright © HarperCollins*Publishers* Ltd 1998
Mapping © Bartholomew Ltd 1985, 1987, 1989, 1992, 1993, 1995, 1997

Based upon the Ordnance Survey Mapping with the permission of The Controller of Her Majesty's Stationery Office © Crown Copyright 399302.

The contents of this publication are believed correct at the time of printing. Nevertheless, the publisher can accept no responsibility for errors or omissions, changes in the detail given, or for any expense or loss thereby caused.

The representation of a road, track or footpath is no evidence of a right of way.

Printed in Italy   ISBN 0 00 448816 4   LI 9887   CDNR

e-mail: roadcheck@harpercollins.co.uk
web site: www.bartholomewmaps.com

Key to map symbols

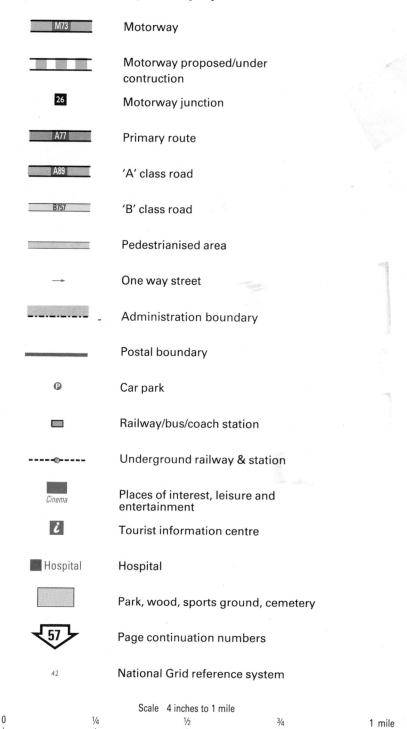

M73	Motorway
	Motorway proposed/under contruction
26	Motorway junction
A77	Primary route
A89	'A' class road
B757	'B' class road
	Pedestrianised area
→	One way street
	Administration boundary
	Postal boundary
℗	Car park
	Railway/bus/coach station
	Underground railway & station
Cinema	Places of interest, leisure and entertainment
𝒊	Tourist information centre
Hospital	Hospital
	Park, wood, sports ground, cemetery
57	Page continuation numbers
42	National Grid reference system

Scale   4 inches to 1 mile

0	¼	½	¾	1 mile
0	500	1000	1500 metres	

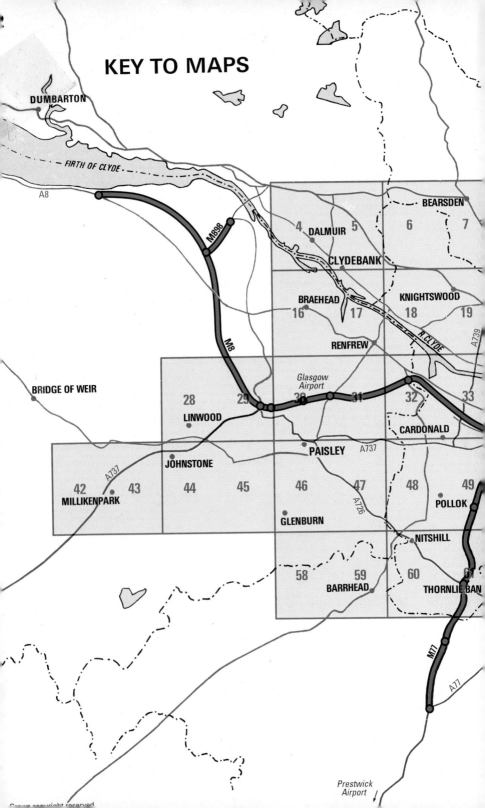

KEY TO MAPS

DUMBARTON

FIRTH OF CLYDE

A8

M898

M8

BEARSDEN

4 DALMUIR 5 6 7

CLYDEBANK

KNIGHTSWOOD

BRAEHEAD

16 17 18 19

R. CLYDE

A739

RENFREW

Glasgow Airport

BRIDGE OF WEIR

28 29 30 31 32 33

LINWOOD

CARDONALD

PAISLEY A737

JOHNSTONE

42 43 44 45 46 47 48 49

MILLIKENPARK

A737

A726

POLLOK

GLENBURN

NITSHILL

58 59 60 61

BARRHEAD

THORNLIE BAN

M77

A77

Prestwick Airport

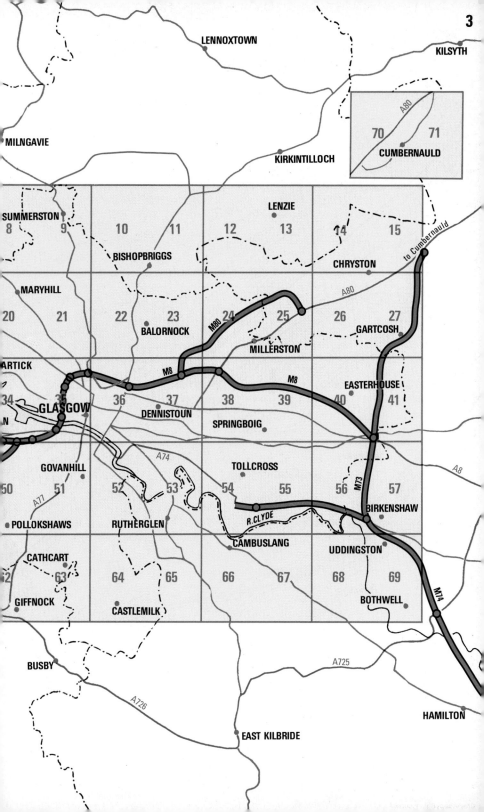

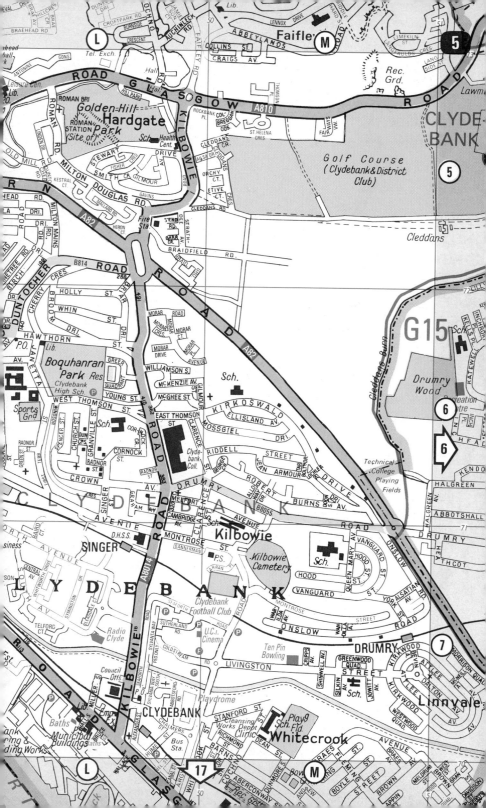

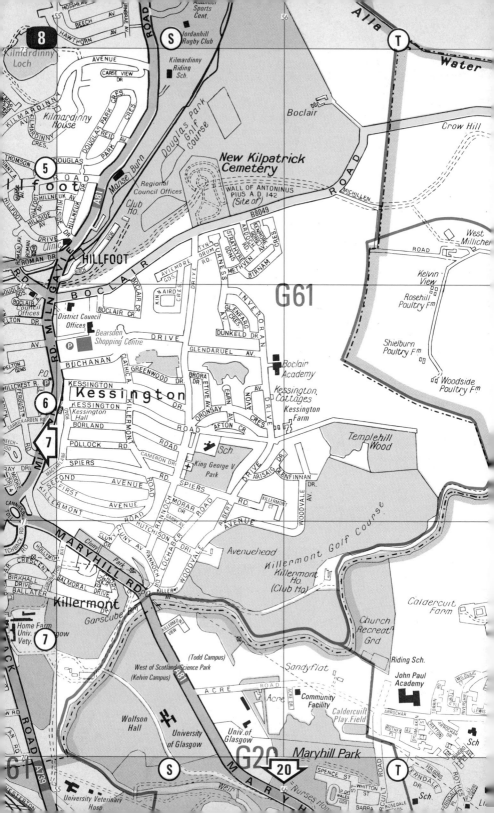

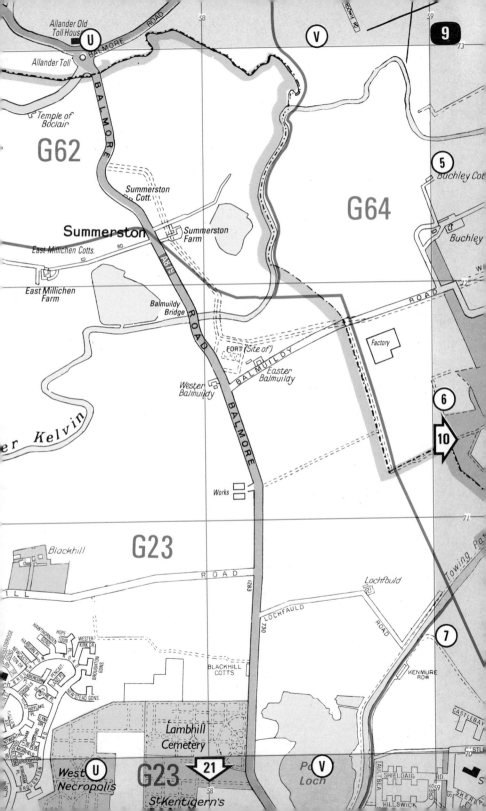

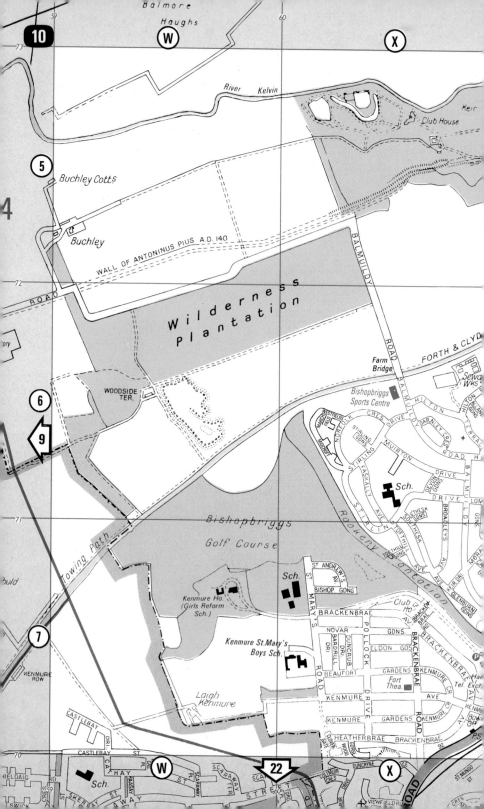

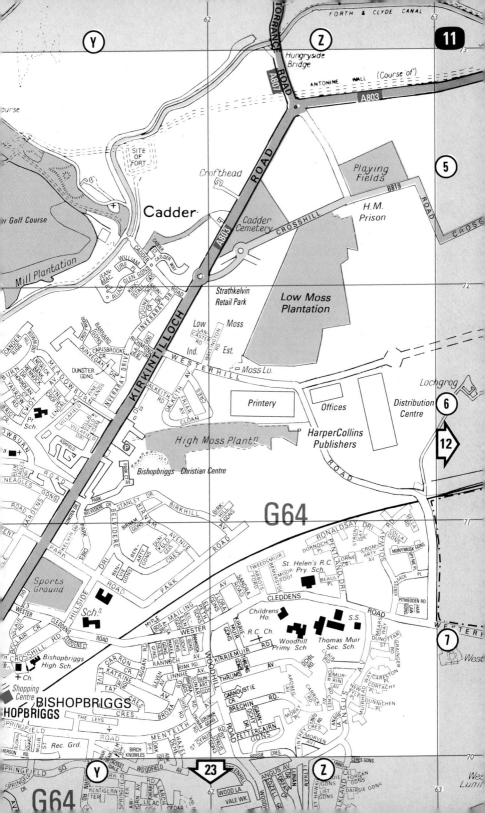

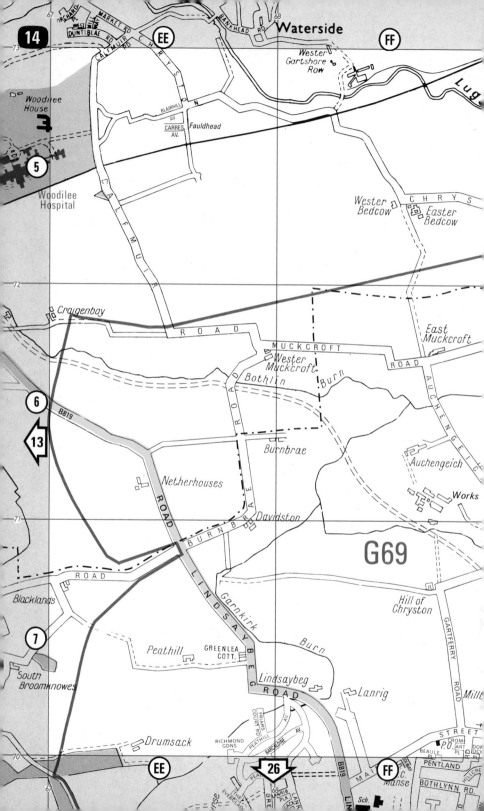

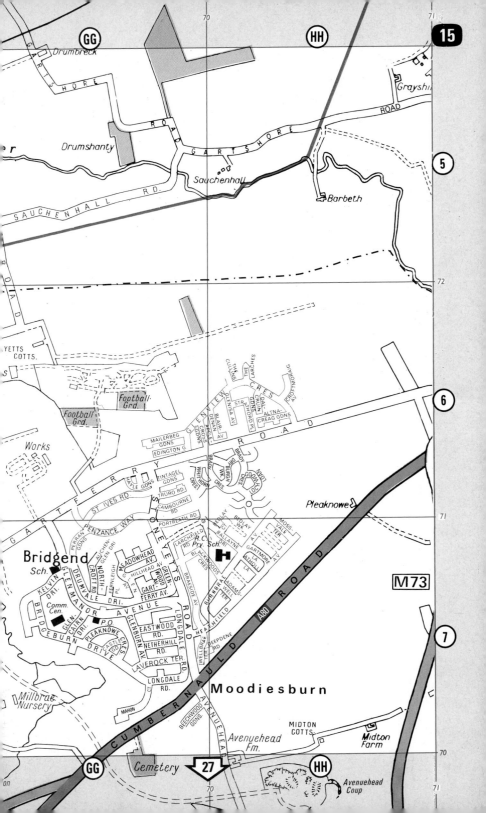

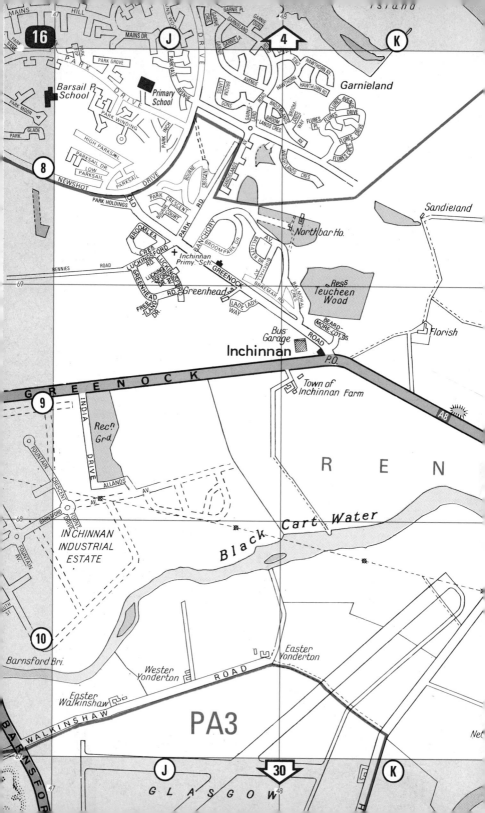

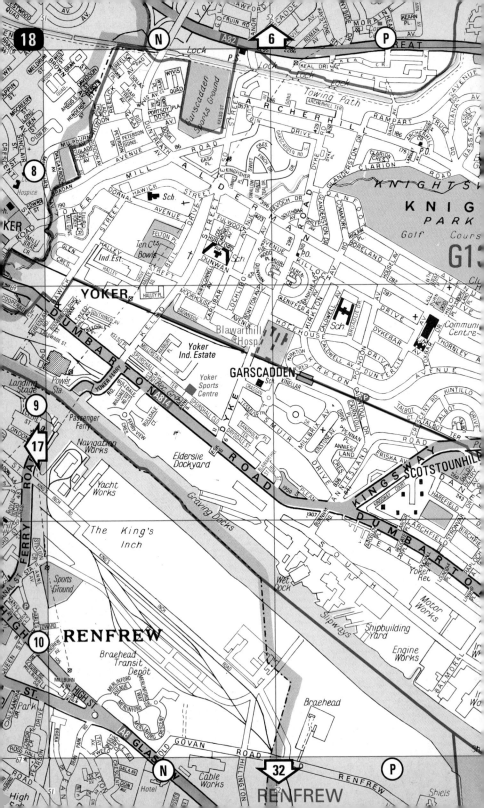

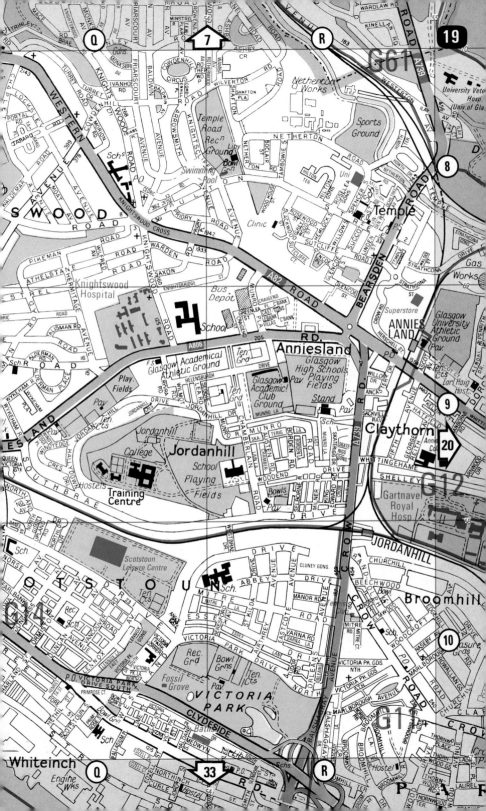

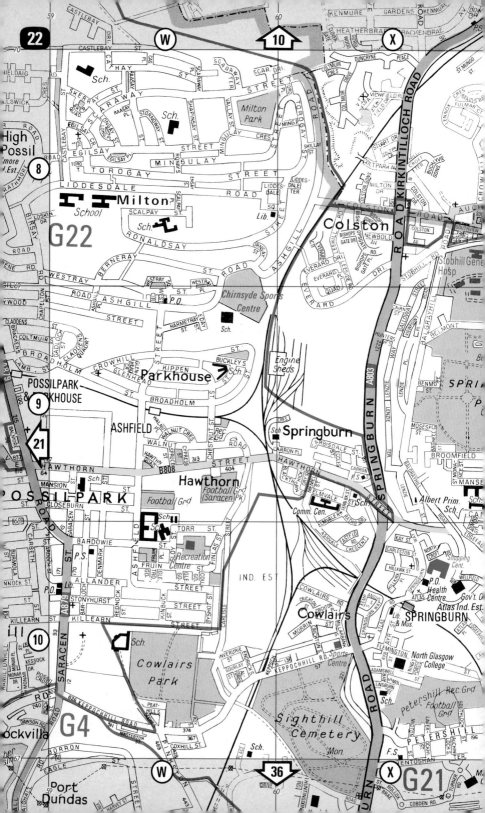

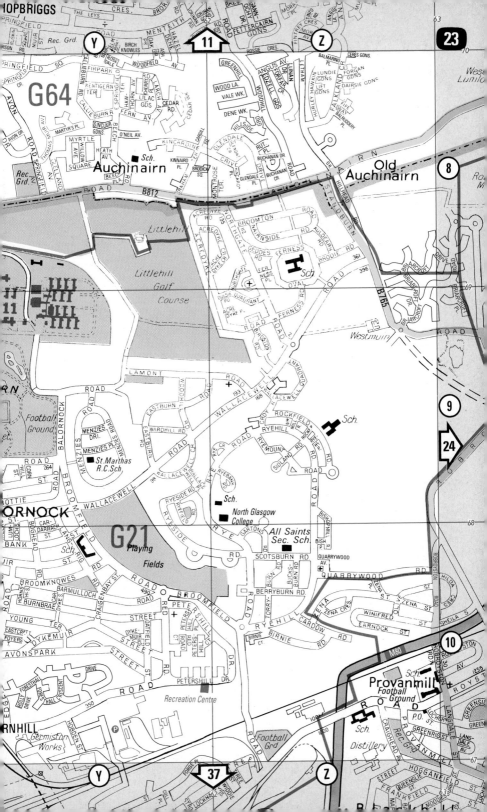

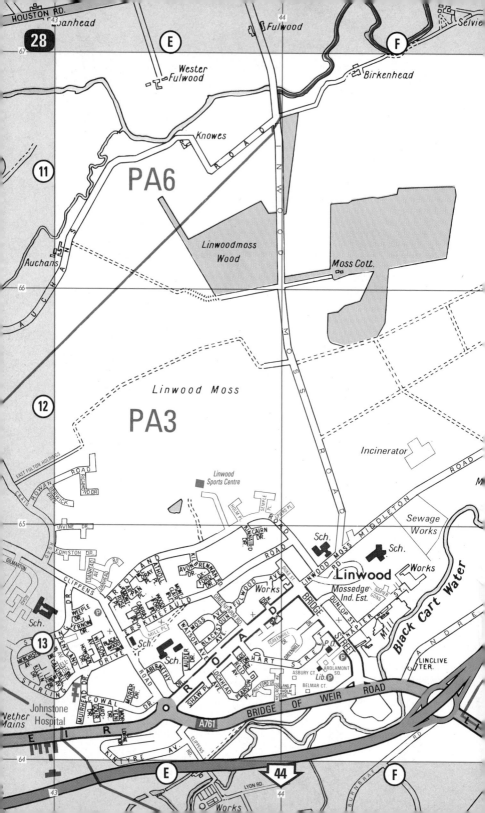

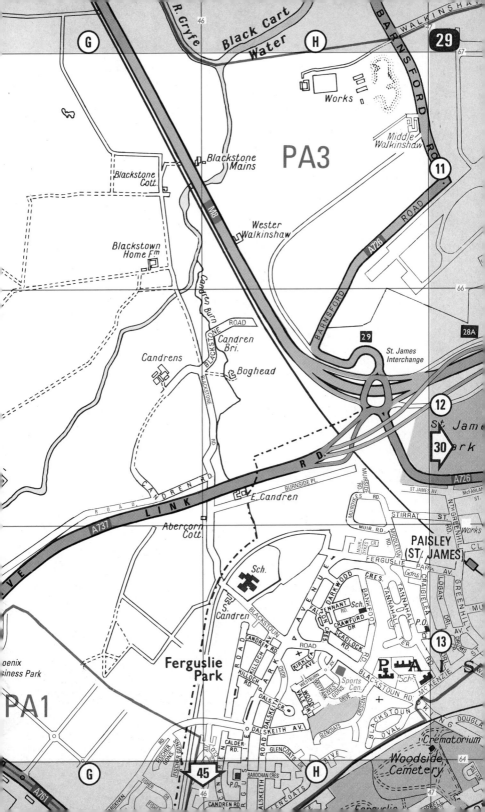

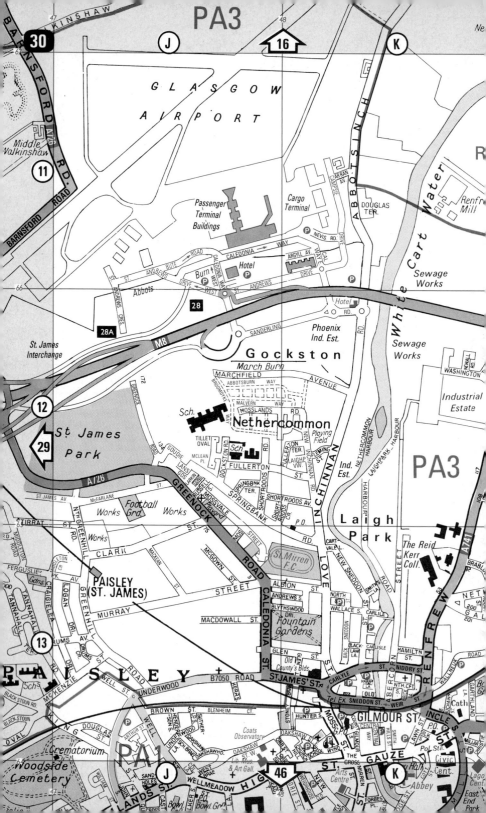

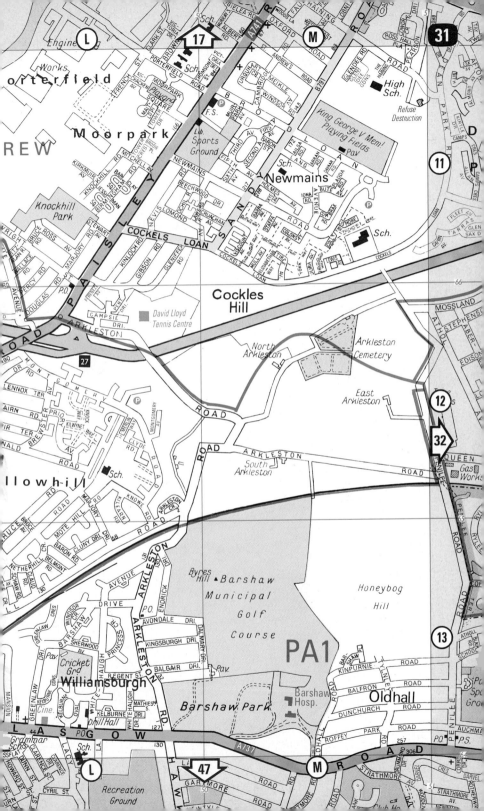

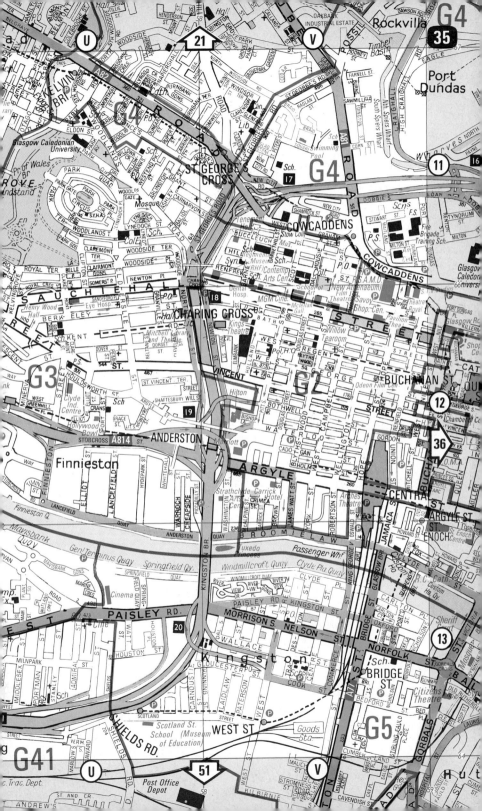

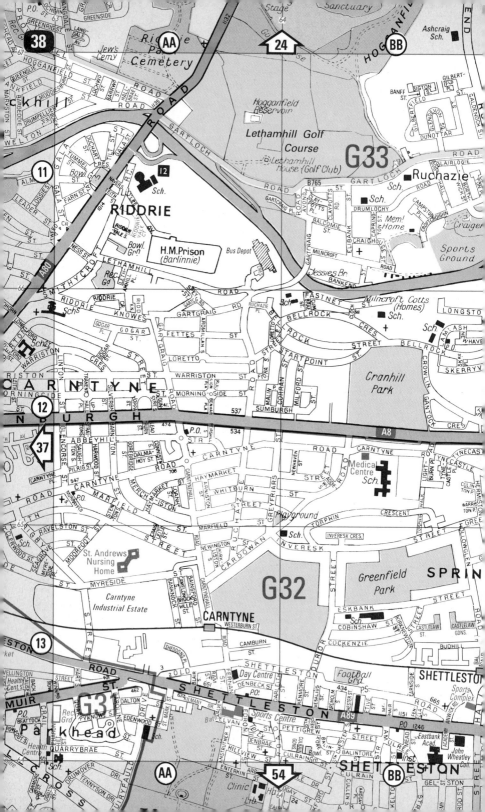

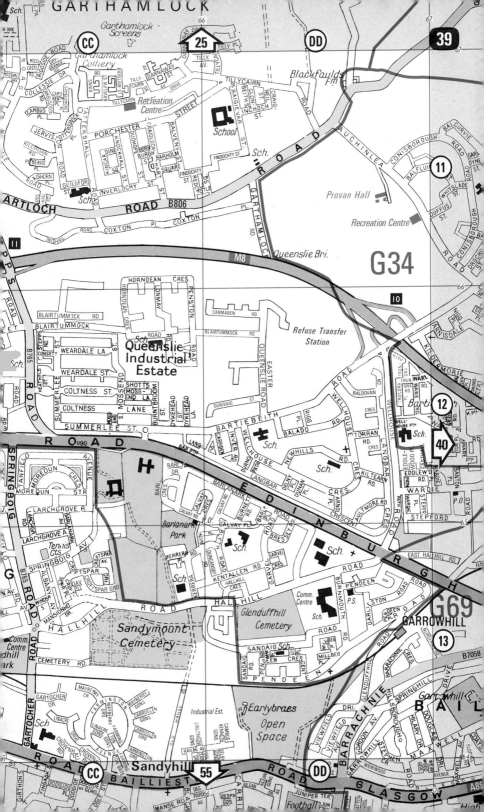

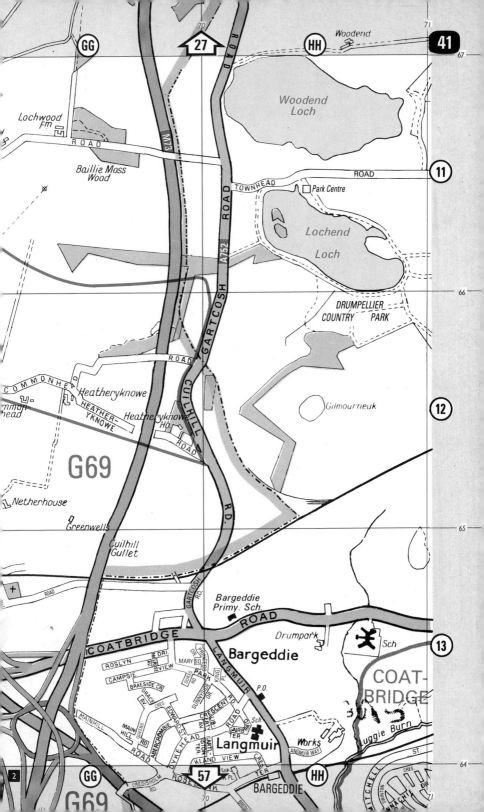

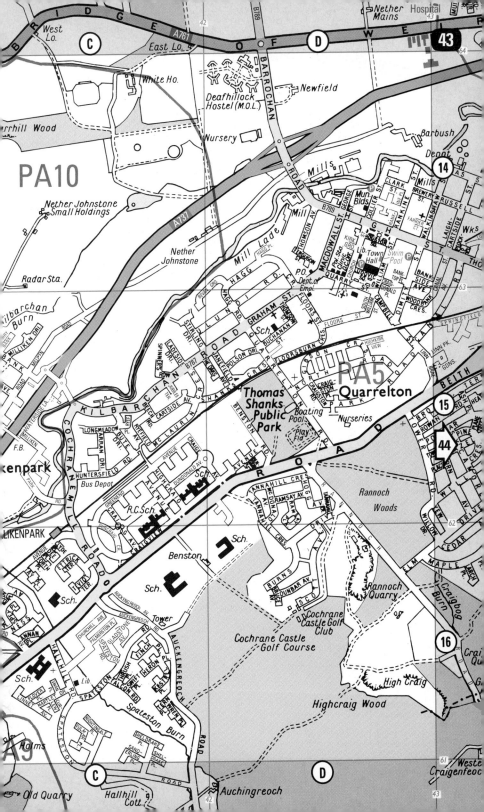

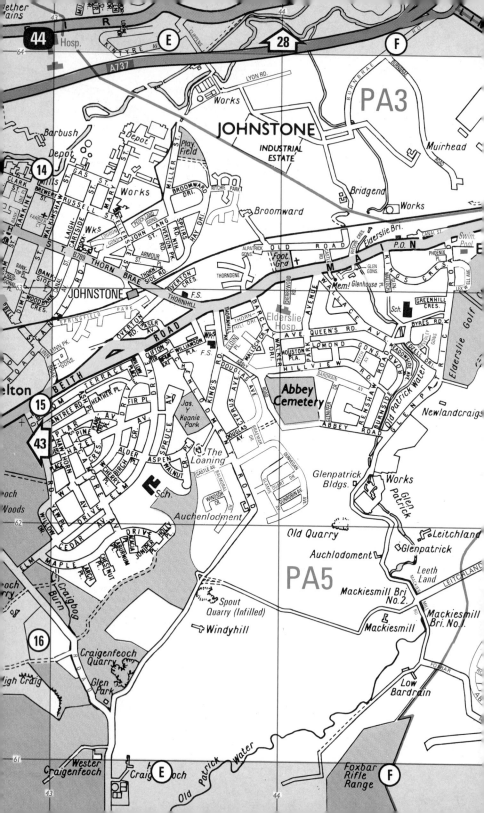

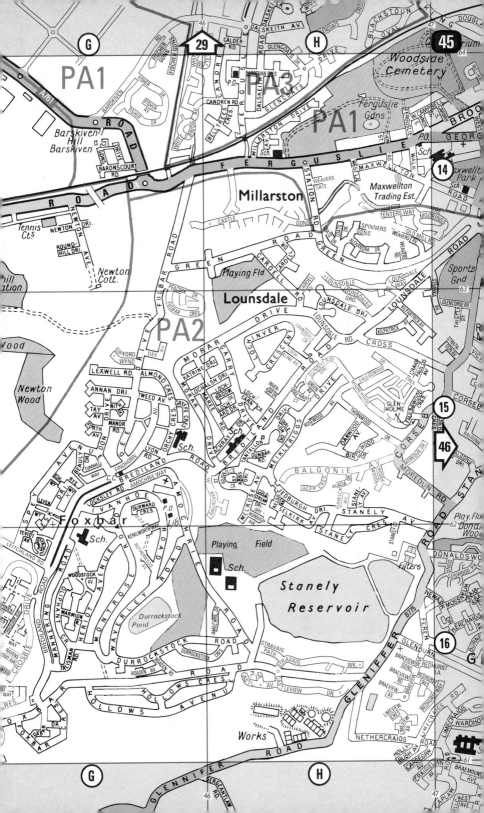

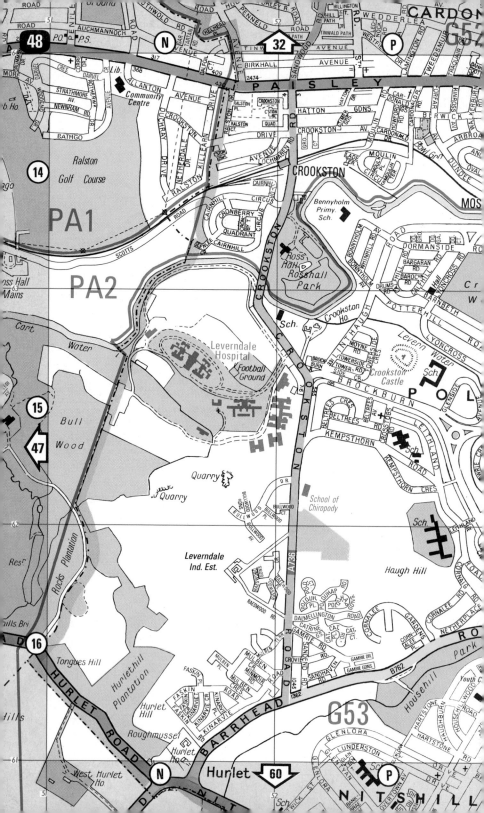

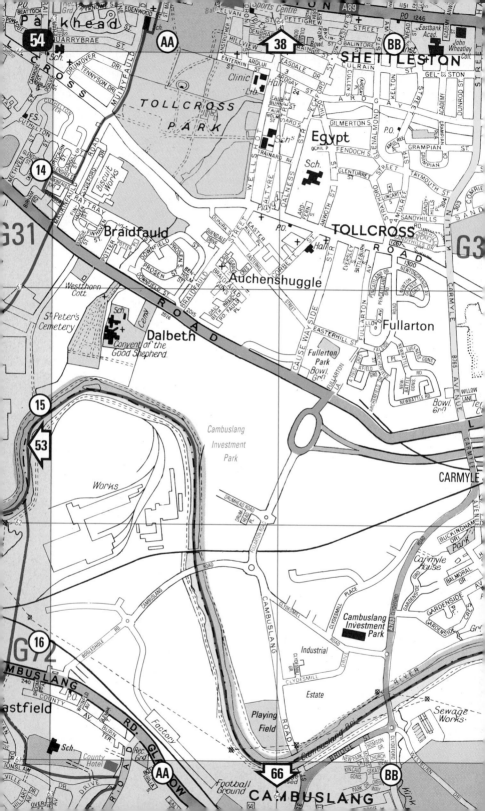

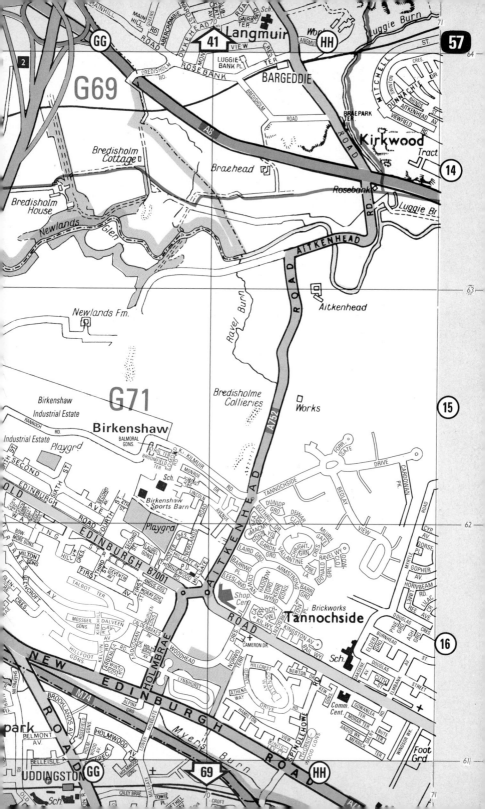

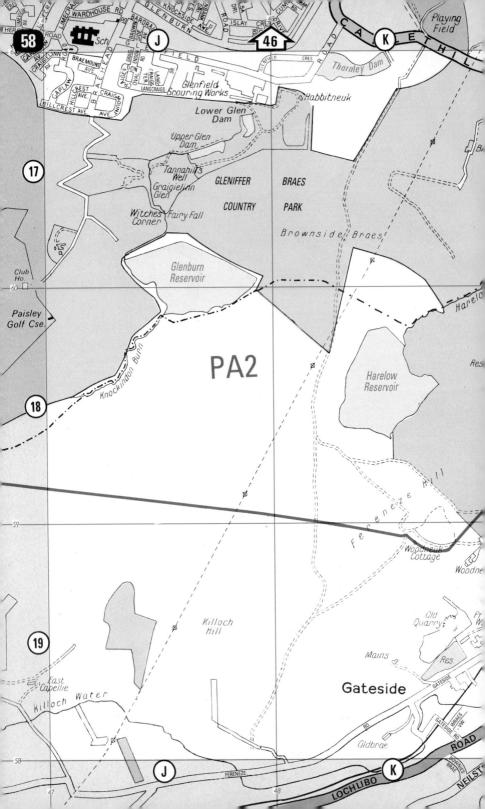

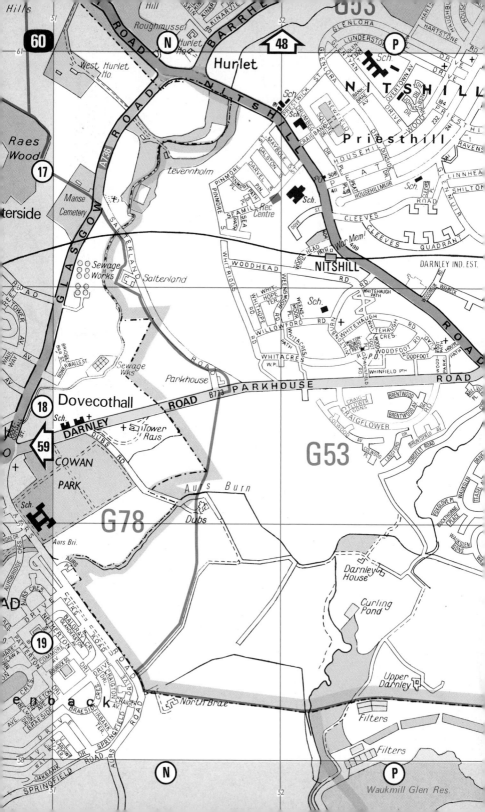

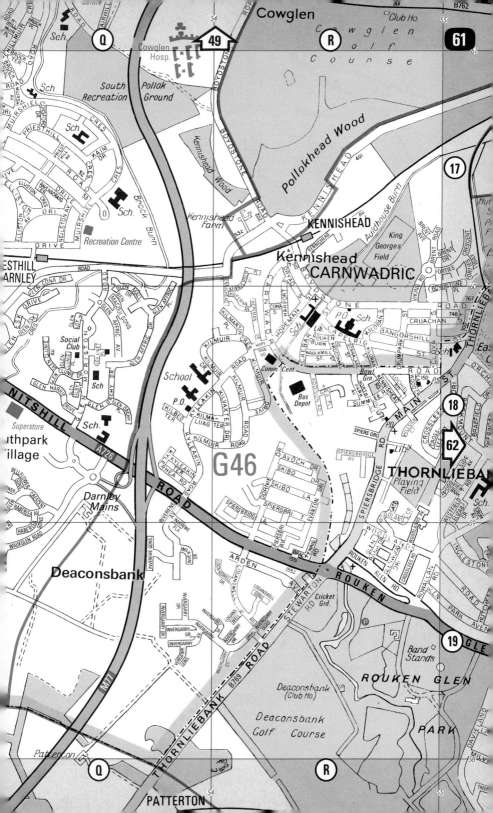

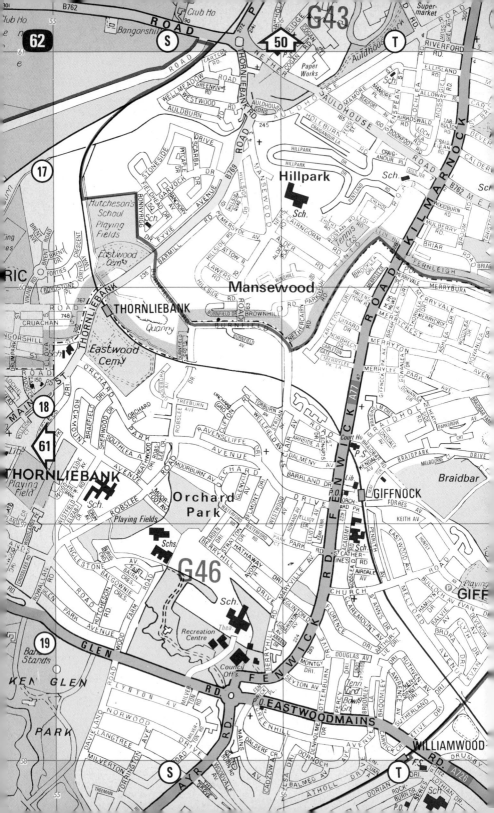

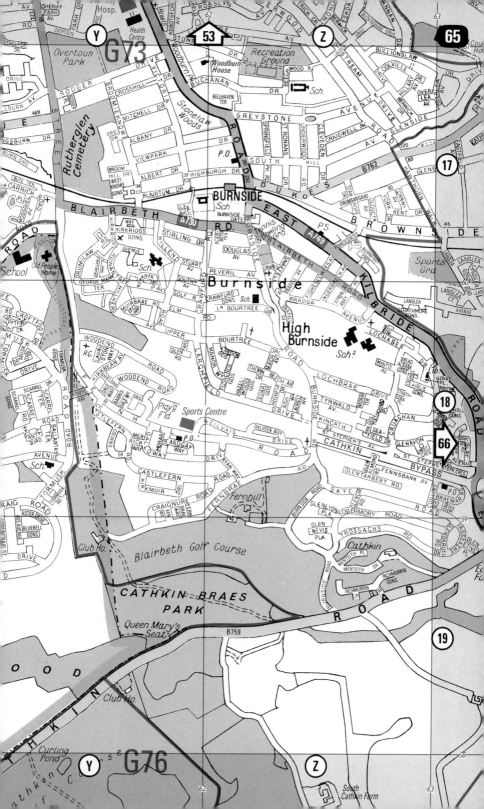

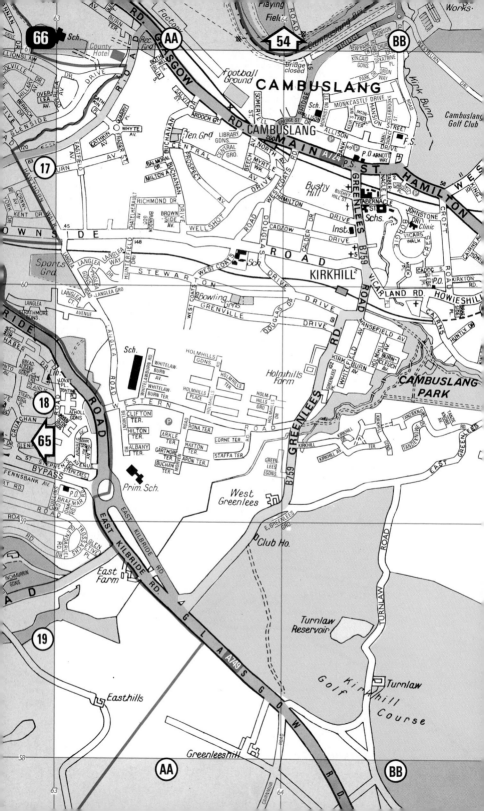

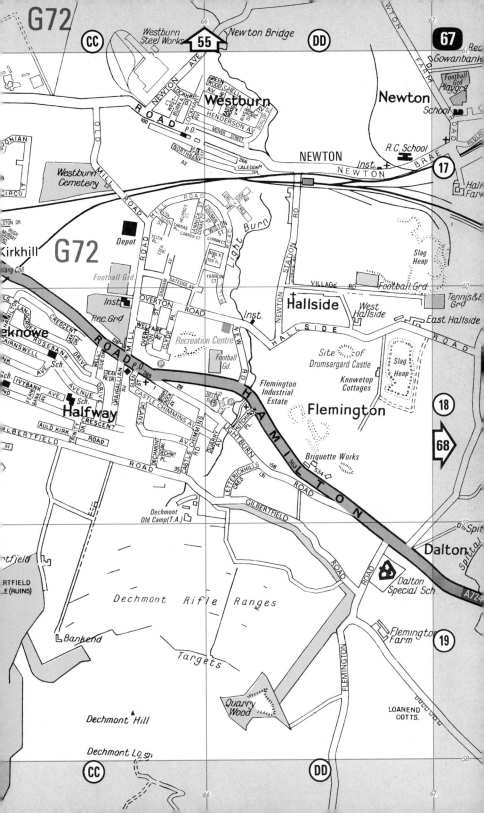

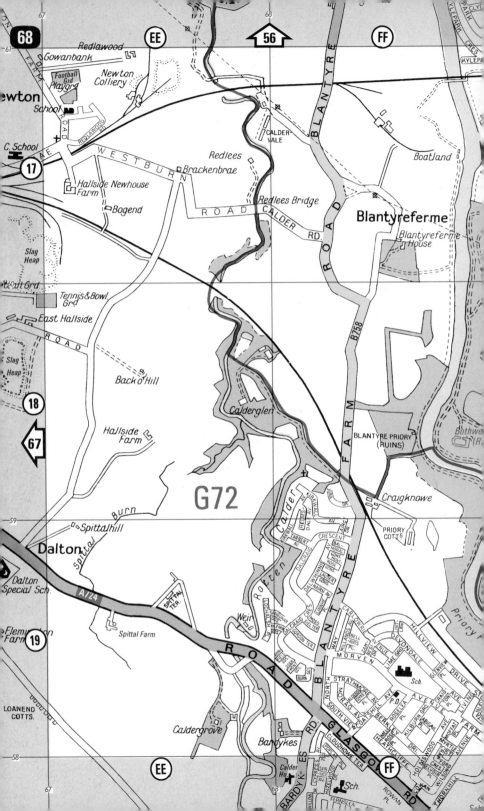

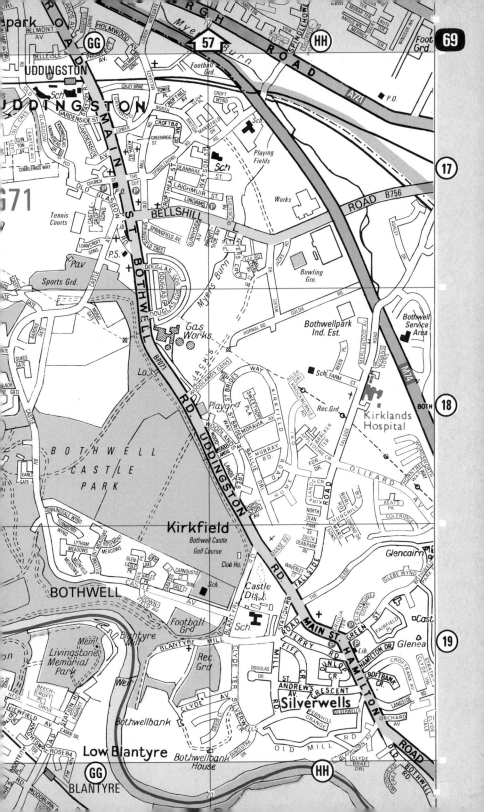

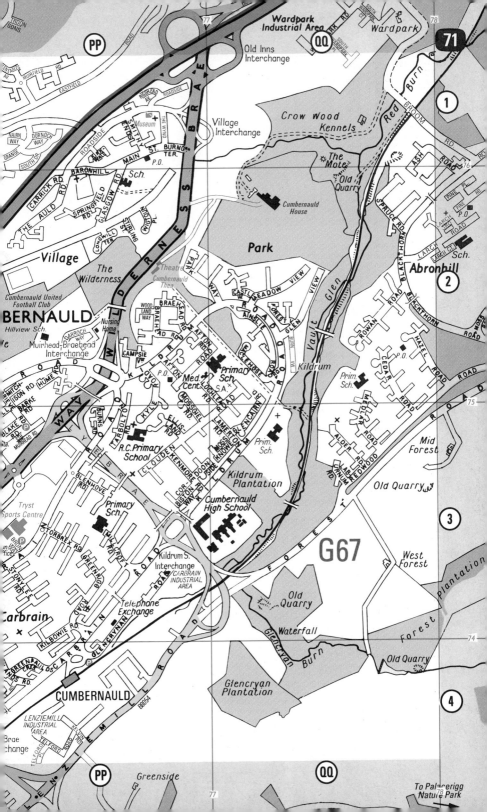

Glasgow

Information

Contents

The City of Glasgow began life as a makeshift hamlet of huts huddled round a 6thC church, built by St. Mungo on the banks of a little salmon river - the Clyde. It was called Gleschow, meaning 'beloved green place' in Celtic. The cathedral was founded in 1136; the university, the second oldest in Scotland, was established in the 15thC; and in 1454 the flourishing medieval city wedged between the cathedral and the river was made a Royal burgh. The city's commercial prosperity dates from the 17thC when the lucrative tobacco, sugar and cotton trade with the New World flourished. The River Clyde, Glasgow's gateway to the Americas, was dredged, deepened and widened in the 18thC to make it navigable to the city's heart.

By the 19thC, Glasgow was the greatest shipbuilding centre in the world. From the 1820s onwards, it grew in leaps and bounds westwards along a steep ridge of land running parallel with the river. The hillside became encased in an undulating grid of streets and squares. Gradually the individualism, expressed in one-off set pieces characteristic of the 18thC and early 19thC, gave way to a remarkable coherent series of terraced squares and crescents of epic proportions - making Glasgow one of the finest of Victorian cities. But the price paid for such rapid industrialisation, the tremendous social problems manifest in the squalor of some of the worst of 19thC slums, was high. Today the city is still the commercial and industrial capital of the West of Scotland. The most notorious of the slums have been cleared but the new buildings lack that sparkling clenchfisted Glaswegian character of the 19thC. Ironically, this character was partially destroyed when the slums were cleared for it wasn't the architecture that had failed, only the bureaucrats, who designated such areas as working class ghettos.

Districts
Little remains of medieval Glasgow, which stood on the wedge of land squeezed between the cathedral and the River Clyde. Its business centre was The Cross, a space formed by the junction of several streets - the tall, square Tolbooth Steeple, 1626, in the middle. Opposite is Trongate, an arch astride a footpath, complete with tower and steeple salvaged from 17thC St. Mary's Church - destroyed by fire in 1793. The centre of 20thC Glasgow is George Square, a tree-lined piazza planned in 1781 and pinned down by more than a dozen statues including an 80 foot high Doric column built in 1837 to carry a statue of Sir Walter Scott. Buildings of interest: the monumental neo-Baroque City Chambers 1883-88 which takes up the east side and the Merchants' House 1874, on the west. To the south of the square, in a huddle of narrow streets, is the old Merchant City. Of interest here is the elegant Trades House, 85 Glassford Street, built by Robert Adam in 1794. An elegant Ionic portico stands on a rusticated ground storey flanked by domed towers. Hutcheson's Hospital, 158 Ingram Street, is an handsome Italianate building designed by David Hamilton in 1805. Nearby is Stirling's Library, originally an 18thC private residence, it became the Royal Exchange in 1827 when the Corinthian portico was added. To the north west is Kelvingrove, Victorian Glasgow at its best. Built around a steep saddle of land, landscaped by Paxton in 1850 and lined along its edge with handsome terraces.

Last but not least are the banks of the River Clyde. From Clyde Walkway on the north bank you can see: the Suspension Bridge of 1871 with its pylons in the form of triumphal arches; 17thC Merchants' Steeple; the Gothic Revival St. Andrew's R.C. Cathedral of 1816; the church, built 1739, in nearby St. Andrew's Square is a typical copy of London's St. Martin-in-the-Fields.

City of Glasgow
Local Information Guide

Useful Information

Area of City 79 sq. miles (approx)

Population (Glasgow City)
1995 618,000

Early Closing Days
Tuesday with alternative of Saturday.
Most of the shops in the central area
operate six-day trading.

Electricity
240 volts A.C.

Emergency Services
Police, Fire and Ambulance. Dial 999
on any telephone.

Licensing Hours
Public Houses
City Centre
Daily except Sundays 11 a.m.-12 p.m.
Sundays 12.30a.m.-12p.m.

Restaurants, Hotels and Public Houses
with catering facililities; same as above
but can be extended for drinks with
meals.

Information Bureau

Tourist Information Centres:
35 St. Vincent Place, Glasgow.
0141 204 4400

Town Hall, Abbey Close, Paisley.
0141 889 0711

Glasgow Airport (Abbotsinch), Paisley.
0141 848 4440

Pier Head, Gourock
(Summer only)
01475 639467

Help & Advice

British Broadcasting Corporation
Queen Margaret Drive, G12 8DG
0141 339 8844

British Council
6 Belmont Crescent, G12 8ES.
0141 339 8651

**British Telecom Scotland
Glasgow Area**
Westergate Chambers,
11 Hope Street,
Glasgow, G2 6AB.
All Enquiries 0141 220 1234
FREEFONE 0800 309 409

Chamber of Commerce
30 George Square, G2 1EQ.
0141 204 2121

Citizens Advice Bureau
87 Bath Street, Glasgow, G2 2EE
0141 331 2345/6/7/8

119 Main Street,
Bridgeton, Glasgow, G40 1QD
0141 554 0336

27 Dougrie Drive, Castlemilk, Glasgow,
G45 9AD
0141 634 0338/9

139 Main Street (Town Hall),
Rutherglen, G73 2JJ
0141 647 5100

216 Main Street, Barrhead, G78 1SN
0141 881 2032

1145 Maryhill Road, Glasgow, G20 9AZ
0141 945 5900

4 Shandwick Square, Easterhouse,
Glasgow, G34 9DS
0141 771 2328

Drumchapel, 49 Dunkenny Square,
G15 8NE
0141 944 2612

1361-1363 Gallowgate
Parkhead
G31 4DN
0141 554 004

Consumer Advice Centre
9 Queen Street,
Glasgow, GL1 3ED
0141 204 0262

Customs and Excise
21 India Street, G2 4PZ 01412213828

H.M. Immigration Office
Public Enquiry Office
Dumbarton Court,
Admin Block D, Argyll Avenue,
Abbotsinch, Paisley
0141 887 2225

Housing Aid and Advice
Shelter, 53 St. Vincent Crescent,
Glasgow, G3 8NQ 0141 221 8895

Legal Aid and Advice
Castlemilk Advice and Law Centre
27 Dougrie Drive, Glasgow, G45 9AD
0141 6340338

Law Centre
32 Dougrie Drive, G45 9AD
0141 634 0313

Lost Property
There is a railway switchboard number
that will put you through to Lost
Property (whichever station).
0141 335 3276

Buses - Office of bus company
Trains - Station of arrival.
Elsewhere in City - Strathclyde Police.
Lost Property Department,
173 Pitt Street, G2 4JS
0141 532 2000

**Registrar of Births, Deaths and
Marriages**
1 Martha Street, G1 1JJ
0141 287 7652

Marriages only:
22 Park Circus, G3 6BE
0141 287 8350
Hours: Monday 9.15 a.m. - 5.00p.m.
Tuesday to Friday 9.15 a.m. - 4.00 p.m.

Births must be registered within twenty
one days, deaths within eights days
and marriages within three days. The
Registrar should be consulted at least
one month before intended date of
marriage.

Children First
31 Burleigh Street, Govan, G51 3LA
0141 445 4541

**RNID - Royal National Institute for
the Deaf**
9 Clairmont Gardens, Glasgow, G3 7LW
0141 332 0343

Samaritans
210 West George Street, Glasgow,
G2 2PQ
0141 248 4488

**Scottish Society for the Mentally
Handicapped**
6th Floor
7 Buchanan Street
Glasgow, G1 3HL
0141 248 4541

Scottish Television
Cowcaddens, G2 3PR
0141 300 3000

**Society for the Prevention of Cruelty
to Animals**
125 Kinnell Avenue, Cardonald G52 3RY
0141 882 3338

Newspapers

Morning Daily
Daily Record
40 Anderston Quay, G3 8DA.
0141 248 7000

The Herald
195 Albion Street, G1 1QP
0141 552 6255

Scottish Daily Express
Park House, Park Circus Place,
G3 6AF
0141 332 9600

The Scotsman
Regent Court, 76 West Regent Street
G2 2QZ
0141 332 6177

Evening Daily
Evening Times
195 Albion Street, G1 1QP
0141 552 6255

Weekly
Scottish Sunday Express
Park House, Park Circus Place, G3 6AF
0141 332 9600

Sunday Mail
40 Anderston Quay, G3 8DA
0141 248 7000

Sunday Post
144 Port Dundas Road, G4 0HZ
0141 332 9933

Parking

Car Parking in the central area of Glasgow is controlled. Parking meters are used extensively and signs indicating restrictions are displayed at kerbsides and on entry to the central area. Traffic Wardens are on duty.

British Rail Car Parks
(Open 24 hours)
Central Station
Queen Street Station

Multi-Storey Car Parks
(Open 24 hours)
Anderston Cross: Cambridge Street: George Street: Mitchell Street: Port Dundas Road: Waterloo Street.

(Limited Opening)
Charing Cross: Cowcaddens Road: St. Enoch Centre: Sauchiehall Street Centre

Surface Car Parks
Cathedral Street (Concert Hall): Dunlop Street: High Street: Ingram Street: King Street: McAlpine Street: Oswald Street: Shuttle Street:

Post Offices

Head Post Office
47 St. Vincent Street, Glasgow G2 5QX
0141 204 3689
Open Monday to Friday 8.30a.m. - 5.45p.m.
Saturdays 9 a.m. - 7.00 p.m.

Branch Offices
228 Hope Street, Glasgow G2 3PN
0141 332 4598

87-91 Bothwell Street, Glasgow
G2 7AA

Taxis

Glasgow has over 1400 traditional London type taxis, all licensed by the Glasgow District Council and all fitted with meters sealed and approved by the Council. A fare card stating the current tariff is displayed in a prominent position within each taxi. At the time of publishing a three mile journey costs approximately £5. The total price of each journey is shown on the meter. Fares are normally reviewed annually by the council. Each taxi can carry a maximum of five passengers.

The major taxi companies in the city offer City tours at fixed prices, listing the places of interest to be visited, leaflets are available at all major hotel reception areas. Tours vary from 2 to 3 hours and in price between £20 and £28. A tour "Glasgow by Night" is also available.

Any passenger wishing to travel to a destination outside the Glasgow District Boundary should ascertain from the driver the fare to be charged or the method of calculating the fare PRIOR to making the journey.

Complaints
Any complaints regarding the conduct of a taxi driver should be addressed to the Taxi Enforcement Officer, City Building Department, 73 Hawthorn Street, Glasgow G22 6HY.
0141 287 3326

Local Government

East Dunbartonshire
PO Box 4, Tom Johnston House, Civic Way, Kirkintilloch, G66 4TJ
0141 776 9000

East Renfrewshire
Council Offices, Eastwood Park, Rouken Glen Road, Giffnock G46 6UG
0141 621 3000

Glasgow City
City Chambers, George Square, Glasgow G2 1DU
0141 287 2000

North Lanarkshire
Civic Centre, Motherwell, ML1 1TW
01698 302222

Renfrewshire
South Buildings, Cotton Street, Paisley, PA1 1BU
0141 842 5000

South Lanarkshire
Council Offices, Almada Street, Hamilton ML3 0AA
01698 454444

West Dunbartonshire
Council Offices
Garshake Road
Dumbarton
G82 3PU
01389 737000

Glasgow Cathedral is a perfect example of pre-Reformation Gothic architecture. Begun in 1238, it has a magnificent choir and handsome nave with shallow projecting transepts. On a windy hill to the east is the Necropolis, a cemetery with a spiky skyline of Victoriana consisting of pillars, temples and obelisks, dominated by an 1825 Doric column carrying the statue of John Knox. Other churches of interest: Landsdowne Church built by J. Honeyman in 1863; St. George's Tron Church by William Stark 1807; Caledonian Road Church, a temple and tower atop a storey-high base, designed by Alexander Thomson in 1857; a similar design is to be found at the United Presbyterian Church, St. Vincent Street, 1858, but on a more highly articulated ground storey; Queen's Cross Church 1897 is an amalgam of Art Nouveau and Gothic Revival by the brilliant Charles Rennie Mackintosh.

Churches within the central area of Glasgow are:

Church of Scotland
Glasgow Cathedral
Castle Street
Renfield St. Stephen's Church
262 Bath Street
St. George's Tron Church
165 Buchanan Street
St. Columba Church (Gaelic)
300 St. Vincent Street

Baptist
Adelaide Place Church
209 Bath Street

Congregational
Hillhead Centre
1 University Avenue

Episcopal Church in Scotland
Cathedral Church of St. Mary
300 Great Western Road

First Church of Christ Scientist
1 La Bell Place, Clifton Street
(off Sauchiehall Street)

Free Church of Scotland
265 St. Vincent Street

German Speaking Congregation
Services held at 7 Hughenden Terrace

Greek Orthodox Cathedral
St. Luke's, 27 Dundonald Road

Jewish Orthodox Synagogue
Garnethill, 29 Garnet Street

Methodist
Woodlands Church
229 Woodlands Road

Roman Catholic
St. Andrew's Cathedral
190 Clyde Street
St. Aloysius' Church
25 Rose Street

Unitarian Church
72 Berkeley Street

United Free
Wynd Church
427 Crown Street

Buildings & Shops

Interesting Buildings

Victorian Glasgow was extremely eclectic architecturally. Good examples of the Greek Revival style are Royal College of Physicians 1845, by W.H. Playfair and the Custom House 1840, by G.L. Taylor. The Queen's Room 1857, by Charles Wilson, is a handsome temple used now as a Christian Science church. The Gothic style is seen at its most exotic in the Stock Exchange 1877, by J. Burnet. The new Victorian materials and techniques with glass, wrought and cast iron were also ably demonstrated in the buildings of the time. Typical are: Gardener's Stores 1856, by J. Baird; the Buck's Head, Argyle Street, an amalgam of glass and cast iron; and the Egyptian Halls of 1873, in Union Street, which has a masonry framework. Both are by Alexander Thomson. The Templeton Carpet Factory 1889, Glasgow Green, by William Leiper, is a Venetian Gothic building complete with battlemented parapet.

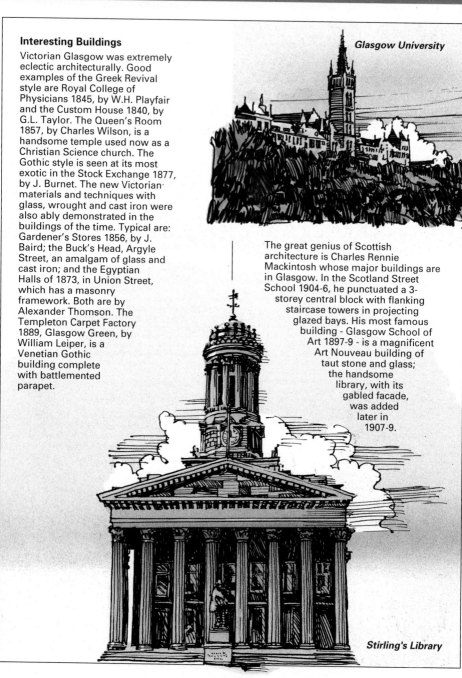

Glasgow University

The great genius of Scottish architecture is Charles Rennie Mackintosh whose major buildings are in Glasgow. In the Scotland Street School 1904-6, he punctuated a 3-storey central block with flanking staircase towers in projecting glazed bays. His most famous building - Glasgow School of Art 1897-9 - is a magnificent Art Nouveau building of taut stone and glass; the handsome library, with its gabled facade, was added later in 1907-9.

Stirling's Library

78

Galleries & museums

Scotland's largest tourist attraction, The Burrell Collection, is situated in Pollok Country Park, Haggs Road and has more than 8,000 objects, housed in an award winning gallery. The Museum and Art Gallery, Kelvingrove Park, Argyle Street, a palatial sandstone building with a glazed central court, has one of the best municipal collections in Britain; superb Flemish, Dutch and French paintings, drawings, prints, also ceramics, silver, costumes and armour, as well as a natural history section. The recently refurbished McLellan Galleries in Sauchiehall Street provide an important venue for touring and temporary art exhibitions. Provand's Lordship c1471, in Castle Street, is Glasgow's oldest house and now a museum of 17th-18thC furniture and household articles. Pollok House, Pollok Country Park, a handsome house designed by William Adam in 1752, has paintings by William Blake and a notable collection of Spanish paintings, including works by El Greco. The Museum of Transport, housed in Kelvin Hall, Bunhouse Road, has a magnificent collection of trams, cars, ships models, bicycles, horse-drawn carriages and 7 steam locos. The People's Palace, The Green built 1898 with a huge glazed Winter Garden, has a lively illustrated history of the city. But the oldest museum in Glasgow is the Hunterian Museum, University of Glasgow, University Avenue, opened in 1807, it has a fascinating collection of manuscripts, early painted books, as well as some fine archaeological and geological exhibits. 400-year old Haggs Castle, St. Andrew's Drive, is now a children's museum with practical demonstrations and exhibits showing how everyday life has changed over the centuries.

Streets & shopping

The Oxford Street of Glasgow is Sauchiehall (meaning 'willow meadow') Street. This together with Buchanan Street, Argyle Street, Princes Square and St. Enoch Centre form the main shopping area. Here you will find the department stores, boutiques and

Old Sheriff Court

general shops. All three streets are partly pedestrianised, but the most exhilarating is undoubtedly Buchanan Street. Of particular interest is the spatially elegant Argyll Arcade 1828, the Venetian Gothic-style Stock Exchange 1877, the picturesque Dutch gabled Buchanan Street Bank building 1896 and the Glasgow Royal Concert Hall (opened 1990). In Glasgow Green is The Barras, the city's famous street market, formed by the junction of London Road and Kent Street. The Market is open weekends. Some parts of the city have early closing on Tuesdays.

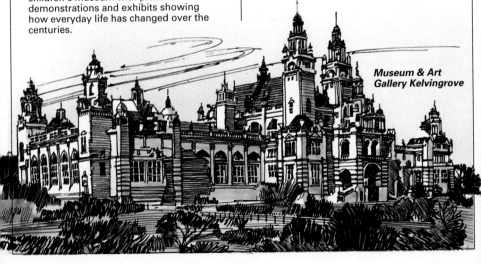

Museum & Art Gallery Kelvingrove

Entertainment

As Scotland's commercial and industrial capital, Glasgow offers a good choice of leisure activities. The city now has many theatres where productions ranging from serious drama to pantomime, pop and musicals are performed. The Theatre Royal, Hope Street is Scotland's only opera house and has been completely restored to its full Victorian splendour. The Royal Scottish National Orchestra gives concerts at the Glasgow Royal Concert Hall every Saturday night in winter and is the venue for the proms in June. Cinemas are still thriving in Glasgow, as are the many public houses, some of which provide meals and live entertainment. In the city centre and Byres Road, West End, there is a fair number of restaurants where traditional home cooking, as well as international cuisines, can be sampled. More night life can be found at the city's discos and dance halls.

Outdoors, apart from the many parks and nature trails, there is Calderpark Zoological Gardens, situated 6 miles from the centre between Mount Vernon and Uddingston. Here you may see white rhinos, black panthers and iguanas among many species. Departing from Stobcross Quay, you can also cruise down the Clyde in 'P.S. Waverley' - the last sea-going paddle- steamer in the world.

Cinemas

ABC Cinema, 380 Clarkston Road
0141 637 2641
ABC Cinema
326 Sauchiehall Street 0141 332 9513
Admin Dept 0141 332 1592
Glasgow Film Theatre
12 Rose Street (Box Office)
0141 332 6535
Grosvenor Cinema
Ashton Lane
0141 339 4298
Kelburne Cinema
(Manager), Glasgow Road, Paisley
PA1 3BD. 0141 889 3612
Odeon Film Centre
56 Renfield Street 0141 332 8701

Virgin Centre
The Forge Shopping Centre
1221 Gallowgate,
G31 4EB
0141 556 4282

Halls

City Halls, Candleriggs
Couper Institute
86 Clarkston Road, G44
Glasgow Royal Concert Hall
2 Sauchiehall Street, G2 3NY
Langside Hall, 5 Langside Avenue
Partick Burgh Hall, 9 Burgh Hall Street,
Pollokshaws Hall
2025 Pollokshaws Road,
Woodside Hall, Glenfarg Street
More information about the above
G.C.C. halls and others contact,
Performing Arts and Venues, Exchange
House, 229 George Street, G1 1QU
0141 287 5008

Theatres

Arches Theatre
30 Midland Street G1 4PR
0141 221 9736
Citizens' Theatre
119 Gorbals Street G5 9DS
0141 429 0022
King's Theatre
297 Bath Street 0141 227 5511
Mitchell Theatre and Moir Hall
Granville Street G3 0141 227 5511
New Athenaeum Theatre
100 Renfrew Street G2 3DB
0141 332 5057
Old Athenaeum Theatre
179 Buchanan Street G1 2JZ
0141 332 2333
Pavilion Theatre
121 Renfield Street G2 3AX
0141 332 1846
Theatre Royal
282 Hope Street G2 3QA
0141 332 9000
Tramway
25 Albert Drive G41 2PE
0141 552 4267
Tron Theatre
63 Trongate, Glasgow G1 5HB
0141 552 4267

The Ticket Centre
Candleriggs, G1 1NQ
Glasgow's Central Box Office for Arches Theatre, Centre for Contemporary Arts, Citizens'
Theatre, City Hall at Candleriggs, King's Theatre, Mitchell Theatre, Tron Theatre, Scottish
Exhibition Centre and Glasgow Royal Concert Hall.
Telephone lines open Mon.- Sat. 9a.m. - 9.00 p.m. Sun. 12.00 - 5 p.m.
0141 227 5511
Counter Service: Mon.- Sat. 9.00 a.m.-6.00 p.m.
Sun. 12.00 - 5.pm

Weather

The City of Glasgow is on the same latitude as the City of Moscow, but because of its close
proximity to the warm Atlantic Shores, and the prevailing westerly winds, it enjoys a more
moderate climate. Summers are generally cool and winters mostly mild, this gives Glasgow
fairly consistent summer and winter temperatures. Despite considerable cloud the City is
sheltered by hills to the south-west and north and the average rainfall for Glasgow is usually
less than 40 inches per year. The following table shows the approximate average figures for
sunshine, rainfall and temperatures to be expected in Glasgow throughout the year.

Weather Forecasts
For the Glasgow Area including Loch Lomond and the Clyde Coast:
Weatherline 0891 232 791 (Recording)
The Glasgow Weather Centre (Meteorological Office), St. Vincent Street, G2 5QD
0141 248 3451

Month	Hours of Sunshine	Inches of Rainfall	Temperature °C		
			Ave. Max.	Ave. Min.	High/Low
January	36	3.8	5.5	0.8	-18
February	62	2.8	6.3	0.8	-15
March	94	2.4	8.8	2.2	21
April	147	2.4	11.9	3.9	22
May	185	2.7	15.1	6.2	26
June	181	2.4	17.9	9.3	30
July	159	2.9	18.6	10.8	29
August	143	3.5	18.5	10.6	31
September	106	4.1	16.3	9.1	-4
October	76	4.1	13.0	6.8	-8
November	47	3.7	8.7	3.3	-11
December	30	4.2	6.5	1.9	-12

For both spectator and participant, football is Glasgow's favourite sport. Both Celtic and Rangers, Scotland's most famous rival teams, have their grounds within the City. Glasgow houses Scotland's national football stadium at Hampden Park.

Badminton

Scottish Badminton Union's Cockburn Centre, 40 Bogmoor Place, G51 4TQ. 0141 445 1218

Bowling Greens

There are greens in all the main Parks. Information about clubs from the Scottish Bowling Association: 50 Wellington Street, G2 6EF. 0141 221 8999

Cricket Grounds

Huntershill Crowhill Road, Bishopbriggs.
Poloc Dawholm, 2060 Pollokshaws Road, G43.
West of Scotland Peel Street, G11.

Football Grounds

Broadwood (Clyde F.C.) Cumbernauld
Celtic Park (Celtic F.C.) 95 Kerrydale Street, G40
Firhill Park (Partick ThistleF.C.) Firhill Road, G20
Hampden Park (Queen's Park F.C.) Somerville Drive, G42
Ibrox Stadium (Rangers F.C.) Edmiston Drive, G51
Kilbowie Park (Clydebank F.C.) Argyll Road, Clydebank
St. Mirren Park (St. Mirren F.C.) Love Street, Paisley

Golf Courses

Glasgow District Council
9 holes
Alexandra Park, Cumbernauld Road, G31
Cambuslang, Westburn Drive, Cambuslang.
King's Park, Carmunnock Road, Croftfoot, G44
Knightswood, Lincoln Avenue,G13

Ruchill, Brassey Street, G20

18 holes
Barshaw, Glasgow Road, Paisley.
Douglaston, Strathblane Road, Milngavie. (Five miles from Glasgow).
Elderslie, Main Road, Johnstone.
Lethamhill, Cumbernauld Road, G33
Littlehill, Auchinairn Road, G64.
Linn Park, Simshill Road,G4
Pollok, Barrhead Road, Pollokshaws, G43

Putting Greens
There are putting greens in some of the main parks.

Pitch & Putt
Courses at Bellahouston Park, Queen's Park, and several others.

Rugby Grounds

Auldhouse (Hutchesons'/Aloysians) Thornliebank
Cartha Queens Park Haggs Road, G41
Garscube Estate Switchback Road, Maryhill, Glasgow, G61
Hughenden (Hillhead High School) Hughenden Road, G12.
New Anniesland (Glasgow Acad.) Helensburgh Drive, G13.
Old Anniesland (Glasgow High School F.P. & Kelvinside Academicals) Crow Road, G11.

Sports Centres

Barrhead, Main Street, Barrhead G78 1SW
0141 881 1900

Bellahouston
31 Bellahouston Drive, G52 1HH.
0141 427 5454
Burnhill 60 Toryglen Road, Rutherglen, G73 1NE.
0141 643 0327
Crownpoint Crownpoint Road, Bridgeton, G40.
0141 554 8274
Linwood, Brediland Road, Linwood PA3 3RA.
01505 329 461
Springburn Key Street, Springburn, G21 1JY.
0141 557 5878
Tryst, Tryst Walk, Cumbernauld G67 1EW.
01236 728138

Swimming Pools

Drumchapel, 199 Drumry Road East, G15 8NS.
0141 944 5812
Easterhouse, Bogbain Road, G34 9LA. 0141 771 7978
Elderslie, 3 Stoddard Square, Elderslie. PA5 9AS
01505 328133
Govan, 1 Harhill Street, G51.
0141 445 1899
Lagoon Leisure Centre, Mill St., Paisley PA1 1LZ.
0141 889 4000
North Woodside, Braid Square, G4 9YB. 0141 332 8102
Pollok Leisure Pool, Cowglen Road, G53. 0141 881 3313
Renfrew, Inchinnan Road, Renfrew PA4 8ND.
0141 886 2088
Scotstown Leisure Centre 72 Danes Drive, Scotstown, G14. 0141 959 4000
Temple, 354 Netherton Road, G13. 0141 954 6537
Tollcross Park Leisure Centre Wellshot Road, Tollcross G32 8TF 0141 763 1222

Tennis

There are courts in some of the main parks. Information about clubs from theSecretary of the West of Scotland Lawn Tennis Association: Mr J Stevenson 01505 812336.

Anniesland College
Hatfield Drive, Glasgow, G12 OYE
0141 357 3969

Ayr College
Dam Park, Ayr, KA8 OEU
01292 265184

Bell College of Technology
Almada Street, Hamilton, Lanarkshire,
ML3 OJB
01698 283100

Cambuslang College
Hamilton Road, Cambuslang, Glasgow,
G72 7BS
0141 641 6600

**Cardonald College of Further
Education**
690 Mosspark Drive, Glasgow, G52 3AY
0141 883 6151

Central College of Commerce
300 Cathedral Street, G1 2TA
0141 552 3941

Clydebank College
Kilbowie Road, Clydebank,
Dunbartonshire, G81 2AA
0141 952 7771

Coatbridge College
Kildonan Street, Coatbridge,
Lanarkshire, ML5 3LS
01236 422316

Cumbernauld College
Town Centre, Cumbernauld, Glasgow,
G67 1HU
01236 731811

Glasgow Caledonian University
Cowcaddens Road, Glasgow G4 0BA
0141 331 3000

**Glasgow College of Building and
Printing**
60 North Hanover Street, Glasgow,
G1 2BP
0141 332 9969

**Glasgow College of Food
Technology**
230 Cathedral Street, Glasgow, G1 2TG
0141 552 3751

Glasgow College of Nautical Studies
21 Thistle Street, Glasgow, G5 9XB
0141 429 3201

James Watt College
Finnart Street, Greenock, Renfrewshire,
PA16 8HF
01475 724433

John Wheatley College
1346-1364 Shettleston Road, Glasgow,
G32 9AT
0141 778 2426

Kilmarnock College
Holehouse Road, Kilmarnock, Ayrshire,
KA3 7AT
01563 23501

Langside College
50 Prospecthill Road, Glasgow, G42 9LB
0141 649 4991

Motherwell College
Dalzell Drive, Motherwell, Lanarkshire,
ML4 2DD
01698 232323

North Glasgow College
110 Flemington Street, Glasgow,
G21 4BX
0141 558 9001

Reid Kerr Gollege, The
Renfrew Road, Paisley, Renfrewshire,
PA13 4DR
0141 889 4225

Stow College
43 Shamrock Street, Glasgow, G4 9LD
0141 332 1786

University of Glasgow
University Avenue, Glasgow
0141 339 8855

University of Paisley
High St, Paisley
0141 848 3000

University of Strathclyde
George Street, Glasgow, G1 1XQ
0141 552 4400

Parks & Gardens

There are over 70 public parks within the city. The most famous is Glasgow Green. Abutting the north bank of the River Clyde, it was acquired in 1662. Of interest are the Winter Gardens attached to the People's Palace. Kelvingrove Park is an 85-acre park laid out by Sir Joseph Paxton in 1852. On the south side of the city is the 148-acre Queen's Park, Victoria Road, established 1857-94. Also of interest: Rouken Glen, Thornliebank, with a spectacular waterfall, walled garden, nature trail and boating facilities; Victoria Park, Victoria Park Drive, with its famous Fossil Grove flower gardens and yachting pond. In Great Western Road are the Botanic Gardens. Founded in 1817, the gardens' 42 acres are crammed with natural attractions, including the celebrated Kibble Palace glasshouse with its fabulous tree ferns, exotic plants and white marble Victorian statues.

Alexandra
671 Alexandra Parade, G31.

Barshaw
Glasgow Road, Paisley.

Bellahouston
Paisley Road West, G52.

Botanic Gardens
730 Great Western Road, G12.

Hogganfield Loch
Cumbernauld Road, G33.

Kelvingrove
Sauchiehall Street, G3.

King's
325 Carmunnock Road, G44.

Linn
Clarkston Road at Netherlee Road, G44.

Pollok Country Park
Pollokshaws Road, G43

Queen's
Victoria Road, G42.

Rouken Glen
Rouken Glen Road, G46.

Springburn
Broomfield Road, G21.

Tollcross
461 Tollcross Road, G32.

Victoria
Victoria Park Drive North, G14.

Kibble Palace

The City of Glasgow has one of the most advanced, fully integrated public transport systems in the whole of Europe. The Strathclyde Transport network consists of: the local railway network, the local bus services and the fully modernised Glasgow Underground, with links to Glasgow Airport and the Steamer and Car Ferry Services.
For information contact:
Strathclyde Transport Travel Centre
St. Enoch Square G1 4BW
0141 226 4826
Open Monday to Saturday 9.30 a.m. - 5.30 p.m.
Phone enquiries Monday to Saturday 9.00 a.m. - 9.00 p.m.
Sunday 9 a.m. - 7.30 p.m.
For City services, ferry services, local train services. Free timetables are available.

Bus Services and Tours

Long Distance Coach Service
0990 505050
Scottish Citylink Coaches Ltd and National Express provide express services to London and most parts of Scotland including Campbeltown, Tarbert, Ardrishaig, Inverary, Oban, Fort William, Skye, Stirling, Perth, Dundee, Arbroath, Montrose, Aberdeen, Aviemore, Inverness and Edinburgh.

Local Bus Services
A comprehensive network of local bus services is provided by a variety of operators within the City of Glasgow and also direct to the following destinations:
Airdrie, Ardrossan, Ayr, Balfron, Barrhead, Bearsden, Beith, Bellshill, Bishopbriggs, Bishopton, Blantyre, Bo'ness, Caldercruix, Cambuslang, Campsie Glen, Carluke, Clydebank, Coatbridge, Cumbernauld, Denny, Drymen, Dunfermline, Duntocher, Eaglesham, East Kilbride, Erskine, Falkirk, Glenrothes, Grangemouth, Hamilton, Irvine, Johnstone, Kilbarchan, Kilbirnie, Killearn, Kilmarnock, Kilsyth, Kirkintilloch, Kirkcaldy, Lanark, Largs, Larkhall, Lennoxtown, Lochwinnoch, Motherwell, Milngavie, Newton Mearns, Old Kilpatrick, Paisley, Prestwick, Renfrew, Saltcoats, Shotts, Stirling, Strathblane, Strathaven,

Uddingston, Wishaw.
These services depart from City Centre bus stops or from Buchanan Bus Station.
0141 332 7133

Coach Hire and Day, Half Day and Extended Tours
Scottish City Link Coaches Ltd
0990 505050
Private hire and seasonal tours
Freephone 0800 080001

Haldane's of Cathcart
12, Delvin Road, G44 3AA
Private hire and tours
0141 637 2234

Strathclyde Buses Ltd.
197 Victoria Road, G42 7AD
0141 636 3190
Private hire and seasonal tours
Freephone 0800 0800 01

Railway Services

Passenger enquiries: 0345 484 950
Sleeper reservations: 0345 5500 33

ScotRail trains serve over 170 stations in Glasgow and Strathclyde (see map). ScotRail services operate to most destinations in Scotland.
East Coast Ltd., West Coast Ltd. and Cross Country Trains Ltd. operate services to England.

Glasgow Queen Street Station
for services to Cumbernauld, Edinburgh, Falkirk, Stirling, Perth, Dundee, Arbroath, Montrose, Aberdeen, Pitlochry, Aviemore, Inverness, Durnbarton, Balloch, Helensburgh, Oban, Fort William, Mallaig, Coatbridge, Airdrie.

Glasgow Central Station
for services to Gourock (ferry connection to Dunoon), Greenock, Wemyss Bay (ferry connection to Rothesay), Paisley, Johnstone, Largs, Ardrossan (ferry connection to Brodick), Irvine, Ayr, Girvan, Stranraer, East Kilbride, Kilmarnock, Dumfries, Motherwell, Hamilton, Lanark, Carlisle, Shotts, Edinburgh, Berwick, Newcastle.
London and destinations on West and East Coast Main Lines.

Strathclyde Transport

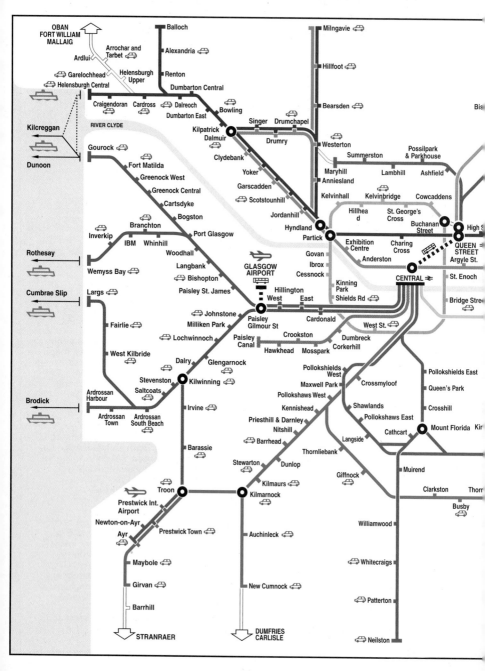

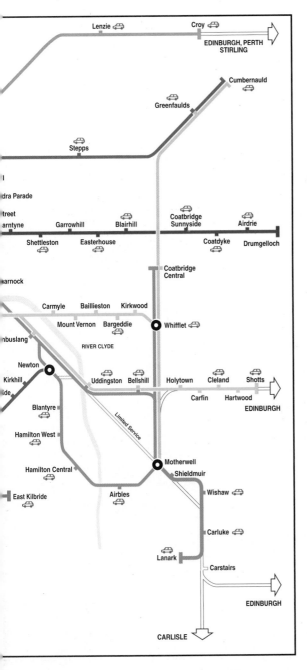

Lenzie
Croy
EDINBURGH, PERTH
STIRLING

Cumbernauld

Greenfaulds

Stepps

dra Parade

treet
arntyne   Garrowhill   Blairhill   Coatbridge   Airdrie
                                         Sunnyside

Shettleston   Easterhouse   Coatdyke   Drumgelloch

arnock   Coatbridge
                                 Central

Carmyle   Baillieston   Kirkwood

Mount Vernon   Bargeddie

nbuslang   RIVER CLYDE   Whifflet

Newton

Kirkhill
de   Uddingston   Bellshill   Holytown   Cleland   Shotts

Blantyre   Carfin   Hartwood
                                                         EDINBURGH

Hamilton West

Hamilton Central   Motherwell

                     Shieldmuir

East Kilbride   Airbles   Wishaw

                  Carluke

            Lanark

                  Carstairs

                            EDINBURGH

            CARLISLE

Limited Service

Rail Interchange

Glasgow Underground

Travelator Link

Other ScotRail Services

Glasgow Airport

Prestwick International
Airport

Interchange with Ferries
(---- Summer Only)

AIRLINK BUS
Glasgow Airport from
Paisley Gilmour Street

Inter-terminal Bus Link

Park-and-Ride
Station car parks

Glasgow Airport

Glasgow Airport is located eight miles west of Glasgow alongside the M8 motorway at Junction 28. It is linked by a bus service to Buchanan Street Bus Station, which runs every 10 minutes from 8.00 a.m.-5.00p.m. Monday to Saturday and less frequently at off peak times. There is a frequent coach service linking the Airport with all major bus and rail terminals in the City. Gilmour Street railway station in Paisley is 2 miles away and is linked by a frequent local bus service or by taxi.

Car parking is available with a graduated scale of charges. The Airport telephone number is 0141 887 1111

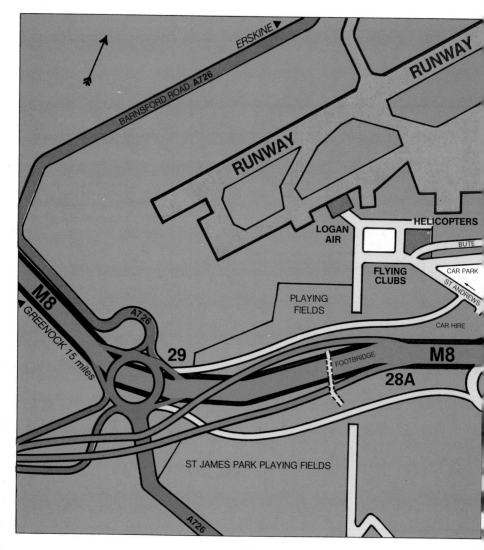

Airlines

Aer Lingus Flights to: Dublin
Reservations 0141 248 4121
Air Canada Flights to: Calgary, Toronto,
Calgary.
Reservations 0345 181313
Air U.K. Flights to: Amsterdam, London
Gatwick, London Stansted.
Reservations 0345 666777
British Airways Flights to: Boston,
New York, Paris, London Heathrow,
Manchester, Birmingham, and Inter
Scottish Routes.
Reservations 0345 222111
British Airways Express Flights to:
Barra, Belfast, Donegal, Islay, Inverness,
Kirkwall, Londonderry, Sumburgh, Tiree.

British Midland Flights to: London
Heathrow, Jersey, Copenhagen, East
Midlands.
Reservations 0345 554554
Business Air Flights to: Aberdeen,
Manchester.
Reservations 01500 340146
Easy Jet Flights to: London Luton.
Reservatons 01582 445566
Icelandair Flights to: Reykjavik.
Reservations 0171 388 5599
Manx Airlines Flights to: Isle of Man
Reservations 0141 221 0162
Sabena Flights to: Brussels
Reservations 0345 125245

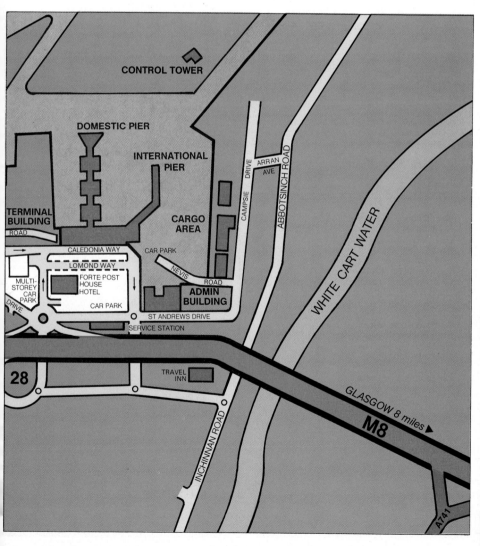

Hospitals

Greater Glasgow Health Board
(Administration)
112 Ingram Street, Glasgow, G1 1ET
0141 201 4444

Acorn Street Psychiatric Day Hospital
23 Acorn Street, Bridgeton, Glasgow,
G40 4AA
0141 556 4789

Baillieston Health Centre
20 Muirside Road, Glasgow, G69 7AD
0141 531 8000

Belvidere Hospital
1362-1452 London Road, Glasgow,
G31 4PG
0141 211 8500

Blawarthill Hospital
129 Holehouse Drive, Knightswood,
Glasgow, G13 3TG
0141 954 9547

Bridgeton Health Centre
201 Abercromby Street, Glasgow,
G40 2AD
0141 531 6500

Canniesburn Hospital
Switchback Road, Bearsden, Glasgow,
G61 1QL
0141 211 5600

Castlemilk Health Centre
Dougrie Drive, Castlemilk, Glasgow,
G45 9AW
0141 531 8500

Charing Cross Clinic
8 Woodside Crescent, Glasgow,
G3 7UL
0141 211 8100

Clydebank Health Centre
Kilbowie Road, Clydebank, G81 2TQ
0141 531 6400

Cowglen Hospital
Boydstone Road, Glasgow, G53 6XJ
0141 632 9106

Douglas Inch Centre
2 Woodside Terrace, Glasgow,
G3 7UY
0141 211 8000

Drumchapel Hospital
129 Drumchapel Road, Glasgow,
G15 6PX
0141 211 6000

Easterhouse Health Centre
9 Auchinlea Road, Glasgow, G34 9QU
0141 531 8100

Gartloch Hospital
Gartloch Road,Glasgow, G69 8EJ
0141 771 0771

Gartnavel General Hospital
1053 Great Western Road, Glasgow,
G12 0YN
0141 211 3000

Gartnavel Royal Hospital
1055 Great Western Road, Glasgow,
G12 0XH
0141 211 3600

Glasgow Dental Hospital and School
378 Sauchiehall Street, Glasgow,
G2 3JZ
0141 211 9600

Glasgow Eye Infirmary
3 Sandyford Place, Glasgow, 63 7NB
0141 211 6767

Glasgow Homeopathic Hospital
1000 Great Western Road, Glasgow,
G12 0AA
0141 211 1600

Glasgow Royal Infirmary
84 Castle Street, Glasgow, G4 0NA
0141 211 4000

Glasgow Royal Maternity Hospital
Rottenrow, Glasgow, G4 0NA
0141 211 3400

Gorbals Health Centre
45 Pine Place, Glasgow, G5 0BQ
0141 429 6291

Govan Health Centre
5 Drumoyne Road, Glasgow G51 4BJ
0141 440 1212

Govanhill Health Centre
233 Calder Street, Glasgow, G42 7DR
0141 531 8300

Knightswood Hospital
125 Knightswood Road, Glasgow,
G13 2XG
0141 211 6900

Lennox Castle Hospital
Lennoxtown, Glasgow, G65 7LB
01360 329200

Lenzie Hospital
Auchinloch Road, Kirkintilloch,
Glasgow, G66 5DF
0141 776 1208

Leverndale Hospital
510 Crookston Road, Glasgow,
G53 7TU
0141 211 6400

Lightburn Hospital
966 Carntyne Road, Glasgow, G32 6ND
0141 774 5102

Maryhill Health Centre
41 Shawpark Street, Glasgow, G20 9DR
0141 531 8700

Mearnskirk Hospital
Newton Mearns, Glasgow, G77 5RZ
0141 201 6000

Parkhead Health Centre
101 Salamanca Street, Glasgow,
G31 5NA
0141 531 9000

Parkhead Hospital
81 Salamanca Street, Glasgow,
G31 5ES
0141 554 7951

Pollock Health Centre
21 Cowglen Road, Glasgow, G53 6EQ
0141 880 8899

Possilpark Health Centre
85 Denmark Street, Glasgow, G22 5EG
0141 531 6120

Queen Mother's Hospital
Yorkhill, Glasgow, 63 8SH
0141 201 0550

Royal Hospital for Sick Children
Yorkhill, Glasgow, G3 8SJ
0141 201 0000

Ruchill Hospital
Bilsland Drive, Glasgow, G20 9NB
0141 946 7120

Rutherglen Health Centre
130 Stonelaw Road, Rutherglen,
Glasgow, G73 2PQ
0141 531 6000

Rutherglen Maternity Hospital
120 Stonelaw Road, Rutherglen,
Glasgow, G73 2PG 0141 201 6060

Shettleston Health Centre
420 Old Shettleston Road, Glasgow,
G32 7JZ
0141 531 6200

Southern General Hospital
1345 Govan Road, Glasgow, G51 4TF
0141 201 1100

Springburn Health Centre
200 Springburn Way, Glasgow, G21 1TR
0141 558 0101

Stobhill General Hospital
133 Balornock Road, Glasgow, G21 3UW
0141 201 3907

Thornliebank Health Centre
20 Kennishead Road, Glasgow, G46 8NY
0141 531 6900

Townhead Health Centre
16 Alexandra Parade, Glasgow, G31 2ES
0141 531 8900

Victoria Geriatric Unit
100 Mansionhouse Road, Glasgow,
G41 3DX
0141 201 6167

Victoria Infirmary
Langside Road, Glasgow, G42 9TY
0141 201 6000

Western Infirmary
Dumbarton Road, Glasgow, G11 6NT
0141 211 2000

Woodilee Hospital
Lenzie, Glasgow, G66 3UG
0141 777 8000

Woodside Health Centre
Barr Street, Glasgow, G20 7LR
0141 531 9200

A selection of leisure, recreational and cultural attractions in Renfrew District:

Barrhead Sports' Centre
The Centre contains swimming pools, sports halls, activity rooms and saunasuite. Bar and restaurant facilities add to the wide range of sporting and leisure activities available.

Barshaw Park, Glasgow Road, Paisley
The park is extensive with formal and informal areas. It adjoins the public golf course and incorporates a boating pond, playgrounds, model "ride-on" railway and a nature corner.

Castle Semple Country Park, Lochwinnoch
Castle Semple Loch is a popular feature for sailing and fishing. Canoes, rowing boats and sailing boards for hire. Fishing permits available. 01505 842882

Coats Observatory
The Observatory has traditionally recorded astronomical and meteorological information since 1882. Now installed with a satellite picture receiver, it is one of the best equipped Observatories in the country. Monday, Tuesday, Thursday 2-8 p.m., Wednesday, Friday, Saturday 10 a.m. - 5 p.m. 0141 889 3151

Erskine Bridge (Toll)
The bridge is an impressive high level structure opened by HRH Princess Anne in 1971 and provides a direct link from Renfrew District to Loch Lomond and the Trossachs. The bridge replaced the Erskine Ferry and affords extensive views up and down river to pedestrian users.

Finlaystone Estate
Off the A8 at Langbank. The Estate is now a garden centre with woodland walks. The house has connections with John Knox and Robert Burns and is open April to August on Sundays from 2.30 - 4.30 p.m. At other times groups by appointment. Estate open all year round. 0147 554 285

Formakin Estate, By Bishopton
A group of buildings and landscaped grounds designed in the Arts and Crafts style at the turn of the century. The estate has a visitor centre, tea room and offers walks, trails, picnic areas and play areas. Open 7 days 11a.m. - 6 p.m. 01505 863400

Gleniffer Braes Country Park, Glenfield Road, Paisley
1,000 breathtaking acres including Glen Park nature trail, picnic and children's play areas. Open dawn till dusk, the park affords extensive walks and spectacular views from this elevated moorland area, and contains an area reserved for model aero flying. 0141 884 3794

Houston Village
Houston was developed in the 18th century as an estate village. The traditional smiddy building, village pubs and terraced houses combine to create a quiet, sleepy atmosphere which has successfully survived the development of extensive modern housing on its periphery.

Inchinnan Bridges
Early 19th century stone bridges over the White Cart and Black Cart rivers close to St. Conval's stone, and the site of the Inchinnan Church which houses the graves of the Knights Templar, whose order was introduced to Scotland in 1153 by King David I.

Johnstone Castle
The remnants of a 1700 building formerly a much larger structure but demolished in the 1950's. The castle has significant historical links with the Cochrane and Houston families, major landowners who were instrumental in the development of the Burgh of Johnstone.

Kilbarchan Village
A good example of an 18th Century weaving village with many original buildings still fronting the narrow streets. A focal point is the steeple building in the square, originally a school and meal market and now used as public meeting rooms. A cycle route/footpath system links it to Glasgow and the Clyde Coast.

Lagoon Leisure Centre, Paisley
Ultra-modern complex housing superb ice rink and extensive "fun" pool featuring artificial wave machine and water slides. Also has cafe/bar facilities. Unique within the area, the complex is easily reached by public transport and has ample parking. Monday - Friday 10 a.m. - 10 p.m., Saturday and Sunday 10 a.m. - 5.00 p.m. 0141 889 4000

Laigh Kirk, Paisley
Originally built in 1738, the Laigh Kirk has been converted to an Arts Centre, with a theatre, workshop, bistro and bar open daily 10 a.m. - 11 p.m. For further information 0141 887 1010

Linwood Sports Centre
A wide range of indoor and outdoor sporting activities include football and rugby pitches, games hall, squash courts, BMX track, fitness trail, tennis courts and conditioning suite.

Lochwinnoch Village
An attractive rural village close to the Castle Semple Water Park, Muirshiel Country Park and the R.S.P.B. nature reserve, Lochwinnoch contains a small local museum with displays reflecting agricultural, social and industrial aspects of village life. Museum open Monday, Wednesday and Friday 10 a.m. - 1 p.m., 2 - 5 p.m. and 6 - 8 p.m. Tuesday and Saturday 10 a.m. - 1 p.m. and 2- 5 p.m. Open most days throughout the year, visitors should telephone 01505 842615

Muirshiel Country Park
Four miles north of Lochwinnoch, the park features trails of varying length radiating from the Information Centre. Open daily 9a.m.-4.30 p.m. (Winter), 9a.m. - 7.30 p.m. (Summer). 01505 842803

Paisley Abbey
Birthplace of the Stewart Dynasty, the Abbey dates, in part, to the 12th century and features regimental flags, relics, the Barochan Cross and beautiful stained glass windows.
Monday - Saturday 10 a.m. - 12.30 p.m., 1.30- 3.30 p.m. 0141 889 3630

Paisley Arts Centre
Converted 18th century church. Performing arts, works by local artists and participatory events and includes bar and bistro. Box office open 7 days 10 a.m. - 8 p.m. Further information 0141 887 1007

Paisley Museum and Art Gallery, High Street, Paisley
In addition to the world famous collection of Paisley shawls, the Museum traces the history of the Paisley pattern, the development of weaving techniques and houses collections of local and natural history, ceramics and paintings. Monday - Saturday 10 a.m - 5 p.m. 0141 8893151

Paisley Town Hall
A Renaissance style building by the River Cart in the heart of Paisley, it features a slim clock tower and houses a Tourist Information Centre. It accommodates many exhibitions during the year and it is also available for conferences and functions. Monday - Saturday 9 a.m. - 5 p.m. 0141 887 1007

Paisley Town Trail
An easy to follow route taking in the town's historic and architecturally significant buildings. Visitors can spend an hour or two walking round the trail and referring to a printed guide and wall plaques on the main buildings.

Renfrew Town Hall
The Town Hall has a "fairy-tale" style to its 105 feet high spire and was the administrative centre of the Royal Burgh of Renfrew. Originally the principal town in the area, Renfrew was strategically placed on the River Clyde, and a passenger ferry continues to operate daily.

Robert Tannahill, Weaver Poet
The works of Tannahill rank with those of Burns. Born in 1774 he took his own life in 1810 and is buried in a nearby graveyard. Visitors can visit his early home, site of his death, and his grave, and read his works in Paisley Library.

Royal Society for Protection of Birds, Lochwinnoch
An interesting visitor centre with observation tower, hides, displays and gift shop. Thursday, Friday, Saturday and Sunday 10a.m. - 5 p.m. Shop open 7 days. 01505 842663

Sma' Shot Cottages, Paisley
Fully restored and furnished artisan's house of the Victorian era; exhibition room displaying photographs plus artefacts of local interest. 18th Century weaver's loomshop with combined living quarters. Open Wednesday & Saturday May - September 1-5 p.m. Group visits arranged by appointment. Tel: 0141 812 2513 or 0141 889 0530

The Clyde Estuary
Visitors travelling along the rural route to the Old Greenock Road above Langbank village at the western end of the District are able to take advantage of extensive views of the upper and lower Clyde Estuary, the Gareloch and the mountains beyond.

Thomas Coats Memorial Church
Open Monday - Friday 9 a.m. - 12 noon. Visitors should check in advance. Another gift from the Coats family to Paisley, the church was built in 1894 and constructed of red sandstone, is one of the finest Baptist Churches in the country. Tel: 0141 889 9980

Wallace Monument, Elderslie
The monument was erected in 1912 and marks the birthplace of the Scottish Patriot, Sir William Wallace. It stands adjacent to the reconstructed foundation plan of the adjacent Wallace Buildings which dated from the 17th Century.

Weaver's Cottage, Kilbarchan
This cottage, built in 1723, houses the last of the village's 800 looms and demonstrations are still given. It contains displays of weaving and domestic utensils, with Cottage garden and refreshments. Open Monday, Tuesday, Thursday, Friday 2 - 5 p.m., Saturday 10 a.m.- 1 p.m. and 2 - 5 p.m.

INDEX TO STREETS

General Abbreviations

Arc.	Arcade	Dr.	Drive	Mans.	Mansions	Sta.	Station
Av.	Avenue	E.	East	Ms.	Mews	Ter.	Terrace
Bk.	Bank	Est.	Estate	N.	North	Trd.	Trading
Bldgs.	Buildings	Ex.	Exchange	Par.	Parade	Twr.	Tower
Boul.	Boulevard	Fm.	Farm	Pas.	Passage	Vill.	Villa
Bri.	Bridge	Gdns.	Gardens	Pk.	Park	Vills.	Villas
Cen.	Centre,Central	Gra.	Grange	Pl.	Place	Vw.	View
Cft.	Croft	Grn.	Green	Quad.	Quadrant	W.	West
Circ.	Circus	Gro.	Grove	Rd.	Road	Wd.	Wood
Clo.	Close	Ho.	House	Ri.	Rise	Wds.	Woods
Cor.	Corner	Ind.	Industrial	S.	South	Wf.	Wharf
Cotts.	Cottages	La.	Lane	Sch.	School	Wk.	Walk
Cres.	Crescent	Ln.	Loan	Sq.	Square		
Ct.	Court	Lo.	Lodge	St.	Street,Saint		

Postal Town Abbreviations

Clyde.	Clydebank	Ersk.	Erskine	Pais.	Paisley
Coat.	Coatbridge	John.	Johnstone	Renf.	Renfrew

District Abbreviations

Abbots.	Abbotsinch	Clark.	Clarkston	Kirk.	Kirkintilloch
Bail.	Baillieston	Cumb.	Cumbernauld	Linw.	Linwood
Barr.	Barrhead	Cumb.V.	Cumbernauld Village	Mill.Pk.	Milliken Park
Bears.	Bearsden	Dunt.	Duntocher	Mood.	Moodiesburn
Bishop.	Bishopbriggs	Elder.	Elderslie	Muir.	Muirhead
Blan.	Blantyre	Gart.	Gartcosh	Old Kil.	Old Kilpatrick
Both.	Bothwell	Giff.	Giffnock	Ruther.	Rutherglen
Camb.	Cambuslang	Inch.	Inchinnan	Thorn.	Thornliebank
Chry.	Chryston	Kilb.	Kilbarchan	Udd.	Uddingston

NOTES

This index contains some street names in standard text which are followed by another street named in italics. In these cases the street in standard text does not actually appear on the map due to insufficient space but can be located close to the street named in italics.

For streets outwith the Glasgow post town area, the appropriate post town abbreviation is used. Thus the post town for Abbey Close is Paisley and it will be found on page 46 in square K14.

94

Airlour Rd. G43 63 U17
Airth Dr. G52 49 R14
Airth La. G52 49 R14
Airth Pl. G52 49 R14
Airthrey Av. G14 19 R10
Airthrey La. G14 19 Q10
  Airthrey Av.
Aitken St. G31 37 Z12
Aitkenhead Av., Coat. ML5 57 HH14
Aitkenhead Rd. (Udd.) G71 57 HH16
Alasdair Ct. (Barr.) G78 59 M19
Albany Av. G32 39 CC13
Albany Cotts. G13 19 R9
  Crow Rd.
Albany Dr. (Ruther.) G73 65 Y17
Albany Pl. (Both.) G71 69 HH19
  Marguerite Gdns.
Albany Quad. G32 39 CC13
  Mansionhouse Dr.
Albany St. G40 53 Y14
Albany Ter. (Camb.) G72 66 AA18
Albany Way, Pais. PA3 30 K12
  Abbotsburn Way
Albert Av. G42 51 U15
Albert Bri. G1 36 W13
Albert Bri. G5 36 W13
Albert Ct. G41 51 U14
  Albert Dr.
Albert Cross G41 51 U14
Albert Dr. G41 50 T15
Albert Dr. (Bears.) G61 8 S7
Albert Dr. (Ruther.) G73 65 Y17
Albert Rd. G42 51 V15
Albert Rd. (Lenzie) G66 13 CC6
Albert Rd., Clyde. G81 5 L6
Albert Rd., Renf. PA4 17 M10
Alberta Ter. G12 20 T10
  Saltoun St.
Albion Gate, Pais. PA3 30 J13
  Mossvale St.
Albion St. G1 36 W12
Albion St. (Bail.) G69 55 DD14
Albion St., Pais. PA3 30 J13
Alcaig Rd. G52 49 R15
Alder Av. (Kirk.) G66 12 BB5
Alder Ct. (Barr.) G78 59 M19
Alder Pl. G43 62 T17
Alder Pl., John. PA5 44 E15
Alder Rd. G43 62 T17
Alder Rd. (Cumb.) G67 71 QQ3
Alder Rd., Clyde. G81 4 K5
Alderman Pl. G13 19 Q9
Alderman Rd. G13 18 N8
Aldersdyke Pl. (Blan.) G72 68 FF19
Alderside Dr. (Udd.) G71 57 GG16
Alexander St., Clyde. G81 5 L7
Alexandra Av. (Stepps) G33 25 CC9
Alexandra Av. (Lenzie) G66 13 CC6
Alexandra Ct. G31 37 Y12
  Roebank St.
Alexandra Cross G31 37 Y12
  Duke St.
Alexandra Dr., Pais. PA2 45 H14
Alexandra Dr., Renf. PA4 17 M10
Alexandra Gdns. (Kirk.) 13 CC6
  G66
Alexandra Par. G31 37 Y12
Alexandra Pk. (Kirk.) G66 13 CC6
Alexandra Pk. St. G31 37 Y12
Alexandra Rd. (Lenzie) G66 13 CC6
Alford St. G21 22 W10
Alfred La. G12 20 T10
  Cecil St.
Algie St. G41 51 U16
Alice St., Pais. PA2 46 K15
Aline Ct. (Barr.) G78 59 L18
Allan Av., Renf. PA4 32 N11
Allan Glen Gdns. (Bishop.) 11 Y6
  G64
Allan Pl. G40 53 Y14
Allan St. G40 53 Y15
Aliander Gdns. (Bishop.) 10 X6
  G64
Allander Rd. (Bears.) G61 7 Q6
Allander St. G22 22 W10
Allands Av. (Inch.), Renf. 16 J9
  PA4
Allanfauld Rd. (Cumb.) G67 70 NN2
Allanton Av., Pais. PA1 48 N14

Allanton Dr. G52 32 P13
Allerdyce Ct. G15 6 N7
Allerdyce Dr. G15 6 N7
Allerdyce Pl. G15 6 N7
Allerdyce Rd. G15 6 N7
Allerton Gdns. (Bail.) G69 55 DD14
  G73
Allison Dr. (Camb.) G72 66 BB17
Allison Pl. G42 51 V15
  Prince Edward St.
Allison Pl. (Gart.) G69 27 GG10
Allison St. G42 51 V15
Allnach Pl. G34 41 GG12
Alloway Av., Pais. PA2 47 L16
Alloway Cres. (Ruther.) 64 X17
  G73
Alloway Cres., Pais. PA2 47 L16
Alloway Dr. (Ruther.) G73 64 X17
Alloway Dr., Clyde. G81 5 M6
Alloway Dr., Pais. PA2 47 L16
Alloway Rd. G43 62 T17
Alma St. G40 37 Y13
Almond Av., Renf. PA4 32 N11
Almond Bk. (Bears.) G61 7 Q7
  Almond Rd.
Almond Cres., Pais. PA2 45 G15
Almond Dr. (Kirk.) G66 12 BB5
Almond Rd. G33 25 CC9
Almond Rd. (Bears.) G61 7 Q7
Almond St. G33 37 Z11
Almond Vale (Udd.) G71 57 HH16
  Hamilton Vw.
Alness Cres. G52 49 R14
Alpatrick Gdns. (Elder.), 44 E14
  John. PA5
Alpine Gro. (Udd.) G71 57 GG16
Alsatian Av., Clyde. G81 5 M7
Alston La. G40 36 X13
  Claythorn St.
Altnacreag Gdns. (Chry.) 15 HH6
  G69
Alton Gdns. G12 20 T10
  Great George St.
Alton Rd., Pais. PA1 47 M14
Altyre St. G32 54 AA14
Alva Gdns. G52 49 R15
Alva Gate G52 49 R15
Alva Pl. (Lenzie) G66 13 DD6
Alyth Gdns. G52 49 R14
Ambassador Way, Renf. 31 M11
  PA4
  Cockels Ln.
Amisfield St. G20 21 U9
Amochrie Dr., Pais. PA2 45 H16
Amochrie Rd., Pais. PA2 45 G15
Amochrie Way, Pais. PA2 45 G15
Amulree Pl. G32 54 BB14
Amulree St. G32 38 BB13
Ancaster Dr. G13 19 R9
Ancaster La. G13 19 Q8
  Great Western Rd.
Anchor Av., Pais. PA1 47 L14
Anchor Cres., Pais. PA1 47 L14
Anchor Dr., Pais. PA1 47 L14
Anchor Wynd, Pais. PA1 47 L14
Ancroft St. G20 21 V10
Anderson Dr., Renf. PA4 17 M10
Anderson Gdns. (Blan.) 69 GG19
  G72
  Station Rd.
Anderson St. G11 34 S11
Anderston Cross Cen. G2 35 V12
Anderston Quay G3 35 U13
Andrew Av. (Lenzie) G66 13 CC6
Andrew Av., Renf. PA4 18 N10
Andrew Dr., Clyde. G81 17 M8
Andrew Sillars Av. (Camb.) 67 CC17
  G72
Andrews St., Pais. PA3 30 J13
Angle Gate G14 19 Q10
Angus Av. G52 48 P14
Angus Av. (Bishop.) G64 23 Z8
Angus Gdns. (Udd.) G71 57 GG16
Angus La. (Bishop.) G64 11 Z7
Angus Oval G52 48 P14
Angus Pl. G52 48 P14
Angus St. G21 22 X10
Angus St., Clyde. G81 18 N8

Angus Wk. (Udd.) G71 57 HH16
Annan Dr. (Bears.) G61 7 Q6
Annan Dr. (Ruther.) G73 53 Z16
Annan Dr., Pais. PA2 45 G15
Annan Pl., John. PA5 43 C16
Annan St. G42 51 V16
Annandale St. G42 51 V14
Annbank Pl. G31 36 X13
  Annbank St.
Annbank St. G31 36 X13
Anne Av., Renf. PA4 17 M10
Anne Cres. (Lenzie) G66 13 CC6
Annette St. G42 51 V15
Annfield Gdns. (Blan.) G72 68 FF19
Annfield Pl. G31 36 X12
Annick Dr. (Bears.) G61 7 Q7
Annick St. G32 38 BB13
Annick St. (Camb.) G72 67 CC17
Anniesdale Av. (Stepps) 25 CC9
  G33
Anniesland Cres. G14 18 P9
Anniesland Mans. G13 19 R9
  Ancaster Dr.
Anniesland Rd. G13 19 Q9
Anniesland Rd. G14 18 P9
Anson St. G40 52 X14
Anson Way, Renf. PA4 31 M11
  Britannia Way
Anstruther St. G32 38 AA13
Anthony St. G2 35 V12
  Cadogan St.
Antonine Gdns., Clyde. G81 5 L5
Antonine Rd. (Bears.) G61 6 P5
Anwoth St. G32 54 BB14
Appin Rd. G31 37 Y12
Appin Ter. (Ruther.) G73 65 Z18
  Lochaber Dr.
Appin Way (Both.) G71 69 HH18
  Bracken Ter.
Appleby St. G22 21 V10
  Eltham St.
Applecross Gdns. (Chry.) 15 GG6
  G69
Applecross St. G22 21 V10
Appledore Cres. (Both.) 69 HH18
  G71
Apsley La. G11 34 S11
Apsley St. G11 34 S11
Aranthrue Cres., Renf. PA4 17 M10
Aranthrue Dr., Renf. PA4 17 M10
Aray St. G20 20 T9
Arbroath Av. G52 48 P14
Arcadia St. G40 36 X13
Arcan Cres. G15 6 P7
Archerfield Av. G32 54 BB15
Archerfield Cres. G32 54 BB15
Archerfield Dr. G32 54 BB15
Archerfield Gro. G32 54 BB15
Archerhill Av. G13 18 N8
Archerhill Cotts. G13 18 P8
  Archerhill Rd.
Archerhill Cres. G13 18 P8
Archerhill Gdns. G13 18 P8
  Archerhill Rd.
Archerhill Rd. G13 18 P8
Archerhill Sq. G13 18 N8
  Kelso St.
Archerhill St. G13 18 P8
  Archerhill Rd.
Archerhill Ter. G13 18 P8
  Archerhill Rd.
Ard Rd., Renf. PA4 17 L10
Ard St. G32 54 BB14
Ardagie Dr. G32 55 CC16
Ardagie Pl. G32 55 CC16
Ardbeg Av. (Bishop.) G64 11 Z7
Ardbeg Av. (Ruther.) G73 66 AA18
Ardbeg La. G42 51 V15
  Coplaw St.
Ardbeg St. G42 51 V15
Ardconnel St. (Thorn.) G46 61 R18
Arden Av. (Thorn.) G46 61 R19
Arden Dr. (Giff.) G46 62 S19
Arden Pl. (Thorn.) G46 61 R19
  Stewarton Rd.
Ardencraig Cres. G45 64 W19
Ardencraig Dr. G45 64 X19
Ardencraig La. G45 64 W19
  Ardencraig Rd.

Ardencraig Quad. G45	64	X19	Arnisdale Pl. G34	40	EE12	Ashley St. G3	35	U11
Ardencraig Rd. G45	64	W19	Arnisdale Rd. G34	40	EE12	Ashmore Rd. G43	63	U17
Ardencraig St. G45	65	Y19	Arnisdale Way (Ruther.)	65	Y18	Ashmore Rd. G44	63	U17
Ardencraig Ter. G45	64	X19	G73			Ashton Gdns. G12	34	T11
Ardenlea Rd. (Udd.) G71	57	GG16	*Shieldaig Dr.*			*University Av.*		
Ardenlea St. G40	53	Y14	Arniston St. G32	38	AA12	Ashton La. G12	34	T11
Ardery St. G11	34	S11	Arnol Pl. G33	39	DD12	*University Av.*		
Apsley St.			Arnold Av. (Bishop.) G64	11	Y7	Ashton La. N. G12	34	T11
Ardessie Pl. G20	20	T9	Arnold St. G20	21	V9	*University Av.*		
Ardessie St. G23	8	T7	Arnott Way (Camb.) G72	66	BB17	Ashton Pl. G12	20	T10
Torrin Rd.			Arnprior Cres. G45	64	W18	*Byres Rd.*		
Ardfern St. G32	54	BB14	Arnprior Gdns. (Chry.) G69	15	GG7	Ashton Rd. G12	34	T11
Ardgay Pl. G32	54	BB14	*Braeside Av.*			*University Av.*		
Ardgay St. G32	54	BB14	Arnprior Quad. G45	64	W18	Ashton Rd. (Ruther.) G73	53	Y15
Ardgay Way (Ruther.) G73	65	Y18	Arnprior Rd. G45	64	W18	Ashton Ter. G12	34	T11
Ardgour Dr. (Linw.), Pais.	28	E13	Arnprior St. G45	64	W18	*University Av.*		
PA3			Arnside Av. (Giff.) G46	62	T18	Ashton Way, Pais. PA2	45	G16
Ardgowan Av., Pais. PA2	46	K14	Arnthern St. (Camb.) G72	67	CC17	Ashtree Rd. G43	50	T16
Ardgowan Dr. (Udd.) G71	57	GG16	Arnwood Dr. G12	20	S9	Ashvale Cres. G21	22	X10
Ardgowan St., Pais. PA2	46	K15	Aron Ter. (Camb.) G72	66	AA18	Aspen Dr. G21	23	Y10
Ardholm St. G32	38	BB13	Aros Dr. G52	49	R15	*Foresthall Dr.*		
Ardhu Pl. G15	6	N6	Aros La. G52	49	Q15	Aspen Pl., John. PA5	44	E15
Ardlamont Sq. (Linw.),	28	F13	*Aros Dr.*			Aster Dr. G45	65	Y18
Pais. PA3			Arran Av. (Abbots.), Pais.	30	K11	Aster Gdns. G53	61	Q18
Ardlaw St. G51	33	R13	PA3			*Waukglen Cres.*		
Ardle Rd. G43	63	U17	Arran Dr. (Giff.) G46	62	S19	Athelstane Dr. (Cumb.) G67	70	MM4
Ardlui St. G32	54	AA14	Arran Dr. G52	49	R14	Athelstane Rd. G13	19	Q8
Ardmaleish Cres. G45	64	X19	Arran Dr. (Cumb.) G67	70	MM4	Athena Way (Udd.) G71	57	HH16
Ardmaleish Rd. G45	64	W19	Arran Dr., John. PA5	43	C15	Athol Av. G52	32	N12
Ardmaleish St. G45	64	X19	Arran Dr., Pais. PA2	46	K16	Athol Ter. (Udd.) G71	57	GG15
Ardmaleish Ter. G45	64	X19	Arran La. (Chry.) G69	15	HH7	Athole Gdns. G12	20	T10
Ardmay Cres. G44	52	W16	*Burnbrae Av.*			Athole La. G12	20	T10
Ardmillan St. G33	38	AA12	Arran Pl., Clyde. G81	5	M7	*Saltoun St.*		
Ardmory Av. G42	52	W16	Arran Pl. (Linw.), Pais. PA3	28	E13	Atholl Cres., Pais. PA1	32	N13
Ardmory La. G42	52	X16	Arran Rd., Renf. PA4	31	M11	Atholl Gdns. (Bishop.) G64	11	Y6
Ardmory Pl. G42	52	X16	Arran Ter. (Ruther.) G73	64	X17	Atholl Gdns. (Ruther.) G73	66	AA18
Ardnahoe Av. G42	52	W16	Arriochmill Rd. G20	20	T10	Atholl La. (Chry.) G69	15	HH7
Ardnahoe Pl. G42	52	W16	*Kelvin Dr.*			Atholl Pl. (Linw.), Pais. PA3	28	E13
Ardneil Rd. G51	33	R13	Arrochar Ct. G23	21	U8	Atlas Pl. G21	22	X10
Ardnish St. G51	33	R12	*Sunningdale Rd.*			Atlas Rd. G21	22	X10
Ardo Gdns. G51	34	S13	Arrochar Dr. G23	8	T7	Atlas Sq. G21	22	X10
Ardoch Gro. (Camb.) G72	66	AA17	Arrochar St. G23	20	T8	*Ayr St.*		
Ardoch Rd. (Bears.) G61	8	S5	Arrol Pl. G40	53	Y14	Atlas St., Clyde. G81	17	L8
Ardoch St. G22	22	W10	Arrol St. G52	32	N12	*Cart St.*		
Ardoch Way (Chry.) G69	15	GG7	Arrowsmith Av. G13	19	Q8	Attlee Av., Clyde. G81	5	M7
Braeside Av.			Arthur Av. (Barr.) G78	59	L19	Attlee Pl., Clyde. G81	5	M7
Ardshiel Rd. G51	33	R12	Arthur Rd., Pais. PA2	46	K16	*Attlee Av.*		
Ardsloy La. G14	18	P10	Arthur St. G3	34	T11	Attow Rd. G43	62	S17
Ardsloy Pl.			Arthur St., Pais. PA1	30	J13	Auburn Dr. (Barr.) G78	59	M19
Ardsloy Pl. G14	18	P10	Arthurlie Av. (Barr.) G78	59	M19	Auchans Rd. (Houston),	28	E11
Ardtoe Cres. G33	25	DD9	Arthurlie Dr. (Giff.) G46	62	T19	John. PA6		
Ardtoe Pl. G33	25	DD9	Arthurlie St. G51	33	R12	Auchencrow St. G34	40	FF12
Arduthie Rd. G51	33	R12	Arthurlie St. (Barr.) G78	59	M19	Auchengeich Rd. (Mood.)	14	FF6
Ardwell Rd. G52	49	R14	Arundel Dr. G42	51	V16	G69		
Argosy Way, Renf. PA4	31	M11	Arundel Dr. (Bishop.) G64	11	Y6	Auchenglen Dr. (Chry.)	15	GG7
Britannia Way			Asbury Ct. (Linw.), Pais.	28	F13	G69		
Argyle St. G2	35	V12	PA3			Auchengreoch Av., John.	43	C16
Argyle St. G3	34	T11	Ascaig Cres. G52	49	R15	PA5		
Argyle St., Pais. PA1	46	J14	Ascog Rd. (Bears.) G61	7	R7	Auchengreoch Rd., John.	43	C16
Argyll Arc. G2	35	V12	Ascog St. G42	51	V15	PA5		
Argyll Av. (Abbots.), Pais.	30	K11	Ascot Av. G12	19	R9	Auchenlodment Rd., John.	44	E15
PA3			Ascot Ct. G12	20	S9	PA5		
Argyll Av., Renf. PA4	17	L10	Ash Gro. (Bishop.) G64	11	Y7	Auchentorlie Quad., Pais.	47	L14
Argyll Av., Clyde. G81	5	M7	Ash Gro. (Kirk.) G66	12	BB5	PA1		
Arisaig Dr. G52	49	R14	Ash Gro. (Bail.) G69	41	GG13	Auchentorlie St. G11	33	R11
Arisaig Dr. (Bears.) G61	8	S6	Ash Gro. (Udd.) G71	57	HH16	*Dumbarton Rd.*		
Arisaig Pl. G52	49	R14	Ash Pl., John. PA5	44	E15	Auchentoshan Av., Clyde.	4	K5
Ark La. G31	36	X12	Ash Rd. (Cumb.) G67	71	QQ1	G81		
Arkle Ter. (Camb.) G72	66	AA18	Ash Rd. (Bail.) G69	56	EE14	Auchentoshan Ter. G21	36	X11
Arkleston Cres., Pais. PA3	31	L12	Ash Rd., Clyde. G81	4	K5	Auchentoshan Cotts.	4	J5
Arkleston Rd., Pais. PA1	31	L13	Ash Wk. (Ruther.) G73	65	Z18	(Old Kil.) G60		
Arkleston Rd., Pais. PA3	31	M12	Ashburton La. G12	20	S9	Auchinairn Rd. (Bishop.)	22	X8
Arkleston Rd., Renf. PA4	31	L12	*Ashburton Rd.*			G64		
Arklet Rd. G51	33	R13	Ashburton Rd. G12	20	S9	Auchinbee Way (Cumb.)	70	MM2
Arlington St. G3	35	U11	Ashby Cres. G13	7	R7	G68		
Armadale Ct. G31	37	Y12	Ashcroft Dr. G44	64	X17	*Eastfield Rd.*		
Townmill Rd.			Ashdale Dr. G52	49	R14	Auchingill Path G34	40	FF11
Armadale Path G31	37	Y12	Ashdene Rd. G22	21	V8	*Auchingill Rd.*		
Armadale Pl. G31	37	Y12	Ashfield (Bishop.) G64	11	Y6	Auchingill Pl. G34	40	FF11
Armadale St. G31	37	Y12	Ashfield St. G22	22	W10	Auchingill Rd. G34	40	FF11
Armaleish Dr. G45	64	X19	Ashgill Pl. G22	22	W9	Auchinlea Rd. G34	39	DD11
Armour Pl., John. PA5	44	E14	Ashgill Rd. G22	21	V9	Auchinleck Av. G33	24	AA9
Armour St. G31	36	X13	Ashgrove (Mood.) G69	41	GG13	Auchinleck Cres. G33	24	AA9
Armour St., John. PA5	44	E14	Ashgrove St. G40	53	Y15	Auchinleck Dr. G33	24	AA9
Armstrong Cres. (Udd.)	57	HH16	Ashkirk Dr. G52	49	R14	Auchinleck Gdns. G33	24	AA9
G71			Ashlea Dr. (Giff.) G46	62	T18	Auchinleck Rd. G33	24	AA8
Arngask Rd. G51	33	R12	Ashley Dr. (Both.) G71	69	HH19	Auchinloch Rd. (Lenzie)	13	CC6
Arnhall Pl. G52	49	R14	Ashley La. G3	35	U11	G66		
Arnholm Pl. G52	49	R14	*Woodlands Rd.*			Auchinloch St. G21	22	X10

Auchmannoch Av., Pais. 32 N13
PA1
Auckland Pl., Clyde. G81 4 J6
Auckland St. G22 21 V10
Auld Kirk Rd. (Camb.) G72 67 CC18
Auld Rd., The (Cumb.) G67 71 PP2
Auld St., Clyde. G81 4 K6
Auldbar Rd. G52 49 R14
Auldbar Ter., Pais. PA2 47 L15
Auldburn Pl. G43 62 S17
Auldburn Rd.
Auldburn Rd. G43 62 S17
Auldearn Rd. G21 23 Z8
Auldgirth Rd. G52 49 R14
Auldhouse Av. G43 62 S17
Thornliebank Rd.
Auldhouse Gdns. G43 62 S17
Auldhouse Rd. G43 62 S17
Auldhouse Ter. G43 62 T17
Auldhouse Rd.
Aultbea St. G22 21 V8
Aultmore Rd. G33 39 DD12
Aurs Cres. (Barr.) G78 59 M19
Aurs Dr. (Barr.) G78 59 M19
Aurs Glen (Barr.) G78 59 M19
Aurs Pl. (Barr.) G78 59 M19
Aurs Rd. (Barr.) G78 59 M18
Aursbridge Cres. (Barr.) 59 M19
G78
Aursbridge Dr. (Barr.) G78 59 M19
Austen La. G13 19 R9
Skaterig La.
Austen Rd. G13 19 R9
Avenel Rd. G13 7 R7
Avenue, The (Kilb.), John. 42 B15
PA10
Low Barholm
Avenue End Rd. G33 24 BB10
Avenue St. G40 37 Y13
Avenue St. (Ruther.) G73 53 Y15
Avenuehead Rd. (Chry.) 15 GG7
G69
Avenuepark St. G20 21 U10
Aviemore Gdns. (Bears.) 8 S5
G61
Aviemore Rd. G52 49 R15
Avoch Dr. (Thorn.) G46 61 R18
Avoch St. G34 40 EE11
Avon Av. (Bears.) G61 8 S6
Avon Dr. (Bishop.) G64 23 Y8
Avon Dr. (Linw.), Pais. PA3 28 E13
Avon Rd. (Giff.) G46 62 S19
Avon Rd. (Bishop.) G64 23 Y8
Avon St. G5 35 U13
Avonbank Rd. (Ruther.) 52 X16
G73
Avondale Dr., Pais. PA1 31 L13
Avondale St. G33 38 BB11
Avonhead Av. (Cumb.) 70 MM4
G67
Avonhead Gdns. (Cumb.) 70 MM4
G67
Avonhead Pl. (Cumb.) G67 70 MM4
Avonhead Rd. (Cumb.) G67 70 MM4
Avonspark St. G21 23 Y10
Aylmer Rd. G43 63 U17
Ayr Rd. (Giff.) G46 62 S19
Ayr St. G21 22 X10
Aytoun Rd. G41 50 T14

B

Back Causeway G31 37 Z13
Back Sneddon St., Pais. 30 K13
PA3
Backmuir Rd. G15 6 P6
Bagnell St. G21 22 X9
Baillie Dr. (Both.) G71 69 HH18
Baillie Wynd (Udd.) G71 57 HH16
Baillieston Rd. G32 55 CC14
Baillieston Rd. (Udd.) G71 56 EE14
Bain Sq. G40 36 X13
Bain St.
Bain St. G40 36 X13
Bainsford St. G32 38 AA13
Baird Av. G52 32 N12
Baird Ct., Clyde. G81 5 L7
North Av.
Baird Dr. (Bears.) G61 7 Q5

Baird St. G4 36 W11
Bairdsbrae G4 21 V10
Possil Rd.
Baker Pl. G41 51 U15
Baker St.
Baker St. G41 51 U15
Bakewell Rd. (Bail.) G69 40 EE13
Balaclava St. G2 35 V13
McAlpine St.
Balado Rd. G33 39 DD12
Balbeg St. G51 33 R13
Balbeggie Pl. G32 55 CC14
Balbeggie St. G32 55 CC14
Balblair Rd. G52 49 R15
Balcarres Av. G12 20 T9
Balcomie St. G33 38 BB11
Balcurvie Rd. G34 40 EE11
Baldinnie Rd. G34 40 EE12
Baldorran Cres. (Cumb.) 70 LL2
G68
Baldovan Cres. G33 39 DD12
Baldovie Rd. G52 49 Q14
Baldragon Rd. G34 40 EE11
Baldric Rd. G13 19 Q9
Baldwin Av. G13 7 Q7
Balerno Dr. G52 49 R14
Balfluig St. G34 39 DD11
Balfour St. G20 20 T9
Balfron Rd. G51 33 R12
Balfron Rd., Pais. PA1 31 M13
Balgair Dr., Pais. PA1 31 L13
Balgair St. G22 21 V9
Balgair Ter. G32 38 BB13
Balglass St. G22 21 V10
Balgonie Av., Pais. PA2 45 H15
Balgonie Dr., Pais. PA2 46 J15
Balgonie Rd. G52 49 R14
Balgonie Wds., Pais. PA2 46 J15
Balgownie Cres. (Thorn.) 62 S19
G46
Balgray Cres. (Barr.) G78 60 N19
Balgraybank St. G21 23 Y10
Balgrayhill Rd. G21 22 X9
Balintore St. G32 38 BB13
Baliol La. G3 35 U11
Woodlands Rd.
Baliol St. G3 35 U11
Ballaig Av. (Bears.) G61 7 Q5
Ballaig Cres. (Stepps) G33 25 CC9
Ballantay Quad. G45 65 Y18
Ballantay Rd. G45 65 Y18
Ballantay Ter. G45 65 Y18
Ballantyne Rd. G52 32 P12
Ballater Dr. (Bears.) G61 7 R7
Ballater Dr., Pais. PA2 47 L15
Ballater Dr. (Inch.), Renf. 16 J8
PA4
Ballater Pl. G5 52 W14
Ballater St. G5 36 W13
Ballayne Dr. (Chry.) G69 15 HH7
Ballindalloch Dr. G31 37 Y12
Ballindarroch La. G31 37 Y12
Meadowpark St.
Balloch Gdns. G52 49 R14
Balloch Loop Rd. (Cumb.) 70 MM3
G68
Balloch Vw. (Cumb.) G67 70 NN3
Ballochmill Rd. (Ruther.) 53 Z16
G73
Ballogie Rd. G44 51 V16
Balmarino Pl. (Bishop.) G64 11 Z7
Balmartin Rd. G23 8 T7
Balmerino Pl. (Bishop.) G64 23 Z8
Angus Av.
Balmoral Cres. G42 51 V15
Queens Dr.
Balmoral Cres. (Inch.), 16 K9
Renf. PA4
Balmoral Dr. G32 54 BB16
Balmoral Dr. (Bears.) G61 8 S7
Balmoral Dr. (Camb.) G72 66 AA17
Balmoral Gdns. (Udd.) G71 57 GG15
Balmoral Gdns. (Blan.) G72 68 FF19
Balmoral Rd. (Elder.), 44 E15
John. PA5
Balmoral St. G14 18 P10
Balmore Pl. G22 21 V9
Balmore Rd.
Balmore Rd. G22 21 V8

Balmore Rd. G23 9 U7
Balmore Rd. (Milngavie) 9 U5
G62
Balmore Sq. G22 21 V9
Balmuildy Rd. G23 9 V6
Balmuildy Rd. (Bishop.) G64 9 V6
Balornock Rd. G21 23 Y9
Balruddery Pl. (Bishop.) 23 Z8
G64
Balshagray Av. G11 19 R10
Balshagray Cres. G14 33 R11
Dumbarton Rd.
Balshagray Dr. G11 19 R10
Balshagray La. G11 19 R10
Balshagray Pl. G11 19 R10
Balshagray Dr.
Baltic Ct. G40 53 Y14
Baltic St.
Baltic La. G40 53 Y14
Baltic Pl. G40 52 X14
Baltic St. G40 53 Y14
Balure St. G31 37 Z12
Balvaird Cres. (Ruther.) G73 53 Y16
Balvaird Dr. (Ruther.) G73 53 Y16
Balveny St. G33 39 CC11
Balvicar Dr. G42 51 U15
Balvicar St. G42 51 U15
Balvie Av. G15 6 P7
Balvie Av. (Giff.) G46 62 T19
Banavie Rd. G11 20 S10
Banchory Av. G43 62 S17
Banchory Av. (Inch.), Renf. 16 J8
PA4
Banchory Cres. (Bears.) G61 8 S7
Banff St. G33 38 BB11
Bangorshill St. (Thorn.) 61 R18
G46
Bank Rd. G32 55 CC16
Bank St. G12 35 U11
Bank St. (Camb.) G72 66 BB17
Bank St. (Barr.) G78 59 M19
Bank St., Pais. PA1 46 K14
Bankbrae Av. G53 60 P17
Bankend St. G33 38 BB11
Bankfoot Dr. G52 48 P14
Bankfoot Rd. G52 48 P14
Bankfoot Rd., Pais. PA3 29 H13
Bankglen Rd. G15 6 P6
Bankhall St. G42 51 V15
Bankhead Av. G13 18 P9
Bankhead Dr. (Ruther.) G73 53 Y16
Bankhead Rd. (Ruther.) G73 64 X17
Bankier St. G40 36 X13
Banknock St. G32 38 AA13
Bankside Av., John. PA5 43 D14
Banktop Pl., John. PA5 43 D14
Banling Grn. Rd. G44 63 V17
Clarkston Rd.
Bannatyne Av. G31 37 Y12
Banner Dr. G13 7 Q7
Banner Rd. G13 7 Q7
Bannercross Av. (Bail.) G69 40 EE13
Bannercross Dr. (Bail.) G69 40 EE13
Bannercross Gdns. (Bail.) 40 EE13
G69
Bannercross Dr.
Bannerman Pl., Clyde. G81 5 M7
Bannerman St., Clyde. G81 5 L7
Bantaskin St. G20 20 T8
Banton Pl. G33 40 EE12
Barassie Ct. (Both.) G71 69 GG19
Barassie Cres. (Cumb.) G68 70 NN1
Barbae Pl. (Both.) G71 69 HH18
Hume Dr.
Barberry Av. G53 60 P19
Barberry Gdns. G53 60 P19
Barberry Av.
Barberry Pl. G53 60 P19
Barberry Av.
Barbreck Rd. G42 51 U15
Pollokshaws Rd.
Barcaldine Av. (Chry.) G69 14 EE7
Barclay Av. (Elder.), John. 44 E15
PA5
Barclay Sq., Renf. PA4 31 L11
Barclay St. G21 22 X9
Balgrayhill Rd.
Barcraigs Dr., Pais. PA2 46 K16
Bard Av. G13 18 P8

97

Street	Page	Grid
Bardowie St. G22	21	V10
Bardrain Av. (Elder.), John. PA5	44	F15
Bardrain Rd., Pais. PA2	46	J16
Bardrill Dr. (Bishop.) G64	10	X7
Bardykes Rd. (Blan.) G72	68	FF19
Barfillan Dr. G52	33	R13
Barfillan Rd. G52	33	R13
Bargaran Rd. G53	48	P14
Bargarron Dr., Pais. PA3	31	L12
Bargeddie St. G33	37	Z11
Barholm Sq. G33	39	CC11
Barke Rd. (Cumb.) G67	71	PP2
Barlanark Av. G32	39	CC12
Barlanark Cres. G33	39	CC12
Barlanark Dr. G33	39	CC12
Barlanark Pl. G32	39	CC13
Hallhill Rd.		
Barlanark Pl. G33	39	DD12
Barlanark Rd. G33	39	CC12
Barlia Dr. G45	64	X18
Barlia St. G45	64	X18
Barlia Ter. G45	64	X18
Barloch St. G22	22	W10
Barlogan Av. G52	33	R13
Barlogan Quad. G52	33	R13
Barmill Rd. G43	62	S17
Barmulloch Rd. G21	23	Y10
Barn Grn. (Kilb.), John. PA10	42	B14
Barnard Gdns. (Bishop.) G64	11	Y6
Barnard Ter. G40	53	Y14
Barnbeth Rd. G53	48	P15
Barnes Rd. G20	21	V9
Barnes St. (Barr.) G78	59	L19
Barnflat St. (Ruther.) G73	53	Y15
Barnhill Dr. G21	23	Y10
Foresthall Dr.		
Barnkirk Av. G15	6	P6
Barns St., Clyde. G81	5	M7
Barnsford Av. (Inch.), Renf. PA4	16	J9
Barnsford Rd. (Abbots.), Pais. PA3	29	H12
Barnsford Rd. (Inch.), Renf. PA4	29	H12
Barnton St. G32	38	AA12
Barnwell Ter. G51	33	R12
Barochan Cres., Pais. PA3	45	H14
Barochan Rd. G53	48	P14
Baron Rd., Pais. PA3	31	L13
Baron St., Renf. PA4	31	M11
Baronald Dr. G12	20	S9
Baronald Gate G12	20	S9
Baronald St. (Ruther.) G73	53	Y15
Baronhill (Cumb.) G67	71	PP2
Barons Gate (Both.) G71	69	GG18
Baronscourt Dr., Pais. PA1	45	G14
Baronscourt Gdns., Pais. PA1	45	G14
Baronscourt Rd., Pais. PA1	45	G14
Barony Dr. (Bail.) G69	40	EE13
Barony Gdns. (Bail.) G69	40	EE13
Barony Wynd (Bail.) G69	41	GG13
Dukes Rd.		
Barr Cres., Clyde. G81	5	L5
Barr Gro. (Udd.) G71	57	HH16
Barr Pl., Pais. PA1	46	J14
Barr St. G20	21	V10
Barra Av., Renf. PA4	31	M11
Barra Cres. (Old Kil.) G60	4	J5
Barra Gdns. (Old Kil.) G60	4	J5
Barra Rd.		
Barra Rd. (Old Kil.) G60	4	J5
Barra St. G20	20	T8
Barrachnie Ct. (Bail.) G69	39	DD13
Barrachnie Cres.		
Barrachnie Cres. (Bail.) G69	39	DD13
Barrachnie Rd. (Bail.) G69	39	DD13
Barrack St. G4	36	X13
Barrhead Rd. G43	49	Q16
Barrhead Rd. G53	48	N16
Barrhead Rd., Pais. PA2	47	L14
Barrhill Cres. (Kilb.), John. PA10	42	B15
Barrie Quad., Clyde. G81	5	L6
Barrie Rd. G52	32	P12
Barrington Dr. G4	35	U11
Barrisdale Rd. G20	20	T8
Barrisdale Way (Ruther.) G73	65	Y18
Barrland Dr. (Giff.) G46	62	T18
Barrland St. G41	51	V14
Barrochan Rd., John. PA5	43	D14
Barrowfield St. G40	37	Y13
Barrwood Pl. (Udd.) G71	57	HH16
Barrwood St. G33	38	AA11
Barscube Ter., Pais. PA2	46	K14
Barshaw Dr., Pais. PA1	31	L13
Barshaw Pl., Pais. PA1	31	M13
Barshaw Rd. G52	32	N13
Barskiven Rd., Pais. PA1	45	G14
Barterholm Rd., Pais. PA2	46	K15
Bartholomew St. G40	53	Y14
Bartiebeith Rd. G33	39	DD12
Basset Av. G13	18	P8
Basset Cres. G13	18	P8
Bath La. G2	35	V12
Blythswood St.		
Bath La. W. G3	35	U12
North St.		
Bath St. G2	35	V12
Bathgate St. G31	37	Y13
Bathgo Av., Pais. PA1	48	N14
Batson St. G42	51	V15
Battle Pl. G41	51	U16
Battleburn St. G32	54	BB14
Battlefield Av. G42	51	V16
Battlefield Cres. G42	51	V16
Battlefield Gdns.		
Battlefield Gdns. G42	51	V16
Battlefield Rd. G42	51	V16
Bavelaw St. G33	39	CC11
Bayfield Av. G15	6	P6
Bayfield Ter. G15	6	P6
Beaconsfield Rd. G12	20	S9
Beard Cres. (Gart.) G69	27	GG9
Beardmore Cotts. (Inch.), Renf. PA4	16	K9
Beardmore St., Clyde. G81	4	J6
Beardmore Way, Clyde. G81	4	J7
Bearford Dr. G52	32	P13
Bearsden Rd. G13	19	R9
Bearsden Rd. (Bears.) G61	19	R9
Beaton Rd. G41	51	U15
Beatson Wynd (Udd.) G71	57	HH15
Beattock St. G31	37	Z13
Beatty St., Clyde. G81	4	J6
Beaufort Av. G43	62	T17
Beaufort Gdns. (Bishop.) G64	10	X7
Beauly Dr., Pais. PA2	45	G15
Beauly Pl. G20	20	T9
Beauly Pl. (Bishop.) G64	11	Z7
Beauly Pl. (Chry.) G69	14	FF7
Beauly Rd. (Bail.) G69	56	EE14
Beaumont Gate G12	34	T11
Bedale Rd. (Bail.) G69	55	DD14
Bedford Av., Clyde. G81	5	M7
Onslow Rd.		
Bedford La. G5	35	V13
Bedford Row G5	35	V13
Dunmore St.		
Bedford St. G5	35	V13
Bedlay Ct. (Chry.) G69	15	HH6
Bedlay St. G21	22	X10
Petershill Rd.		
Bedlay Vw. (Udd.) G71	57	HH15
Bedlay Wk. (Chry.) G69	15	HH6
Beech Av. G41	50	S14
Beech Av. (Bail.) G69	40	EE13
Beech Av. (Camb.) G72	66	AA17
Beech Av. (Ruther.) G73	65	Z18
Beech Av. (Elder.), John. PA5	44	F15
Beech Av., Pais. PA2	47	L15
Beech Dr., Clyde. G81	5	L5
Beech Gdns. (Bail.) G69	40	EE13
Beech Pl. (Bishop.) G64	23	Y8
Beech Rd. (Bishop.) G64	23	Y8
Beech Rd. (Lenzie) G66	13	CC5
Beech Rd., John. PA5	43	C15
Beechcroft Pl. (Blan.) G72	69	GG19
Beeches Av., Clyde. G81	4	K5
Beeches Rd., Clyde. G81	4	K5
Beeches Ter., Clyde. G81	4	K5
Beechgrove St. G40	53	Y15
Beechlands Av. G44	63	U19
Beechmount Cotts. G14	18	N9
Dumbarton Rd.		
Beechmount Rd. (Lenzie) G66	13	CC6
Beechwood Av. G11	19	R10
Beechwood Dr.		
Beechwood Av. (Ruther.) G73	65	Z17
Beechwood Ct. (Bears.) G61	7	R6
Beechwood Dr. G11	19	R10
Beechwood Dr., Renf. PA4	31	L11
Beechwood Gdns. (Mood.) G69	15	GG7
Beechwood Gro. (Barr.) G78	59	M19
Arthurlie Av.		
Beechwood La. (Bears.) G61	7	R6
Beechwood Ct.		
Beechwood Pl. G11	19	R10
Beechwood Dr.		
Beechwood Rd. (Cumb.) G67	70	NN3
Beil Dr. G13	18	N8
Beith Rd., John. PA5	44	E15
Beith Rd. (Mill.Pk.), John. PA10	42	B16
Beith St. G11	34	S11
Belgrave La. G12	21	U10
Belgrave Ter.		
Belgrave Ter. G12	21	U10
Belhaven Cres. La. G12	20	T10
Lorraine Rd.		
Belhaven Ter. G12	20	T10
Belhaven Ter. La. G12	20	T10
Belhaven Ter. W. G12	20	T10
Belhaven Ter. W. La. G12	20	T10
Westbourne Gdns. S.		
Bell St. G1	36	W12
Bell St. G4	36	W13
Bell St., Clyde. G81	17	M8
Bell St., Renf. PA4	17	M10
Bellahouston Dr. G52	49	R14
Bellahouston La. G52	49	R14
Bellairs Pl. (Blan.) G72	68	FF19
Belleisle Av. (Udd.) G71	57	GG16
Belleisle St. G42	51	V15
Bellevue Pl. G21	36	X11
Bellfield Ct. (Barr.) G78	59	L18
Bellfield Cres. (Barr.) G78	59	L18
Bellfield St. G31	37	Y13
Bellflower Av. G53	61	Q18
Bellflower Gdns. G53	61	Q18
Bellflower Pl. G53	61	Q18
Bellgrove St. G31	36	X13
Bellhaven Ter. (Ruther.) G73	65	Z17
Bellrock Cres. G33	38	BB12
Bellrock St. G33	38	BB12
Bellscroft Av. (Ruther.) G73	52	X16
Bellshaugh Gdns. G12	20	T9
Bellshaugh La. G12	20	T9
Bellshaugh Pl. G12	20	T9
Bellshaugh Rd. G12	20	T9
Bellshill Rd. (Udd.) G71	69	GG17
Belltrees Cres., Pais. PA3	45	H14
Bellwood St. G41	51	U16
Belmar Ct. (Linw.), Pais. PA3	28	F13
Belmont Av. (Udd.) G71	57	GG16
Belmont Cres. G12	21	U10
Belmont Dr. (Giff.) G46	62	S18
Belmont Dr. (Ruther.) G73	53	Y16
Belmont Dr. (Barr.) G78	59	M19
Belmont La. G12	21	U10
Great Western Rd.		
Belmont Rd. G21	22	X9
Belmont Rd. (Camb.) G72	66	AA18
Belmont Rd., Pais. PA3	31	L13
Belmont St. G12	21	U10
Belmont St., Clyde. G81	17	L8
Belses Dr. G52	33	Q13
Belses Gdns. G52	33	Q13
Belstane Pl. (Both.) G71	69	HH18
Appledore Cres.		
Belsyde Av. G15	6	P7
Beltane St. G3	35	U12
Beltrees Av. G53	48	P15

Beltrees Cres. G53	48	P15
Beltrees Rd. G53	48	P15
Belvidere Cres. (Bishop.) G64	11	Y6
Bemersyde (Bishop.) G64	11	Z7
Bemersyde Av. G43	62	S17
Bemersyde Rd., Pais. PA2	45	G16
Ben Alder Dr., Pais. PA2	47	M15
Ben Buie Way, Pais. PA2	47	M15
Ben Lawers Dr. (Cumb.) G68	70	MM3
Balloch Loop Rd.		
Ben Ledi Av., Pais. PA2	47	M15
Ben Lui Dr., Pais. PA2	47	M15
Ben Macdui Gdns. G53	61	Q18
Ben More Dr., Pais. PA2	47	M15
Ben Nevis Rd., Pais. PA2	47	M15
Ben Venue Way, Pais. PA2	47	M15
Ben Wyvis Dr., Pais. PA2	47	M15
Benalder St. G11	34	T11
Benarty Gdns. (Bishop.) G64	11	Y7
Bencroft Dr. G44	64	X17
Bengairn St. G31	37	Z12
Bengal Pl. G43	50	T16
Christian St.		
Bengal St. G43	50	T16
Shawbridge St.		
Benhar Pl. G33	38	AA12
Benholm St. G32	54	AA14
Benhope Av., Pais. PA2	47	M15
Benlawers Dr., Pais. PA2	47	M15
Benloyal Av., Pais. PA2	47	M15
Benmore St. G21	22	X9
Bennan Sq. G42	52	W15
Benny Lynch Ct. G5	36	W13
Benston Pl., John. PA5	43	D15
Benston Rd., John. PA5	43	D15
Benthall St. G5	52	W14
Bentinck St. G3	35	U11
Bents Rd. (Bail.) G69	40	EE13
Benvane Av., Pais. PA2	47	M15
Benvie Gdns. (Bishop.) G64	11	Y7
Benview St. G20	21	U10
Benview Ter., Pais. PA2	47	L15
Berelands Cres. (Ruther.) G73	52	X16
Berelands Pl. (Ruther.) G73	52	X16
Beresford Av. G14	19	R10
Berkeley St. G3	35	U12
Berkeley Ter. La. G3	35	U11
Elderslie St.		
Berkley Dr. (Blan.) G72	68	FF19
Bernard Path G40	53	Y14
Bernard St. G40	53	Y14
Bernard Ter. G40	53	Y14
Berneray St. G22	22	W8
Berridale Av. G44	63	V17
Berryburn Rd. G21	23	Z10
Berryhill Dr. (Giff.) G46	62	S19
Berryhill Rd. (Giff.) G46	62	S19
Berryhill Rd. (Cumb.) G67	70	NN3
Berryknowes Av. G52	33	Q13
Berryknowes La. G52	33	Q13
Berryknowes Rd. G52	49	Q14
Berryknowes Rd. (Chry.) G69	26	FF8
Bertram St. G41	51	U15
Bertrohill Ter. G33	39	CC12
Stepps Rd.		
Bervie St. G51	33	R13
Berwick Av. (Cumb.) G68	70	NN1
Berwick Cres. (Linw.), Pais. PA3	28	E12
Berwick Dr. G52	48	P14
Berwick Dr. (Ruther.) G73	53	Z16
Betula Dr., Clyde. G81	5	L5
Bevan Av., John. PA5	43	C15
Beverley Rd. G43	62	T17
Bevin Av., Clyde. G81	5	M7
Bideford Cres. G32	55	CC14
Biggar St. G31	37	Y13
Bigton St. G33	38	BB11
Bilsland Ct. G20	21	V9
Bilsland Dr.		
Bilsland Dr. G20	21	U9
Binend Rd. G53	49	Q16
Binnie Pl. G40	36	X13
Binniehill Rd. (Cumb.) G68	70	MM2
Binns Rd. G33	39	CC11
Birch Cres., John. PA5	44	E15
Birch Dr. (Lenzie) G66	13	CC5
Birch Gro. (Udd.) G71	57	HH16
Burnhead St.		
Birch Knowle (Bishop.) G64	11	Y7
Birch Rd., Clyde. G81	5	L5
Birch St. G5	52	W14
Silverfir St.		
Birch Vw. (Bears.) G61	8	S5
Birchfield Dr. G14	18	P10
Birchlea Dr. (Giff.) G46	62	T18
Birchwood Av. G32	55	DD14
Birchwood Dr., Pais. PA2	45	H15
Birchwood Pl. G32	55	DD14
Birdston Rd. G21	23	Z9
Birgidale Av. G45	64	W19
Birgidale Rd. G45	64	W19
Birgidale Ter. G45	64	W19
Birkdale Ct. (Both.) G71	69	GG19
Birken Rd. (Lenzie) G66	13	DD6
Birkenshaw St. G31	37	Y12
Birkenshaw Way, Pais. PA3	30	K12
Abbotsburn Way		
Birkhall Av. G52	48	N14
Birkhall Av. (Inch.), Renf. PA4	16	J8
Birkhall Dr. (Bears.) G61	7	R7
Birkhill Av. (Bishop.) G64	11	Y6
Birkhill Gdns. (Bishop.) G64	11	Z6
Birkmyre Rd. G51	33	R13
Birks Rd., Renf. PA4	31	L11
Tower Dr.		
Birkwood St. G40	53	Y15
Birmingham Rd., Renf. PA4	31	L11
Birnam Av. (Bishop.) G64	11	Y6
Birnam Cres. (Bears.) G61	8	S5
Birnam Gdns. (Bishop.) G64	11	Y7
Birnam Rd. G31	53	Z14
Birness Dr. G43	50	T16
Birness St. G43	50	T16
Birnie Ct. G21	23	Z10
Birnie Rd. G21	23	Z10
Birnock Av., Renf. PA4	32	N11
Birsay Rd. G22	21	V8
Bishop Gdns. (Bishop.) G64	10	X7
Bishop St. G3	35	V12
Bishopmill Pl. G21	23	Z10
Bishopmill Rd. G21	23	Z10
Bishopsgate Dr. G21	22	X8
Bishopsgate Gdns. G21	22	X8
Bishopsgate Pl. G21	22	X8
Bishopsgate Rd. G21	22	X8
Bisset Cres., Clyde. G81	4	K5
Black St. G4	36	W11
Blackburn Sq. (Barr.) G78	59	M19
Blackburn St. G51	34	T13
Blackbyres Rd. (Barr.) G78	59	M17
Blackcraig Av. G15	6	P6
Blackcroft Gdns. G32	55	CC14
Blackcroft Rd. G32	55	CC14
Blackfaulds Rd. (Ruther.) G73	52	X16
Blackford Cres. G32	55	CC14
Blackford Pl. G32	55	CC14
Blackford Rd., Pais. PA2	47	L15
Blackfriars St. G1	36	W12
Blackhall La., Pais. PA1	46	K14
Blackhall St., Pais. PA1	46	K14
Blackhill Cotts. G23	9	V7
Blackhill Pl. G33	37	Z11
Blackhill Rd. G23	8	T7
Blackie St. G3	34	T11
Blacklands Pl. (Lenzie) G66	13	DD6
Blacklaw La., Pais. PA3	30	K13
Blackstone Av. G53	49	Q16
Blackstone Cres. G53	49	Q15
Blackstone Rd., Pais. PA3	29	H12
Blackstoun Av. (Linw.), Pais. PA3	28	E13
Blackstoun Oval, Pais. PA3	29	H13
Blackstoun Rd., Pais. PA3	29	H13
Blackthorn Av. (Kirk.) G66	12	BB5
Blackthorn Gro. (Kirk.) G66	12	BB5
Blackthorn Rd. (Cumb.) G67	71	QQ2
Blackthorn St. G22	22	X9
Blackwood Av. (Linw.), Pais. PA3	28	E13
Blackwood St. G13	19	R8
Blackwood St. (Barr.) G78	59	L19
Blackwoods Cres. (Mood.) G69	15	GG7
Blacurvie Rd. G34	40	EE11
Bladda La., Pais. PA1	46	K14
Blades Ct. (Gart.) G69	27	HH9
Bladnoch Dr. G15	7	Q7
Moraine Av.		
Blaeloch Av. G45	64	W19
Blaeloch Dr. G45	64	W19
Blaeloch Ter. G45	64	W19
Blair Cres. (Bail.) G69	56	EE14
Blair Rd., Pais. PA1	32	N13
Blair St. G32	38	AA13
Blairatholl Av. G11	20	S10
Blairatholl Gdns. G11	20	S10
Blairbeth Dr. G44	51	V16
Blairbeth Rd. (Ruther.) G73	65	Y17
Blairbeth Ter. (Ruther.) G73	65	Y18
Blairdardie Rd. G13	7	Q7
Blairdardie Rd. G15	6	P7
Blairdenan Av. (Chry.) G69	15	HH6
Blairdenon Dr. (Cumb.) G68	70	MM2
Blairgowrie Rd. G52	49	Q14
Blairhall Av. G41	51	U16
Blairhill Av. (Kirk.) G66	14	EE5
Blairlogie St. G33	38	BB11
Blairston Av. (Both.) G71	69	HH19
Blairston Gdns. (Both.) G71	69	HH19
Blairston Av.		
Blairtum Dr. (Ruther.) G73	65	Y17
Blairtummock Rd. G33	39	CC12
Blake Rd. (Cumb.) G67	71	PP3
Blane St. G4	36	W11
Blantyre Fm. Rd. (Blan.) G72	68	FF19
Blantyre Mill Rd. (Both.) G71	69	GG19
Blantyre Rd. (Both.) G71	69	HH19
Blantyre St. G3	34	T11
Blaven Ct. (Bail.) G69	56	FF14
Bracadale Rd.		
Blawarthill St. G14	18	N9
Blenheim Av. (Stepps) G33	25	CC9
Blenheim Ct. (Stepps) G33	25	DD9
Blenheim Av.		
Blenheim Ct., Pais. PA1	30	J13
Blenheim La. (Stepps) G33	25	DD9
Blesdale Ct., Clyde. G81	5	L7
Blochairn Rd. G21	37	Y11
Bluebell Gdns. G45	65	Y19
Bluevale St. G31	37	Y13
Blyth Pl. G33	39	CC13
Blyth Rd. G33	39	DD13
Blythswood Av., Renf. PA4	17	M10
Blythswood Ct. G2	35	V12
Cadogan St.		
Blythswood Dr., Pais. PA3	30	J13
Blythswood Rd., Renf. PA4	17	M9
Blythswood Sq. G2	35	V12
Blythswood St. G2	35	V12
Boclair Av. (Bears.) G61	7	R6
Boclair Cres. (Bears.) G61	8	S6
Boclair Cres. (Bishop.) G64	11	Y7
Boclair Rd. (Bishop.) G64	11	Y7
Boclair St. G13	19	R8
Boden St. G40	53	Y14
Bodmin Gdns. (Chry.) G69	15	GG6
Gartferry Rd.		
Bogany Ter. G45	64	X19
Bogbain Rd. G34	40	EE12
Boggknowe (Udd.) G71	56	FF16
Old Edinburgh Rd.		
Boghall Rd. (Udd.) G71	56	EE15
Boghall St. G33	38	BB11
Boghead Rd. G21	23	Y10
Boghead Rd. (Kirk.) G66	12	BB6
Bogleshole Rd. (Camb.) G72	54	AA16
Bogmoor Rd. G51	33	Q12
Bogside Pl. (Bail.) G69	40	FF12
Whamflet Av.		
Bogside Rd. G33	24	BB9
Bogside St. G40	53	Y14
Bogton Av. G44	63	U18

Bogton Av. La. G44	63	U18	
Bogton Av.			
Boleyn Rd. G41	51	U15	
Bolivar Ter. G42	52	W16	
Bolton Dr. G42	51	V16	
Bon Accord Sq., Clyde. G81	17	L8	
Bonawe St. G20	21	U10	
Boness St. G40	53	Y14	
Bonhill St. G22	21	V10	
Bonnar St. G40	53	Y14	
Bonnaughton Rd. (Bears.)	6	P5	
G61			
Bonnyholm Av. G53	48	P14	
Bonnyrigg Dr. G43	62	S17	
Bonyton Av. G13	18	N9	
Boon Dr. G15	6	P7	
Boquhanran Pl., Clyde. G81	5	L6	
Albert Rd.			
Boquhanran Rd., Clyde. G81	4	K7	
Borden La. G13	19	R9	
Borden Rd. G13	19	R9	
Boreland Dr. G13	18	P8	
Boreland Pl. G13	18	P9	
Borgie Cres. (Camb.) G72	66	BB17	
Borland Rd. (Bears.) G61	8	S6	
Borron St. G4	22	W10	
Borthwick St. G33	38	BB11	
Boswell Ct. G42	51	U16	
Boswell Sq. G52	32	N12	
Botanic Cres. G20	20	T10	
Bothlyn Cres. (Gart.) G69	27	GG8	
Bothlynn Dr. (Stepps) G33	25	CC9	
Bothlynn Rd. (Chry.) G69	26	FF8	
Bothwell La. G2	35	V12	
West Campbell St.			
Bothwell Pk. Rd. (Both.)	69	HH19	
G71			
Bothwell Rd. (Udd.) G71	69	GG17	
Bothwell St. G2	35	V12	
Bothwell St. (Camb.) G72	66	AA17	
Bothwell Ter. G12	35	U11	
Bank St.			
Bothwellpark Ind. Est.	69	HH18	
(Udd.) G71			
Bothwick Way, Pais. PA2	45	G16	
Boundary Rd. (Ruther.) G73	52	X15	
Rutherglen Rd.			
Bourne Ct. (Inch.), Renf.	16	J8	
PA4			
Bourne Cres. (Inch.), Renf.	16	J8	
PA4			
Bourock Sq. (Barr.) G78	60	N19	
Bourtree Dr. (Ruther.) G73	65	Z18	
Bouverie St. G14	18	N9	
Bouverie St. (Ruther.) G73	52	X16	
Bowden Dr. G52	32	P13	
Bower St. G12	21	U10	
Bowerwalls St. (Barr.) G78	60	N18	
Bowes Cres. (Bail.) G69	55	DD14	
Bowfield Av. G52	32	N13	
Bowfield Cres. G52	32	N13	
Bowfield Dr. G52	32	N13	
Bowfield Pl. G52	32	N13	
Bowfield Ter. G52	32	N13	
Bowfield Cres.			
Bowhouse Way (Ruther.)	65	Y18	
G73			
Bowling Grn. La. G14	19	Q10	
Westland Dr.			
Bowling Grn. Rd. G14	19	Q10	
Bowling Grn. Rd. G32	55	CC14	
Bowling Grn. Rd. G44	63	V17	
Bowling Grn. Rd. (Chry.)	26	FF8	
G69			
Bowman St. G42	51	V15	
Bowmont Gdns. G12	20	T10	
Bowmont Hill (Bishop.) G64	11	Y6	
Bowmont Ter. G12	20	T10	
Bowmore Gdns. (Udd.)	57	GG16	
G71			
Bowmore Gdns. (Ruther.)	66	AA18	
G73			
Bowmore Rd. G52	33	R13	
Boyd St. G42	51	V15	
Boydstone Pl. (Thorn.) G46	61	R17	
Boydstone Rd. G43	61	R17	
Boydstone Rd. (Thorn.)	61	R17	
G46			
Boydstone Rd. G53	61	R17	

Boyle St., Clyde. G81	17	M8	
Boylestone Rd. (Barr.) G78	59	L18	
Boyndie Path G34	40	EE12	
Boyndie St. G34	40	EE12	
Brabloch Cres., Pais. PA3	30	K13	
Bracadale Dr. (Bail.) G69	56	FF14	
Bracadale Gdns. (Bail.) G69	56	FF14	
Bracadale Gro. (Bail.) G69	56	FF14	
Bracadale Rd. (Bail.) G69	56	FF14	
Bracken St. G22	21	V9	
Bracken Ter. (Both.) G71	69	HH18	
Brackenbrae Av. (Bishop.)	10	X7	
G64			
Brackenbrae Rd. (Bishop.)	10	X7	
G64			
Brackenrig Rd. (Thorn.)	61	R19	
G46			
Brackla Av. G13	18	N8	
Brackla Av., Clyde. G81	18	N8	
Bracora Pl. G20	20	T9	
Glenfinnan Dr.			
Bradan Av. G13	18	N8	
Bradan Av., Clyde. G81	18	N8	
Bradda Av. (Ruther.) G73	65	Z18	
Bradfield Av. G12	20	T9	
Brady Cres. (Mood.) G69	15	HH6	
Braeface Rd. (Cumb.) G67	70	NN3	
Braefield Dr. (Thorn.) G46	62	S18	
Braefoot Cres., Pais. PA2	46	K16	
Braehead Rd. (Cumb.) G67	71	PP2	
Braehead Rd., Pais. PA2	58	J17	
Braehead St. G5	52	W14	
Braemar Av., Clyde. G81	4	K6	
Braemar Cres. (Bears.) G61	7	R7	
Braemar Cres., Pais. PA2	46	K16	
Braemar Dr. (Elder.), John.	44	E15	
PA5			
Braemar Rd. (Ruther.) G73	66	AA18	
Braemar Rd. (Inch.), Renf.	16	J8	
PA4			
Braemar St. G42	51	U16	
Braemar Vw., Clyde. G81	4	K5	
Braemount Av., Pais. PA2	58	J17	
Braes Av., Clyde. G81	17	M8	
Braeside Av. (Chry.) G69	15	GG7	
Braeside Av. (Ruther.) G73	53	Z16	
Braeside Cres. (Bail.) G69	41	GG13	
Braeside Cres. (Barr.) G78	60	N19	
Braeside Dr. (Barr.) G78	59	M19	
Braeside Pl. (Camb.) G72	66	BB18	
Braeside St. G20	21	U10	
Braeview Av., Pais. PA2	45	H16	
Braeview Dr., Pais. PA2	45	H16	
Braeview Gdns., Pais. PA2	45	H16	
Braeview Rd., Pais. PA2	45	H16	
Braid Sq. G4	35	V11	
Braid St. G4	35	V11	
Braidbar Fm. Rd. (Giff.) G46	62	T18	
Braidbar Rd. (Giff.) G46	62	T18	
Braidcraft Pl. G53	49	Q16	
Braidcraft Rd. G53	49	Q15	
Braidfauld Gdns. G32	54	AA14	
Braidfauld Pl. G32	54	AA15	
Braidfauld St. G32	54	AA15	
Braidfield Gro., Clyde. G81	5	L5	
Braidfield Rd., Clyde. G81	5	L5	
Braidholm Cres. (Giff.) G46	62	T18	
Braidholm Rd. (Giff.) G46	62	T18	
Braidpark Cres. (Giff.) G46	62	T18	
Braidpark Dr. (Giff.) G46	62	T18	
Braids Rd., Pais. PA2	46	K15	
Bramley Pl. (Lenzie) G66	13	DD6	
Branchock Av. (Camb.) G72	67	CC18	
Brand Pl. G51	34	T13	
Brand St. G51	34	T13	
Brandon Gdns. (Camb.)	66	AA17	
G72			
Brandon St. G31	36	X13	
Branscroft (Kilb.), John.	42	B14	
PA10			
Brassey St. G20	21	U9	
Breadalbane Gdns.	65	Z18	
(Ruther.) G73			
Breadalbane St. G3	35	U12	
St. Vincent St.			
Brechin Rd. (Bishop.) G64	11	Z7	
Brechin St. G3	35	U12	
Breck Av., Pais. PA2	44	F16	
Brediland Rd., Pais. PA2	45	G15	

Brediland Rd. (Linw.), Pais.	28	E13	
PA3			
Bredisholm Dr. (Bail.) G69	56	FF14	
Bredisholm Rd. (Bail.) G69	56	FF14	
Bredisholm Ter. (Bail.) G69	56	FF14	
Brenfield Av. G44	63	U18	
Brenfield Dr. G44	63	U18	
Brenfield Rd. G44	63	U18	
Brent Av. (Thorn.) G46	61	R17	
Brent Dr. (Thorn.) G46	61	R17	
Brent Rd. (Thorn.) G46	61	R17	
Brentwood Av. G53	60	P18	
Brentwood Dr. G53	60	P18	
Brentwood Sq. G53	60	P18	
Brentwood Dr.			
Brereton St. G42	52	W15	
Bressey Rd. G33	39	DD13	
Brewery St., John. PA5	43	D14	
Brewster Av., Pais. PA3	31	L12	
Briar Dr., Clyde. G81	5	L6	
Briar Gdns. G43	62	T17	
Briar Gro. G43	62	T17	
Briar Neuk (Bishop.) G64	23	Y8	
Briar Rd. G43	62	T17	
Briarcroft Dr. G33	23	Z8	
Briarcroft Pl. G33	24	AA9	
Briarcroft Rd. G33	23	Z9	
Briarlea Dr. (Giff.) G46	62	T18	
Briarwood Ct. G32	55	DD15	
Briarwood Gdns. G32	55	DD15	
Woodend Rd.			
Brick La., Pais. PA3	30	K13	
Bridge of Weir Rd. (Linw.),	28	E13	
Pais. PA3			
Bridge St. G5	35	V13	
Bridge St. (Camb.) G72	66	BB17	
Bridge St., Clyde. G81	4	K6	
Bridge St., Pais. PA1	46	K14	
Bridge St. (Linw.), Pais.	28	F13	
PA3			
Bridgebar St. (Barr.) G78	60	N18	
Bridgeburn Dr. (Chry.) G69	15	GG7	
Bridgegate G1	36	W13	
Bridgeton Cross G40	36	X13	
Brigham Pl. G23	21	U8	
Broughton Rd.			
Bright St. G21	36	X11	
Brighton Pl. G51	34	S13	
Brighton St. G51	34	S13	
Brightside Av. (Udd.) G71	69	HH17	
Brisbane Ct. (Giff.) G46	62	T18	
Braidpark Dr.			
Brisbane St. G42	51	V16	
Brisbane St., Clyde. G81	4	J6	
Britannia Way, Renf. PA4	31	M11	
Briton St. G51	34	S13	
Broad Pl. G40	36	X13	
Broad St.			
Broad St. G40	36	X13	
Broadford St. G4	36	W11	
Harvey St.			
Broadholm St. G22	21	V9	
Broadleys Av. (Bishop.)	10	X6	
G64			
Broadlie Dr. G13	18	P9	
Broadloan, Renf. PA4	31	M11	
Broadwood Dr. G44	63	V17	
Brock Oval G53	61	Q17	
Brock Pl. G53	49	Q16	
Brock Rd. G53	49	Q16	
Brock Ter. G53	61	Q17	
Brock Way (Cumb.) G67	71	PP3	
North Carbrain Rd.			
Brockburn Rd. G53	48	P15	
Brockburn Ter. G53	49	Q16	
Brockville St. G32	38	AA13	
Brodick Sq. (Bishop.) G64	23	Y8	
Brodick St. G21	37	Y11	
Brodie Pk. Av., Pais. PA2	46	K15	
Brodie Pk. Cres., Pais. PA2	46	J15	
Brodie Pk. Gdns., Pais. PA2	46	K15	
Brodie Pl., Renf. PA4	31	L11	
Brodie Rd. G21	23	Z8	
Brogknowe (Udd.) G71	56	FF16	
Glasgow Rd.			
Bron Way (Cumb.) G67	71	PP3	
Brook St. G40	36	X13	
Brooklands Av. (Udd.) G71	57	GG16	
Brooklea Dr. (Giff.) G46	62	T17	

Brookside St. G40 37 Y13
Broom Cres. (Barr.) G78 59 L17
Broom Dr., Clyde. G81 5 L6
Broom Gdns. (Kirk.) G66 12 BB5
Broom Path (Bail.) G69 55 DD14
Tudor St.
Broom Rd. G43 62 T17
Broom Rd. (Cumb.) G67 71 QQ1
Broom Ter., John. PA5 43 D15
Broomdyke Way, Pais. PA3 30 J12
Broomfield Av. G21 23 Y10
Broomfield Rd.
Broomfield Av. (Camb.) G72 53 Z16
Broomfield La. G21 22 X9
Broomfield Rd.
Broomfield Pl. G21 22 X9
Broomfield Rd.
Broomfield Rd. G21 22 X9
Broomfield Ter. (Udd.) G71 57 GG15
Broomhill Av. G11 33 R11
Broomhill Av. G32 54 BB16
Broomhill Cres. G11 19 R10
Broomhill Dr. G11 19 R10
Broomhill Dr. (Ruther.) G73 65 Y17
Broomhill Gdns. G11 19 R10
Broomhill La. G11 19 R10
Broomhill Path G11 33 R11
Broomhill Ter.
Broomhill Pl. G11 19 R10
Broomhill Rd. G11 33 R11
Broomhill Ter. G11 33 R11
Broomieknowe Dr. 65 Y17
(Ruther.) G73
Broomieknowe Rd. 65 Y17
(Ruther.) G73
Broomielaw G1 35 V13
Broomknowe (Cumb.) G68 70 MM2
Broomknowe Pl. (Lenzie) 13 DD6
G66
Broomknowes Rd. G21 23 Y10
Broomlands Av., Ersk. PA8 16 J8
Broomlands Cres., Ersk. 16 J8
PA8
Broomlands Gdns., Ersk. 16 J8
PA8
Broomlands Rd. (Cumb.) 71 PP4
G67
Broomlands St., Pais. PA1 46 J14
Broomlands Way, Ersk. 16 K8
PA8
Broomlea Cres. (Inch.), 16 J8
Renf. PA4
Bromley Dr. (Giff.) G46 62 T19
Bromley La. (Giff.) G46 62 T19
Broomloan Ct. G51 34 S13
Broomloan Pl. G51 34 S13
Broomloan Rd. G51 34 S13
Broompark Circ. G31 36 X12
Broompark Dr. G31 36 X12
Broompark Dr. (Inch.), 16 J8
Renf. PA4
Broompark La. G31 36 X12
Craigpark
Broompark St. G31 36 X12
Broomton Rd. G21 23 Z8
Broomward Dr., John. PA5 44 E14
Brora Dr. (Giff.) G46 62 T19
Brora Dr. (Bears.) G61 8 S6
Brora Dr., Renf. PA4 18 N10
Brora Gdns. (Bishop.) G64 11 Y7
Brora La. G33 37 Z11
Brora St.
Brora Rd. (Bishop.) G64 11 Y7
Brora St. G33 37 Z11
Broughton Dr. G23 21 U8
Broughton Gdns. G23 9 U7
Broughton Rd. G23 21 U8
Brown Av., Clyde. G81 17 M8
Brown Pl. (Camb.) G72 66 BB17
Allison Dr.
Brown Rd. (Cumb.) G67 70 NN3
Brown St. G2 35 V12
Brown St., Pais. PA1 30 J13
Brown St., Renf. PA4 31 L11
Brownhill Rd. G43 62 S18
Brownlie St. G42 51 V16
Browns La., Pais. PA1 46 K14
Brownsdale Rd. (Ruther.) 52 X16
G73

Brownside Av. (Camb.) 66 AA17
G72
Brownside Av. (Barr.) G78 59 L17
Brownside Av., Pais. PA2 46 J16
Brownside Cres. (Barr.) 59 L17
G78
Brownside Dr. G13 18 N9
Brownside Dr. (Barr.) G78 59 L17
Brownside Gro. (Barr.) G78 59 L17
Brownside Rd. (Camb.) 65 Z17
G72
Brownside Rd. (Ruther.) 65 Z17
G73
Bruce Av., John. PA5 43 D16
Bruce Av., Pais. PA3 31 L12
Bruce Rd. G41 51 U14
Bruce Rd., Pais. PA3 31 L13
Bruce Rd., Renf. PA4 31 L11
Bruce St., Clyde. G81 5 L7
Bruce Ter. (Blan.) G72 69 GG19
Brucefield Pl. G34 40 FF12
Brunstane Rd. G34 40 EE11
Brunswick Ho., Clyde. G81 4 J5
Perth Cres.
Brunswick La. G1 36 W12
Brunswick St.
Brunswick St. G1 36 W12
Brunton St. G44 63 V17
Brunton Ter. G44 63 U18
Bruntsfield Av. G53 60 P18
Bruntsfield Gdns. G53 60 P18
Bruntsfield Av.
Brydson Pl. (Linw.), Pais. 28 E13
PA3
Fulwood Av.
Buccleuch Av. G52 32 N12
Buccleuch La. G3 35 V11
Scott St.
Buccleuch St. G3 35 V11
Buchan St. G5 35 V13
Norfolk St.
Buchan Ter. (Camb.) G72 66 AA18
Buchanan Cres. (Bishop.) 23 Z8
G64
Buchanan Dr. (Bears.) G61 8 S6
Buchanan Dr. (Bishop.) 23 Z8
G64
Buchanan Dr. (Lenzie) G66 13 CC6
Buchanan Dr. (Camb.) G72 66 AA17
Buchanan Dr. (Ruther.) 65 Y17
G73
Buchanan Gdns. G32 55 DD15
Buchanan Gro. (Bail.) G69 40 EE13
Buchanan St. G1 35 V12
Buchanan St. (Bail.) G69 56 EE14
Buchanan St., John. PA5 43 D15
Buchley (Bishop.) G64 10 W5
Buchlyvie Gdns. (Bishop.) 22 X8
G64
Buchlyvie Path G34 40 EE12
Buchlyvie Rd., Pais. PA1 32 N13
Buchlyvie St. G34 40 EE12
Buckingham Bldgs. G12 20 T10
Great Western Rd.
Buckingham Dr. G32 54 BB16
Buckingham Dr. (Ruther.) 53 Z16
G73
Buckingham St. G12 20 T10
Buckingham Ter. G12 20 T10
Bucklaw Gdns. G52 49 Q14
Bucklaw Pl. G52 49 Q14
Bucklaw Ter. G52 49 Q14
Buckley St. G22 22 W9
Bucksburn Rd. G21 23 Z10
Buckthorne Pl. G53 60 P18
Buddon St. G40 53 Z14
Budhill Av. G32 38 BB13
Bulldale Ct. G14 18 N9
Bulldale Rd. G14 18 N9
Bulldale St. G14 18 N9
Bullionslaw Dr. (Ruther.) 65 Z17
G73
Bulloch Av. (Giff.) G46 62 T19
Bullwood Av. G53 48 N15
Bullwood Ct. G53 48 N15
Bullwood Dr. G53 48 N15
Bullwood Gdns. G53 48 N15
Bullwood Pl. G53 48 N15
Bunessan St. G52 33 R13

Bunhouse Rd. G3 34 T11
Burgh Hall La. G11 34 S11
Fortrose St.
Burgh Hall St. G11 34 S11
Burgh La. G12 20 T10
Vinicombe St.
Burghead Dr. G51 33 R12
Burghead Pl. G51 33 R12
Burgher St. G31 37 Z13
Burleigh Rd. (Both.) G71 69 HH18
Burleigh St. G51 34 S12
Burlington Av. G12 20 S9
Burmola St. G22 21 V10
Burn Gdns. (Blan.) G72 68 FF19
Burn Pl. (Camb.) G72 54 AA16
Burn Ter.
Burn Ter. (Camb.) G72 54 AA16
Burn Vw. (Cumb.) G67 71 QQ2
Burnacre Gdns. (Udd.) G71 57 GG16
Burnbank Dr. (Barr.) G78 59 M19
Burnbank Gdns. G20 35 U11
Burnbank Pl. G4 36 X12
Drygate
Burnbank Ter. G20 35 U11
Burnbrae, Clyde. G81 5 L5
Burnbrae Av. (Mood.) G69 15 HH7
Burnbrae Av. (Linw.), Pais. 28 F13
PA3
Bridge St.
Burnbrae Ct. (Lenzie) G66 13 CC6
Auchinloch Rd.
Burnbrae Dr. (Ruther.) G73 65 Z17
East Kilbride Rd.
Burnbrae Rd. (Kirk.) G66 13 DD7
Burnbrae Rd. (Chry.) G69 14 EE7
Burnbrae Rd. (Linw.), Pais. 44 F14
PA3
Burnbrae St. G21 23 Y10
Burncleuch Av. (Camb.) 66 BB18
G72
Burncrooks Ct., Clyde. G81 4 K5
Burndyke Ct. G51 34 T12
Burndyke Sq. G51 34 T12
Burndyke St. G51 34 S12
Burnett Rd. G33 39 DD12
Burnfield Av. (Thorn.) G46 62 S18
Burnfield Cotts. (Thorn.) 62 S18
G46
Burnfield Dr. G43 62 S18
Burnfield Gdns. (Giff.) G46 62 T18
Burnfield Rd.
Burnfield Rd. G43 62 S17
Burnfield Rd. (Thorn.) G46 62 S18
Burnfoot Cres. (Ruther.) 65 Z17
G73
Burnfoot Cres., Pais. PA2 46 J16
Burnfoot Dr. G52 32 P13
Burngreen Ter. (Cumb.) G67 71 PP1
Burnham Rd. G14 18 P10
Burnham Ter. G14 18 P10
Burnham Rd.
Burnhead Rd. G43 63 U17
Burnhead Rd. (Cumb.) G68 70 MM3
Burnhead St. (Udd.) G71 57 HH16
Burnhill Quad. (Ruther.) 52 X16
G73
Burnhill St. (Ruther.) G73 52 X16
Burnhouse St. G20 20 T9
Kelvindale Rd.
Burnmouth Ct. G33 39 DD13
Pendeen Rd.
Burnmouth Rd. G33 39 DD13
Burnpark Av. (Udd.) G71 56 FF16
Burns Dr., John. PA5 43 D16
Burns Gro. (Thorn.) G46 62 S19
Burns Rd. (Cumb.) G67 71 PP3
Burns St. G4 35 V11
Burns St., Clyde. G81 4 K6
Burnside Av. (Barr.) G78 59 L18
Burnside Ct., Clyde. G81 4 K6
Scott St.
Burnside Gdns. (Mill.Pk.), 42 B15
John. PA10
Burnside Gate (Ruther.) 65 Z17
G73
Burnside Gro., John. PA5 43 D15
Quarrelton Rd.
Burnside Pl., Pais. PA3 29 H12
Burnside Rd. (Ruther.) G73 65 Z17

Street	Page	Grid
Burnside Rd. (Elder.), John. PA5	44	F15
Burntbroom Dr. (Bail.) G69	55	DD14
Burntbroom Gdns. (Bail.) G69	55	DD14
Burntbroom St. G33	39	CC12
Burntshields Rd. (Kilb.), John. PA10	42	A15
Burr Gdns. (Bishop.) G64	11	Z6
Solway Rd.		
Burrells La. G4	36	X12
High St.		
Burrelton Rd. G43	63	U17
Burton La. G42	51	V15
Langside Rd.		
Bushes Av., Pais. PA2	46	J15
Busheyhill St. (Camb.) G72	66	BB17
Bute Av., Renf. PA4	31	M11
Bute Cres. (Bears.) G61	7	R7
Bute Cres., Pais. PA2	46	J16
Bute Dr., John. PA5	43	C15
Bute Gdns. G12	34	T11
Bute Gdns. G44	63	U18
Bute La. G12	34	T11
Great George St.		
Bute Rd. (Abbots.), Pais. PA3	30	J11
Bute Ter. (Udd.) G71	57	HH16
Bute Ter. (Ruther.) G73	65	Y17
Butterbiggins Rd. G42	51	V14
Butterfield Pl. G41	51	U15
Pollokshaws Rd.		
Byrebush Rd. G53	49	Q15
Byres Av., Pais. PA3	31	L13
Byres Cres., Pais. PA3	31	L13
Byres Rd. G11	34	T11
Byres Rd. G12	34	T11
Byres Rd. (Elder.), John. PA5	44	F15
Byron Ct. (Both.) G71	69	HH19
Shelley Dr.		
Byron St. G11	33	R11
Byron St., Clyde. G81	4	K6
Byshot St. G22	22	W10

C

Street	Page	Grid
Cable Depot Rd., Clyde. G81	4	K7
Cadder Ct. (Bishop.) G64	11	Y5
Cadder Gro. G20	21	U8
Cadder Rd.		
Cadder Pl. G20	21	U8
Cadder Rd. G20	21	U8
Cadder Rd. G23	21	U8
Cadder Rd. (Bishop.) G64	11	Y5
Cadder Way (Bishop.) G64	11	Y5
Cadoc St. (Camb.) G72	66	BB17
Cadogan St. G2	35	V12
Cadzow Dr. (Camb.) G72	66	AA17
Cadzow St. G2	35	V12
Cadogan St.		
Caird Dr. G11	34	S11
Cairn Av., Renf. PA4	32	N11
Cairn Dr. (Linw.), Pais. PA3	28	E13
Cairn La., Pais. PA3	30	J12
Mosslands Rd.		
Cairn St. G21	22	X9
Cairnban St. G51	33	Q13
Cairnbrook Rd. G34	40	FF12
Cairncraig St. G31	53	Z14
Cairndow Av. G44	63	U18
Cairndow Ct. G44	63	U18
Cairngorm Cres. (Bears.) G61	6	P5
Cairngorm Cres. (Barr.) G78	59	M19
Cairngorm Cres., Pais. PA2	46	K15
Cairngorm Rd. G43	62	T17
Cairnhill Circ. G52	48	N14
Cairnhill Dr. G52	48	N14
Cairnhill Pl. G52	48	N14
Cairnhill Circ.		
Cairnhill Rd. (Bears.) G61	7	R7
Cairnlea Dr. G51	34	S13
Cairnoch Hill (Cumb.) G68	70	MM3
Cairns Av. (Camb.) G72	66	BB18
Cairns Rd. (Camb.) G72	66	BB18
Cairnsmore Rd. G15	6	N7
Cairnswell Av. (Camb.) G72	67	CC18
Cairnswell Pl. (Camb.) G72	67	CC18
Cairntoul Ct. (Cumb.) G68	70	MM3
Cairntoul Dr. G14	18	P9
Cairntoul Pl. G14	18	P9
Caithness St. G20	21	U10
Calcots Path G34	40	FF11
Auchingill Rd.		
Calcots Pl. G34	40	FF11
Caldarvan St. G22	21	V10
Calder Av. (Barr.) G78	59	M19
Calder Dr. (Camb.) G72	66	BB17
Calder Gate (Bishop.) G64	10	X6
Calder Pl. (Bail.) G69	56	EE14
Calder Rd. (Udd.) G71	68	EE17
Calder Rd., Pais. PA3	29	H13
Calder St. G42	51	V15
Calderbank Vw. (Bail.) G69	56	FF14
Calderbraes Av. (Udd.) G71	57	GG16
Caldercuilt Rd. G20	20	T8
Caldercuilt Rd. G23	20	T8
Calderpark Av. (Udd.) G71	56	EE15
Calderpark Cres. (Udd.) G71	56	EE15
Caldervale (Udd.) G71	68	FF17
Calderwood Av. (Bail.) G69	56	EE14
Calderwood Dr. (Bail.) G69	56	EE14
Calderwood Gdns. (Bail.) G69	56	EE14
Calderwood Rd. G43	62	T17
Calderwood Rd. (Ruther.) G73	53	Z16
Caldwell Av. G13	18	P9
Caldwell Av. (Linw.), Pais. PA3	28	E13
Caledon La. G12	34	T11
Highburgh Rd.		
Caledon St. G12	34	T11
Caledonia Av. G5	52	W14
Caledonia Av. (Ruther.) G73	53	Y16
Caledonia Ct., Pais. PA3	30	J13
Mossvale St.		
Caledonia Dr. (Bail.) G69	56	EE14
Caledonia Rd. G5	52	W14
Caledonia Rd. (Bail.) G69	56	EE14
Caledonia St. G5	52	W14
Caledonia St., Clyde. G81	4	K7
Caledonia St., Pais. PA3	30	J13
Caledonia Way E. (Abbots.), Pais. PA3	30	K11
Caledonia Way W. (Abbots.), Pais. PA3	30	J11
Caledonian Circuit (Camb.) G72	67	CC17
Caledonian Cres. G12	35	U11
Caledonian Mans. G12	20	T10
Great Western Rd.		
Caledonian Pl. (Camb.) G72	67	DD17
Caley Brae (Udd.) G71	69	GG17
Calfhill Rd. G53	48	P14
Calfmuir Rd. (Kirk.) G66	14	EE5
Calfmuir Rd. (Chry.) G69	14	EE5
Calgary St. G4	36	W11
Callander St. G20	21	V10
Callieburn Rd. (Bishop.) G64	23	Y8
Cally Av. G15	6	P6
Calside, Pais. PA2	46	K15
Calside Av., Pais. PA2	46	J14
Calton Entry G40	36	X13
Gallowgate		
Calvay Cres. G33	39	CC12
Calvay Pl. G33	39	DD13
Calvay Rd. G33	39	CC12
Cambourne Rd. (Chry.) G69	15	GG6
Cambridge Av., Clyde. G81	5	L6
Cambridge Dr. G20	20	T9
Glenfinnan Dr.		
Cambridge La. G3	35	V11
Cambridge St.		
Cambridge Rd., Renf. PA4	31	M11
Cambridge St. G2	35	V12
Cambridge St. G3	35	V12
Camburn St. G32	38	AA13
Cambus Pl. G33	39	CC11
Cambusdoon Rd. G33	39	CC11
Cambuskenneth Gdns. G32	39	DD13
Cambuskenneth Pl. G33	39	CC11
Cambuslang Rd. G32	54	AA16
Cambuslang Rd. (Camb.) G72	53	Z16
Cambuslang Rd. (Ruther.) G73	53	Y15
Cambusmore Pl. G33	39	CC11
Camden St. G5	52	W14
Camelon St. G32	38	AA13
Cameron Dr. (Bears.) G61	8	S6
Cameron Dr. (Udd.) G71	57	HH16
Cameron Sq., Clyde. G81	5	M5
Glasgow Rd.		
Cameron St. G20	21	V10
Cameron St. G52	32	N12
Cameron St., Clyde. G81	17	M8
Camlachie St. G31	37	Y13
Camp Rd. (Bail.) G69	40	EE13
Camp Rd. (Ruther.) G73	52	X15
Campbell Cres. (Both.) G71	69	HH18
Campbell Dr. (Bears.) G61	7	Q5
Campbell Dr. (Barr.) G78	59	M19
Campbell St. G20	20	T8
Campbell St., John. PA5	43	D15
Campbell St., Renf. PA4	17	M10
Camperdown St. G20	21	V10
Garscube Rd.		
Camphill, Pais. PA1	46	J14
Camphill Av. G41	51	U16
Camps Cres., Renf. PA4	32	N11
Campsie Av. (Barr.) G78	59	M19
Campsie Dr., Pais. PA2	46	J16
Campsie Dr. (Abbots.), Pais. PA3	30	K11
Campsie Dr., Renf. PA4	31	L12
Campsie Pl. (Chry.) G69	26	FF8
Campsie St. G21	22	X9
Campsie Vw. (Stepps) G33	25	CC10
Campsie Vw. (Cumb.) G67	71	PP2
Campsie Vw. (Bail.) G69	41	GG13
Campsie Vw. (Chry.) G69	26	FF8
Campsie Vw. (Udd.) G71	57	HH16
Campston Pl. G33	38	BB11
Camstradden Dr. E. (Bears.) G61	7	Q6
Camstradden Dr. W. (Bears.) G61	7	Q6
Camus Pl. G15	6	N6
Canal Av., John. PA5	44	E15
Canal Rd., John. PA5	43	D15
Canal St. G4	36	W11
Canal St., Clyde. G81	17	L8
Canal St., John. PA5	44	E14
Canal St. (Elder.), John. PA5	44	E14
Canal St., Pais. PA1	46	J14
Canal St., Renf. PA4	17	M10
Canal Ter., Pais. PA1	46	J14
Canberra Av., Clyde. G81	4	J6
Canberra Ct. (Giff.) G46	62	T18
Braidpark Dr.		
Cander Rigg (Bishop.) G64	11	Y6
Candleriggs G1	36	W13
Candren Rd., Pais. PA3	45	H14
Candren Rd. (Linw.), Pais. PA3	28	F13
Canmore Pl. G31	53	Z14
Canmore St. G31	53	Z14
Cannich Dr., Pais. PA2	47	L15
Canniesburn Rd. (Bears.) G61	7	Q6
Canniesburn Sq. (Bears.) G61	7	R7
Macfarlane Rd.		
Canniesburn Toll (Bears.) G61	7	R6
Canonbie St. G34	40	FF11
Canting Way G51	34	T12
Capelrig St. (Thorn.) G46	61	R18
Caplaw Rd., Pais. PA2	58	J17
Caplethill Rd. (Barr.) G78	46	K16
Caplethill Rd., Pais. PA2	46	K16
Caprington St. G33	38	BB11
Cara Dr. G51	33	R12
Caravelle Way, Renf. PA4	31	M11
Friendship Way		
Carberry Rd. G41	50	T15
Carbeth St. G22	21	V10
Carbisdale St. G22	22	X9
Carbost St. G23	8	T7
Torgyle St.		
Carbrook St. G21	37	Y11
Carbrook St., Pais. PA1	46	J14

Cardarrach St. G21	23	Y10
Cardell Av., Pais. PA2	45	H14
Cardell Dr., Pais. PA2	45	H14
Cardell Rd., Pais. PA2	45	H14
Carding La. G3	35	U12
Argyle St.		
Cardonald Dr. G52	48	P14
Cardonald Gdns. G52	48	P14
Cardonald Pl. Rd. G52	48	P14
Cardow Rd. G21	23	Z10
Cardowan Dr. (Stepps) G33	25	CC9
Cardowan Pk. (Udd.) G71	57	HH15
Cardowan Rd. G32	38	AA13
Cardowan Rd. (Stepps) G33	25	DD9
Cardrona St. G33	24	BB10
Cardross Ct. G31	36	X12
Cardross St. G31	36	X12
Cardwell St. G41	51	V14
Cardyke St. G21	23	Y10
Careston Pl. (Bishop.) G64	11	Z7
Carfin St. G42	51	V15
Carfrae St. G3	34	T12
Cargill Sq. (Bishop.) G64	23	Y8
Cargill St. G31	54	AA14
Carham Cres. G52	33	Q13
Carham Dr. G52	33	Q13
Carillon Rd. G51	34	T13
Carisbrooke Cres. (Bishop.) G64	11	Y6
Carlaverock Rd. G43	62	T17
Carleith Av., Clyde. G81	4	K5
Carleith Quad. G51	33	Q12
Carleith Ter., Clyde. G81	4	K5
Carleith Av.		
Carleston St. G21	22	X10
Atlas Rd.		
Carleton Dr. (Giff.) G46	62	T18
Carleton Gate (Giff.) G46	62	T18
Carlibar Av. G13	18	N9
Carlibar Dr. (Barr.) G78	59	M18
Carlibar Gdns. (Barr.) G78	59	M18
Commercial Rd.		
Carlibar Rd. (Barr.) G78	59	L18
Carlile La., Pais. PA3	30	K13
New Sneddon St.		
Carlile Pl., Pais. PA3	30	K13
Carlisle St. G21	22	W10
Carlisle Ter., Pais. PA3	30	K13
Carlowrie Av. (Blan.) G72	68	FF19
Carlton Ct. G5	35	V13
Carlton Pl. G5	35	V13
Carlton Ter. G20	21	U10
Wilton St.		
Carlyle Av. G52	32	N12
Carlyle St., Pais. PA3	30	K13
Carlyle Ter. (Ruther.) G73	53	Y15
Carmaben Rd. G33	39	DD12
Carment Dr. G41	50	T16
Carment La. G41	50	T16
Carmichael Pl. G42	51	U16
Carmichael St. G51	34	S13
Carmunnock La. G44	63	V17
Madison Av.		
Carmunnock Rd. G44	51	V16
Carmunnock Rd. G45	64	W17
Carmunnock Rd. (Clark.) G76	64	W19
Carmyle Av. G32	54	BB15
Carna Dr. G44	64	W17
Carnarvon St. G3	35	U11
Carnbooth Ct. G45	64	X19
Carnbroe St. G20	35	V11
Carnegie Rd. G52	32	P13
Carnock Cres. (Barr.) G78	59	L19
Carnock Rd. G53	49	Q16
Carnoustie Ct. (Both.) G71	69	GG19
Carnoustie Cres. (Bishop.) G64	11	Z7
Carnoustie St. G5	35	U13
Carntyne Gdns. G32	38	AA12
Abbeyhill St.		
Carntyne Pl. G32	37	Z12
Carntyne Rd. G31	37	Z13
Carntyne Rd. G32	38	AA12
Carntynehall Rd. G32	38	AA12
Carnwadric Rd. (Thorn.) G46	61	R18
Carnwath Av. G43	63	U17
Caroline St. G31	38	AA13
Carolside Dr. G15	6	P6
Carradale Gdns. (Bishop.) G64	11	Z7
Thrums Av.		
Carradale Pl. (Linw.), Pais. PA3	28	E13
Carrbridge Dr. G20	20	T9
Glenfinnan Dr.		
Carresbrook Av. (Kirk.) G66	14	EE5
Carriagehill Av., Pais. PA2	46	K15
Carriagehill Dr., Pais. PA2	46	K15
Carrick Cres. (Giff.) G46	62	T19
Carrick Dr. G32	55	DD14
Carrick Dr. (Ruther.) G73	65	Y17
Carrick Gro. G32	55	DD14
Carrick Rd. (Bishop.) G64	11	Z7
Carrick Rd. (Cumb.) G67	71	PP2
Carrick Rd. (Ruther.) G73	64	X17
Carrick St. G2	35	V12
Carrickarden Rd. (Bears.) G61	7	R6
Carrickstone Rd. (Cumb.) G68	70	NN1
Carrickstone Vw. (Cumb.) G68	70	NN1
Carriden Pl. G33	39	DD12
Carrington St. G4	35	U11
Carroglen Gdns. G32	39	CC13
Carroglen Gro. G32	39	CC13
Carron Ct. (Camb.) G72	67	CC17
Carron Cres. G22	22	W9
Carron Cres. (Bears.) G61	7	Q6
Carron Cres. (Bishop.) G64	11	Y7
Carron Cres. (Lenzie) G66	13	DD6
Carron La., Pais. PA3	31	L12
Kilearn Rd.		
Carron Pl. G22	22	X9
Carron St. G22	22	X9
Carrour Gdns. (Bishop.) G64	10	X7
Carsaig Dr. G52	33	R13
Carse Vw. Dr. (Bears.) G61	8	S5
Carsebrook Av. (Kirk.) G66	14	EE5
Chryston Rd.		
Carsegreen Av., Pais. PA2	45	H16
Carstairs St. G40	53	Y15
Carswell Gdns. G41	51	U15
Cart St., Clyde. G81	17	L8
Cartcraigs Rd. G43	62	S17
Cartha Cres., Pais. PA2	47	L14
Cartha St. G41	51	U16
Cartside Av., John. PA5	43	C15
Cartside Quad. G42	51	V16
Cartside Ter. (Mill.Pk.), John. PA10	43	C15
Kilbarchan Rd.		
Cartvale La., Pais. PA3	30	K13
Cartvale Rd. G42	51	U16
Caskie Dr. (Blan.) G72	69	GG19
Cassley Av., Renf. PA4	32	N11
Castle Av. (Udd.) G71	69	GG17
Castle Av. (Elder.), John. PA5	44	E15
Castle Chimmins Av. (Camb.) G72	67	CC18
Castle Chimmins Rd. (Camb.) G72	67	CC18
Castle Cres. N. Ct. G1	36	W12
Royal Ex. Sq.		
Castle Gait, Pais. PA1	46	J14
Castle Gdns. (Chry.) G69	15	GG7
Castle Gdns., Pais. PA2	45	H14
Castle Gate (Udd.) G71	69	GG17
Castle Pl. (Udd.) G71	69	GG17
Ferry Rd.		
Castle Rd. (Elder.), John. PA5	44	F14
Castle Sq., Clyde. G81	4	K6
Castle St. G4	36	X12
Castle St. G11	34	T11
Benalder St.		
Castle St. (Bail.) G69	56	EE14
Castle St. (Ruther.) G73	53	Y16
Castle St., Clyde. G81	4	K6
Castle St., Pais. PA1	46	J14
Castle Vw., Clyde. G81	5	L6
Granville St.		
Castle Way (Cumb.) G67	71	QQ2
Castle Way (Bail.) G69	41	GG13
Dukes Rd.		
Castlebank Ct. G13	19	R9
Castlebank Cres. G11	34	S11
Meadowside St.		
Castlebank Gdns. G13	19	R9
Castlebank St. G11	33	R11
Castlebank Vills. G13	19	R9
Castlebay Dr. G22	10	W7
Castlebay Pl. G22	22	W8
Castlebay St. G22	22	W8
Castlecroft Gdns. (Udd.) G71	69	GG17
Castlefern Rd. (Ruther.) G73	65	Y18
Castlehill Cres., Renf. PA4	17	M10
Ferry Rd.		
Castlehill Rd. (Bears.) G61	6	P5
Castlelaw Gdns. G32	38	BB13
Castlelaw Pl. G32	38	BB13
Castlelaw St. G32	38	BB13
Castlemilk Cres. G44	64	X17
Castlemilk Dr. G45	64	X18
Castlemilk Ms. G44	64	X17
Castlemilk Rd.		
Castlemilk Rd. G44	52	X16
Castleton Av. (Bishop.) G64	22	X8
Colston Rd.		
Castleton Ct. G45	64	X19
Castleview Av., Pais. PA2	45	H16
Castleview Dr., Pais. PA2	45	H16
Castleview Pl., Pais. PA2	45	H16
Cathay St. G22	22	W8
Cathcart Cres., Pais. PA2	47	L14
Cathcart Pl. (Ruther.) G73	52	X16
Cathcart Rd. G42	51	V16
Cathcart Rd. (Ruther.) G73	52	X16
Cathedral Ct. G4	36	W12
Rottenrow E.		
Cathedral La. G4	36	W12
Cathedral St.		
Cathedral Sq. G4	36	X12
Cathedral St. G1	36	W12
Cathedral St. G4	36	W12
Catherine Pl. G3	35	U12
Hydepark St.		
Cathkin Av. (Camb.) G72	66	AA17
Cathkin Av. (Ruther.) G73	52	Z16
Cathkin Bypass (Ruther.) G73	65	Z18
Cathkin Ct. G45	64	X19
Cathkin Gdns. (Udd.) G71	57	GG15
Cathkin Pl. (Camb.) G72	66	AA17
Cathkin Rd. G42	51	U16
Cathkin Rd. (Udd.) G71	57	GG15
Cathkin Rd. (Ruther.) G73	65	Y19
Cathkin Rd. (Clark.) G76	65	Y19
Cathkin Vw. G32	54	BB16
Cathkinview Pl. G42	51	V16
Cathkinview Rd. G42	51	V16
Catrine Ct. G53	48	P16
Catrine Gdns. G53	48	P16
Catrine Pl. G53	48	P16
Catrine Rd. G53	48	P16
Causewayside St. G32	54	BB15
Causeyside St., Pais. PA1	46	K14
Cavendish Pl. G5	51	V14
Cavendish St. G5	51	V14
Cavin Dr. G45	64	X18
Cavin Rd. G45	64	X18
Cayton Gdns. (Bail.) G69	55	DD14
Cecil Pl. G51	35	U13
Paisley Rd. W.		
Cecil St. G12	20	T10
Cedar Av., Clyde. G81	4	J6
Cedar Av., John. PA5	44	E16
Cedar Ct. G20	35	V11
Cedar Ct. (Kilb.), John. PA10	42	B14
Cedar Dr. (Lenzie) G66	13	CC5
Cedar Gdns. (Ruther.) G73	65	Z18
Cedar Pl. (Blan.) G72	68	FF19
Cedar Pl. (Barr.) G78	59	M19
Cedar Rd. (Bishop.) G64	23	Y8
Cedar Rd. (Cumb.) G67	71	QQ2
Cedar St. G20	35	V11
Cedar Wk. (Bishop.) G64	23	Y8
Cedric Pl. G13	19	Q8

Cedric Rd. G13 19 Q8
Celtic St. G20 20 T8
Cemetery Rd. G52 49 Q14
Paisley Rd. W.
Centenary Ct., Clyde. G81 5 L7
Bruce St.
Central Av. G11 33 R11
Broomhill Ter.
Central Av. G32 55 CC14
Central Av. (Camb.) G72 66 AA17
Central Av., Clyde. G81 5 L7
Central Chambers G2 35 V12
Hope St.
Central Gro. (Camb.) G72 66 AA17
Central Path G32 55 DD14
Central Rd., Pais. PA1 30 K13
Central Sta. G1 35 V12
Central Way (Cumb.) G67 70 NN4
Central Way, Pais. PA1 30 K13
Centre, The (Barr.) G78 59 L19
Centre St. G5 35 V13
Centre Way (Barr.) G78 59 L18
Ceres Gdns. (Bishop.) G64 11 Z7
Cessnock Rd. G33 24 BB9
Cessnock St. G51 34 T13
Chachan Dr. G51 33 R12
Skipness Dr.
Chalmers Ct. G40 36 X13
Chalmers Gate G40 36 X13
Claythorn St.
Chalmers Pl. G40 36 X13
Claythorn St.
Chalmers St. G40 36 X13
Chalmers St., Clyde. G81 5 L7
Chamberlain La. G13 19 R9
Chamberlain Rd. G13 19 R9
Chancellor St. G11 34 S11
Chapel Rd., Clyde. G81 5 L5
Chapel St. G20 21 U9
Chapel St. (Ruther.) G73 52 X16
Chapelhill Rd., Pais. PA2 47 L15
Chapelton Av. (Bears.) G61 7 R6
Chapelton Gdns. (Bears.) 7 R6
G61
Chapelton St. G22 21 V9
Chaplet Av. G13 19 Q8
Chapman St. G42 51 V15
Allison St.
Chappell St. (Barr.) G78 59 L18
Charing Cross G2 35 U11
Charing Cross La. G3 35 U12
Granville St.
Charles Av., Renf. PA4 17 M10
Charles Cres. (Lenzie) G66 13 CC6
Charles St. G21 36 X11
Charlotte La. G1 36 W13
London Rd.
Charlotte La. S. G1 36 W13
Charlotte St.
Charlotte Pl., Pais. PA2 46 K15
Charlotte St. G1 36 W13
Chatelherault Av. (Camb.) 66 AA17
G72
Chatton St. G23 8 T7
Cheapside St. G3 35 U12
Chelmsford Dr. G12 20 S9
Cherry Bk. (Kirk.) G66 12 BB5
Cherry Cres., Clyde. G81 5 L6
Cherry Pl. (Bishop.) G64 23 Y8
Cherry Pl., John. PA5 44 E15
Cherrybank Rd. G43 63 U17
Cherrywood Rd. (Elder.), 44 F15
John. PA5
Chester St. G32 38 BB13
Chesterfield Av. G12 20 S9
Chesters Pl. (Ruther.) G73 53 Y16
Chesters Rd. (Bears.) G61 7 Q6
Chestnut Dr. (Kirk.) G66 12 BB5
Chestnut Dr., Clyde. G81 5 L5
Chestnut Pl., John. PA5 44 E16
Chestnut St. G22 22 W9
Cheviot Av. (Barr.) G78 59 M19
Cheviot Rd. G43 62 T17
Cheviot Rd., Pais. PA2 46 K16
Chirnside Pl. G52 32 P13
Chirnside Rd. G52 32 P13
Chisholm St. G1 36 W13
Crighton Grn. (Udd.) G71 57 HH16
Christian St. G43 50 T16

Christie La., Pais. PA3 30 K13
New Sneddon St.
Christie Pl. (Camb.) G72 66 BB17
Christie St., Pais. PA1 30 K13
Christopher St. G21 37 Y11
Chryston Rd. (Kirk.) G66 14 FF5
Chryston Rd. (Chry.) G69 26 FF8
Church Av. (Stepps) G33 25 CC9
Church Av. (Ruther.) G73 65 Z17
Church Dr. (Kirk.) G66 13 CC5
Church Hill, Pais. PA1 30 K13
Church La. G42 51 V15
Victoria Rd.
Church Rd. (Giff.) G46 62 T19
Church Rd. (Muir.) G69 26 FF8
Church St. G11 34 T11
Church St. (Bail.) G69 56 FF14
Church St. (Udd.) G71 69 GG17
Church St., Clyde. G81 5 L6
Church St., John. PA5 43 D14
Church St. (Kilb.), John. 42 B14
PA10
Church Vw. (Camb.) G72 54 BB16
Churchill Av., John. PA5 43 C16
Churchill Cres. (Both.) G71 69 HH18
Churchill Dr. G11 19 R10
Churchill Pl. (Kilb.), John. 42 B14
PA10
Churchill Way (Bishop.) G64 10 X7
Kirkintilloch Rd.
Circus Dr. G31 36 X12
Circus Pl. G31 36 X12
Circus Pl. La. G31 36 X12
Circus Pl.
Cityford Cres. (Ruther.) 52 X16
G73
Cityford Dr. (Ruther.) G73 52 X16
Clachan Dr. G51 33 R12
Skipness Dr.
Claddens Pl. (Lenzie) G66 13 DD6
Claddens Quad. G22 22 W9
Claddens St. G22 21 V9
Claddens Wynd (Kirk.) G66 13 DD6
Claddon Vw., Clyde. G81 5 M6
Kirkoswald Dr.
Clair Rd. (Bishop.) G64 11 Z7
Clairmont Gdns. G3 35 U11
Clare St. G21 37 Y11
Claremont Pas. G3 35 U11
Claremont Ter.
Claremont Pl. G3 35 U11
Claremont Ter.
Claremont St. G3 35 U12
Claremont Ter. G3 35 U11
Claremont Ter. La. G3 35 U11
Clifton St.
Claremount Av. (Giff.) G46 62 T19
Clarence Dr. G11 20 S10
Clarence Dr. G12 20 S10
Clarence Dr., Pais. PA1 47 L14
Clarence Gdns. G11 20 S10
Clarence La. G12 20 S10
Hyndland Rd.
Clarence St., Clyde. G81 5 M6
Clarence St., Pais. PA1 31 L13
Clarendon La. G20 35 V11
Clarendon St.
Clarendon Pl. G20 35 V11
Clarendon St. G20 35 V11
Clarion Cres. G13 18 P8
Clarion Rd. G13 18 P8
Clark St. G41 35 U13
Tower St.
Clark St., Clyde. G81 4 K6
Clark St., John. PA5 43 D14
Clark St., Pais. PA3 30 J13
Clark St., Renf. PA4 17 L10
Clarkston Av. G44 63 U18
Clarkston Rd. G44 63 U18
Clarkston Rd. (Clark.) G76 63 U19
Clathic Av. (Bears.) G61 8 S6
Claud Rd., Pais. PA3 31 L13
Claude Av. (Camb.) G72 67 DD18
Claudhall Av. (Gart.) G69 27 GG8
Clavens Rd. G52 32 N13
Claverhouse Pl., Pais. PA2 47 L14
Claverhouse Rd. G52 32 N12
Clavering St. E., Pais. PA1 30 J13
Well St.

Clavering St. W., Pais. PA1 30 J13
King St.
Clayhouse Rd. G33 25 DD9
Claypotts Pl. G33 38 BB11
Claypotts Rd. G33 38 BB11
Clayslaps Rd. G3 34 T11
Argyle St.
Claythorn Av. G40 36 X13
Claythorn Circ. G40 36 X13
Claythorn Av.
Claythorn Ct. G40 36 X13
Claythorn Pk.
Claythorn Pk. G40 36 X13
Claythorn St. G40 36 X13
Claythorn Ter. G40 36 X13
Claythorn Pk.
Clayton Ter. G31 36 X12
Cleddans Cres., Clyde. G81 5 M5
Cleddans Rd., Clyde. G81 5 M5
Cleddens Ct. (Bishop.) G64 11 Y7
Cleeves Pl. G53 60 P17
Cleeves Quad. G53 60 P17
Cleeves Rd. G53 60 P17
Cleghorn St. G22 21 V10
Cleland La. G5 36 W13
Cleland St.
Cleland St. G5 36 W13
Clelland Av. (Bishop.) G64 23 Y8
Clerwood St. G32 37 Z13
Cleveden Cres. G12 20 S9
Cleveden Cres. La. G12 20 S9
Cleveden Dr.
Cleveden Dr. G12 20 S9
Cleveden Dr. (Ruther.) G73 65 Z17
Cleveden Gdns. G12 20 T9
Cleveden La. G12 20 S9
Burlington Av.
Cleveden Pl. G12 20 S9
Cleveden Rd. G12 20 S9
Cleveland St. G3 35 U12
Cliff Rd. G3 35 U11
Clifford Gdns. G51 34 S13
Clifford La. G51 34 T13
North Gower St.
Clifford Pl. G51 34 T13
Clifford St.
Clifford St. G51 34 S13
Clifton Pl. G3 35 U11
Clifton St.
Clifton Rd. (Giff.) G46 62 S18
Clifton St. G3 35 U11
Clifton Ter. (Camb.) G72 66 AA18
Clifton Ter., John. PA5 44 E15
Clincart Rd. G42 51 V16
Clincarthill Rd. (Ruther.) 53 Y16
G73
Clinton Av. (Udd.) G71 69 GG17
Clippens Rd. (Linw.), Pais. 28 E13
PA3
Cloan Av. G15 6 P7
Cloan Cres. (Bishop.) G64 11 Y6
Cloberhill Rd. G13 7 Q7
Cloch St. G33 38 BB12
Clochoderick Av. (Mill.Pk.), 42 B15
John. PA10
Mackenzie Dr.
Clonbeith St. G33 39 DD11
Closeburn St. G22 22 W9
Cloth St. (Barr.) G78 59 M19
Clouden Rd. (Cumb.) G67 71 PP3
Cloudhowe Ter. (Blan.) 68 FF19
G72
Clouston Ct. G20 21 U10
Clouston La. G20 20 T10
Clouston St.
Clouston St. G20 20 T10
Clova Pl. (Udd.) G71 69 GG17
Clova St. (Thorn.) G46 61 R18
Clover Av. (Bishop.) G64 10 X7
Cloverbank St. G21 37 Y11
Clovergate (Bishop.) G64 10 X7
Clunie Rd. G52 49 R14
Cluny Av. (Bears.) G61 8 S7
Cluny Dr. (Bears.) G61 8 S7
Cluny Dr., Pais. PA3 31 L13
Cluny Gdns. G14 19 R10
Cluny Gdns. (Bail.) G69 56 EE14
Cluny Vills. G14 19 Q10
Westland Dr.

Clutha St. G51 35 U13
Paisley Rd. W.
Clyde Av. (Both.) G71 69 GG19
Clyde Av. (Barr.) G78 59 M19
Clyde Ct., Clyde. G81 4 K6
Little Holm
Clyde Pl. G5 35 V13
Clyde Pl. (Camb.) G72 67 CC18
Clyde Pl., John. PA5 43 C16
Clyde Rd., Pais. PA3 31 L12
Clyde St. G1 35 V13
Clyde St., Clyde. G81 17 L8
Clyde St., Renf. PA4 17 M9
Clyde Ter. (Both.) G71 69 HH19
Clyde Tunnel G14 33 R11
Clyde Tunnel G51 33 R11
Clyde Tunnel Expressway 33 Q12
G51
Clyde Vale (Both.) G71 69 HH19
Clyde Vw., Pais. PA2 47 L15
Clydebrae Dr. (Both.) G71 69 HH19
Clydebrae St. G51 34 S12
Clydeford Dr. G32 54 AA14
Clydeford Dr. (Udd.) G71 56 FF16
Clydeford Rd. (Camb.) G72 54 BB16
Clydeholm Rd. G14 33 Q11
Clydeholm Ter., Clyde. G81 17 M8
Clydeneuk Dr. (Udd.) G71 56 FF16
Clydesdale Av., Pais. PA3 31 L11
Clydeside Expressway G3 34 T11
Clydeside Expressway G14 19 Q10
Clydeside Rd. (Ruther.) 52 X15
G73
Clydesmill Dr. G32 54 BB16
Clydesmill Gro. G32 54 BB16
Clydesmill Pl. G32 54 BB16
Clydesmill Rd. G32 54 BB16
Clydeview G11 34 S11
Dumbarton Rd.
Clydeview La. G11 33 R11
Broomhill Ter.
Clydeview Ter. G32 55 CC16
Clydeview Ter. G40 52 X14
Newhall St.
Clynder St. G51 34 S13
Clyth Dr. (Giff.) G46 62 T19
Coalhill St. G31 37 Y13
Coatbridge Rd. (Bail.) G69 41 GG13
Coatbridge Rd. (Gart.) G69 27 GG10
Coates Cres. G53 49 Q16
Coats Cres. (Bail.) G69 40 EE13
Coats Dr., Pais. PA2 45 H14
Coatshill Av. (Blan.) G72 68 FF19
Cobblerigg Way (Udd.) 69 GG17
G71
Cobden Rd. G21 36 X11
Cobinshaw St. G32 38 BB13
Cobinton Pl. G33 38 BB11
Coburg St. G5 35 V13
Cochno St., Clyde. G81 17 M8
Cochran St., Pais. PA1 46 K14
Cochrane St. G1 36 W12
Cochrane St. (Barr.) G78 59 L19
Cochranemill Rd., John. 43 C15
PA5
Cockels Ln., Renf. PA4 31 L11
Cockenzie St. G32 38 BB13
Cockmuir St. G21 23 Y10
Cogan Rd. G43 62 T17
Cogan St. G43 50 T16
Cogan St. (Barr.) G78 59 L19
Colbert St. G40 52 X14
Colbreggan Ct., Clyde. G81 5 M5
St. Helena Cres.
Colbreggan Gdns., Clyde. 5 M5
G81
Colchester Dr. G12 20 S9
Coldingham Av. G14 18 N9
Coldstream Dr. (Ruther.) 65 Z17
G73
Coldstream Dr., Pais. PA2 45 H15
Coldstream Pl. G21 22 W10
Keppochhill Rd.
Coldstream Rd., Clyde. G81 5 L7
Colebrook La. G12 21 U10
Colebrooke St.
Colebrooke Pl. G12 21 U10
Belmont St.

Colebrooke St. G12 21 U10
Colebrooke Ter. G12 21 U10
Colebrooke St.
Coleridge (Both.) G71 69 HH18
Colfin St. G34 40 FF11
Colgrain St. G20 21 V9
Colgrave Cres. G32 54 AA14
Colinbar Circle (Barr.) G78 59 L19
Colinslee Av., Pais. PA2 46 K15
Colinslee Cres., Pais. PA2 46 K15
Colinslee Dr., Pais. PA2 46 K15
Colinslie Rd. G53 49 Q16
Colinton Pl. G32 38 BB12
Colintraive Av. G33 24 AA10
Colintraive Cres. G33 24 AA10
Coll Av., Renf. PA4 31 M11
Coll Pl. G21 37 Y11
Coll St. G21 37 Y11
Colla Gdns. (Bishop.) G64 11 Z7
College La. G1 36 W13
High St.
College La., Pais. PA1 46 J14
College St. G1 36 W12
Collessie Dr. G33 39 CC11
Collier St., John. PA5 43 D14
Collina St. G20 20 T9
Collins St. G4 36 X12
Collylin Rd. (Bears.) G61 7 R6
Colmonell Av. G13 18 N8
Colonsay Av., Renf. PA4 31 M11
Colonsay Rd. G52 33 R13
Colonsay Rd., Pais. PA2 46 J16
Colquhoun Av. G52 32 P12
Colquhoun Dr. (Bears.) G61 7 Q5
Colston Av. (Bishop.) G64 22 X8
Colston Dr. (Bishop.) G64 22 X8
Colston Gdns. (Bishop.) 22 X8
G64
Colston Path (Bishop.) G64 22 X8
Colston Gdns.
Colston Pl. (Bishop.) G64 22 X8
Colston Rd.
Colston Rd. (Bishop.) G64 22 X8
Coltmuir Av. (Bishop.) G64 22 X8
Coltmuir Dr.
Coltmuir Cres. (Bishop.) 22 X8
G64
Coltmuir Dr. (Bishop.) G64 22 X8
Coltmuir Gdns. (Bishop.) 22 X8
G64
Coltmuir Dr.
Coltmuir St. G22 21 V9
Coltness La. G33 39 CC12
Coltness St. G33 39 CC12
Coltpark Av. (Bishop.) G64 22 X8
Coltpark La. (Bishop.) G64 22 X8
Coltsfoot Dr. G53 60 P18
Columba Path, Clyde. G81 5 M7
Onslow Rd.
Columba St. G51 34 S12
Colvend Dr. (Ruther.) G73 65 Y18
Colvend St. G40 52 X14
Colville Dr. (Ruther.) G73 65 Z17
Colwood Av. G53 60 P18
Colwood Gdns. G53 60 P18
Colwood Av.
Colwood Path G53 60 P18
Parkhouse Rd.
Colwood Pl. G53 60 P18
Colwood Sq. G53 60 P18
Colwood Av.
Comedie Rd. G33 25 DD10
Comely Pk. St. G31 37 Y13
Comley Pl. G31 37 Y13
Gallowgate
Commerce St. G5 35 V13
Commercial Ct. G5 36 W13
Commercial Rd. G5 52 W14
Commercial Rd. (Barr.) 59 M18
G78
Commonhead Rd. G34 40 FF12
Commore Av. (Barr.) G78 59 M19
Commore Dr. G13 18 P8
Comrie Rd. G33 25 CC9
Comrie St. G32 54 BB14
Cona St. (Thorn.) G46 61 R18
Conan Ct. (Camb.) G72 67 CC17
Condorrat Ring Rd. 70 MM4
(Cumb.) G67

Congleton St. G53 60 N17
Nitshill Rd.
Congress Rd. G3 35 U12
Conifer Pl. (Kirk.) G66 12 BB5
Conisborough Path G34 39 DD11
Balfluig St.
Conisborough Rd. G34 39 DD11
Conistone Cres. (Bail.) G69 55 DD14
Connal St. G40 53 Y14
Conniston St. G32 38 AA12
Connor Rd. (Barr.) G78 59 L18
Conon Av. (Bears.) G61 7 Q6
Consett La. G33 39 CC12
Consett St. G33 39 CC12
Consett La.
Contin Pl. G12 20 T9
Convair Way, Renf. PA4 31 M11
Lismore Av.
Conval Way, Pais. PA3 30 J12
Abbotsburn Way
Cook St. G5 35 V13
Cooperage Ct. G14 17 M9
Coopers Well La. G11 34 T11
Dumbarton Rd.
Coopers Well St. G11 34 T11
Dumbarton Rd.
Copland Pl. G51 34 S13
Copland Quad. G51 34 S13
Copland Rd. G51 34 S13
Coplaw St. G42 51 V14
Copperfield La. (Udd.) G71 57 HH16
Hamilton Vw.
Corbett St. G32 54 BB14
Corbiston Way (Cumb.) 71 PP3
G67
Cordiner St. G44 51 V16
Corkerhill Gdns. G52 49 R14
Corkerhill Pl. G52 49 Q15
Corkerhill Rd. G52 49 Q15
Corlaich Av. G42 52 X16
Corlaich Dr. G42 52 X16
Corn St. G4 35 V11
Cornaig Rd. G53 48 P16
Cornalee Gdns. G53 48 P16
Cornalee Pl. G53 48 P16
Cornalee Rd. G53 48 P16
Cornhill St. G21 23 Y9
Cornoch St. G23 8 T7
Torrin Rd.
Cornock Cres., Clyde. G81 5 L6
Cornock St., Clyde. G81 5 L6
Cornwall Av. (Ruther.) G73 65 Z17
Cornwall St. G41 34 T13
Coronation Pl. (Gart.) G69 27 GG8
Coronation Way (Bears.) 8 S7
G61
Corpach Pl. G34 40 FF11
Corran St. G33 38 AA12
Corrie Dr., Pais. PA1 48 N14
Corrie Gro. G44 63 U18
Corrie Pl. (Lenzie) G66 13 DD6
Corrour Rd. G43 50 T16
Corse Rd. G52 32 N13
Corsebar Av., Pais. PA2 46 J15
Corsebar Cres., Pais. PA2 46 J15
Corsebar Dr., Pais. PA2 46 J15
Corsebar La., Pais. PA2 45 H15
Balgonie Av.
Corsebar Rd., Pais. PA2 45 H15
Corsebar Way, Pais. PA2 46 J14
Corseford Av., John. PA5 43 C16
Corsehill Pl. G34 40 FF12
Corsehill St. G34 40 FF12
Corselet Rd. G53 60 P18
Corsewall Av. G32 55 DD14
Corsford Dr. G53 61 Q17
Corsock St. G31 37 Z12
Corston St. G33 37 Z12
Cortachy Pl. (Bishop.) G64 11 Z7
Coruisk Way, Pais. PA2 45 G16
Spencer Dr.
Corunna St. G3 35 U12
Coshneuk Rd. G33 24 BB9
Cottar St. G20 21 U8
Cotton Av. (Linw.), Pais. 28 E13
PA3
Cotton St. G40 53 Y15
Cotton St., Pais. PA1 46 K14
Coulin Gdns. G22 22 W10

Coulters La. G40 36 X13
Countess Way (Bail.) G69 41 HH13
 Park Rd.
County Av. (Camb.) G72 53 Z16
County Pl., Pais. PA1 30 K13
 Moss St.
County Sq., Pais. PA1 30 K13
Couper St. G4 36 W11
Courthill (Bears.) G61 7 Q5
Courthill Av. G44 63 V17
Coustonhill St. G43 50 T16
 Pleasance St.
Coustonholm Rd. G43 50 T16
Coventry Dr. G31 37 Y12
Cowal Dr. (Linw.), Pais. PA3 28 E13
Cowal Rd. G20 20 T8
Cowal St. G20 20 T8
Cowan Clo. (Barr.) G78 59 M18
Cowan Cres. (Barr.) G78 59 M19
Cowan La. G12 35 U11
 Cowan St.
Cowan Rd. (Cumb.) G68 70 MM3
Cowan St. G12 35 U11
Cowan Wilson Av. (Blan.) 68 FF19
 G72
Cowan Wynd (Udd.) G71 57 HH16
Cowcaddens Rd. G4 35 V11
Cowcaddens St. G2 35 V12
 Renfield St.
Cowden Dr. (Bishop.) G64 11 Y6
Cowden St. G51 33 Q12
Cowdenhill Circ. G13 19 Q8
Cowdenhill Pl. G13 19 Q8
Cowdenhill Rd. G13 19 Q8
Cowdray Cres., Renf. PA4 17 M10
Cowell Vw., Clyde. G81 5 L6
 Granville St.
Cowglen Pl. G53 49 Q16
 Cowglen Rd.
Cowglen Rd. G53 49 Q16
Cowglen Ter. G53 49 Q16
Cowlairs Rd. G21 22 X10
Coxhill St. G21 22 W10
Coxton Pl. G33 39 CC11
Coylton Rd. G43 63 U17
Craggan Dr. G14 18 N9
Crags Av., Pais. PA2 46 K15
Crags Cres., Pais. PA2 46 K15
Crags Rd., Pais. PA2 46 K15
Craig Rd. G44 63 V17
Craigallian Av. (Camb.) 67 CC18
 G72
Craiganour La. G43 62 T17
Craiganour Pl. G43 62 T17
Craigard Pl. (Ruther.) G73 66 AA18
 Inverclyde Gdns.
Craigbank Dr. G53 60 P17
Craigbank St. G22 22 W10
Craigbarnet Cres. G33 24 BB10
Craigbo Av. G23 8 T7
Craigbo Ct. G23 20 T8
Craigbo Dr. G23 20 T8
Craigbo Pl. G23 20 T8
Craigbo Rd. G23 20 T8
Craigbo St. G23 8 T7
Craigbog Av., John. PA5 43 C15
Craigdonald Pl., John. PA5 43 D14
Craigellan Rd. G43 62 T17
Craigenbay Cres. (Lenzie) 13 CC5
 G66
Craigenbay Rd. (Lenzie) 13 CC6
 G66
Craigenbay St. G21 23 Y10
Craigencart Ct., Clyde. G81 4 K5
 Gentle Row
Craigend Pl. G13 19 R9
Craigend St. G13 19 R9
Craigendmuir Rd. G33 25 DD10
Craigendmuir St. G33 37 Z11
Craigendon Oval, Pais. PA2 58 J17
Craigendon Rd., Pais. PA2 58 J17
Craigends Dr. (Kilb.), John. 42 B14
 PA10
 High Barholm
Craigenfeoch Av., John. 43 C15
 PA5
Craigfaulds Av., Pais. PA2 45 H15
Craigflower Gdns. G53 60 P18
Craigflower Rd. G53 60 P18

Craighalbert Rd. (Cumb.) 70 MM2
 G68
Craighalbert Way (Cumb.) 70 MM2
 G68
Craighall Rd. G4 35 V11
Craighead Av. G33 23 Z10
Craighead St. (Barr.) G78 59 L19
Craighead Way (Barr.) G78 59 L19
Craighouse St. G33 38 BB11
Craigie Pk. (Lenzie) G66 13 DD5
Craigie St. G42 51 V15
Craigiebar Dr., Pais. PA2 46 J16
Craigieburn Gdns. G20 20 S8
Craigieburn Rd. (Cumb.) 70 NN3
 G67
Craigiehall Pl. G51 34 T13
Craigiehall St. G51 35 U13
 Craigiehall Pl.
Craigielea Dr., Pais. PA3 29 H13
Craigielea Pk., Renf. PA4 17 L10
Craigielea Rd., Renf. PA4 17 M10
Craigielea St. G31 37 Y12
Craigielinn Av., Pais. PA2 58 J17
Craigievar St. G33 39 DD11
Craigleith St. G32 38 AA13
Craiglockhart St. G33 39 CC11
Craigmaddie Ter. La. G3 35 U12
 Derby St.
Craigmillar Rd. G42 51 V16
Craigmont Dr. G20 21 U9
Craigmont St. G20 21 U9
Craigmore St. G31 37 Z13
Craigmount Av., Pais. PA2 58 J17
Craigmuir Cres. G52 32 N13
Craigmuir Pl. G52 32 N13
 Craigmuir Rd.
Craigmuir Rd. G52 32 N13
Craigneil St. G33 39 DD11
Craignestock Pl. G40 36 X13
 London Rd.
Craignestock St. G40 36 X13
 Lawrie St.
Craignure Rd. (Ruther.) G73 65 Y18
Craigpark G31 37 Y12
Craigpark Dr. G31 37 Y12
Craigpark Ter. G31 37 Y12
 Craigpark
Craigpark Way (Udd.) G71 57 HH16
 Newton Dr.
Craigs Av., Clyde. G81 5 M5
Craigston Pl., John. PA5 43 D15
Craigston Rd., John. PA5 43 D15
Craigton Av. (Barr.) G78 60 N19
Craigton Dr. G51 33 R13
Craigton Dr. (Barr.) G78 60 N19
Craigton Pl. G51 33 R13
 Craigton Dr.
Craigton Pl. (Blan.) G72 68 FF19
Craigton Rd. G51 33 R13
Craigvicar Gdns. G32 39 CC13
 Hailes Av.
Craigview Av., John. PA5 43 C16
Craigwell Av. (Ruther.) 65 Z17
 G73
Crail St. G31 37 Z13
Cramond Av., Renf. PA4 32 N11
Cramond St. G5 52 W15
Cramond Ter. G32 38 BB13
Cranborne Rd. G12 20 S9
Cranbrooke Dr. G20 20 T8
Cranston St. G3 35 U12
 Great George St.
Cranworth La. G12 20 T10
 Great George St.
Cranworth St. G12 20 T10
Crarae Av. (Bears.) G61 7 R7
Crathie Dr. G11 34 S11
Crathie La. G11 34 S11
 Exeter Dr.
Craw Rd., Pais. PA2 46 J14
Crawford Av. (Lenzie) G66 13 DD6
Crawford Ct. (Giff.) G46 62 S19
 Milverton Rd.
Crawford Cres. (Udd.) G71 57 GG16
Crawford Cres. (Blan.) G72 68 FF19
Crawford Dr. G15 6 N7
Crawford La. G11 34 S11
Crawford Path G11 34 S11
 Crawford St.

Crawford St. G11 34 S11
Crawfurd Dr., Pais. PA3 29 H13
Crawfurd Gdns. (Ruther.) 65 Y18
 G73
Crawfurd Rd. (Ruther.) G73 65 Y18
Crawriggs Av. (Kirk.) G66 13 CC5
Crebar Dr. (Barr.) G78 59 M19
Crebar St. (Thorn.) G46 61 R18
Credon Gdns. (Ruther.) 65 Z18
 G73
Cree Av. (Bishop.) G64 11 Z7
Cree Gdns. G32 38 AA13
 Kilmany Dr.
Creran Dr., Renf. PA4 17 L10
Creran St. G40 36 X13
 Tobago St.
Crescent Ct., Clyde. G81 4 K6
 Swindon St.
Crescent Rd. G13 18 P9
Crescent Rd. G14 18 P9
Cresswell La. G12 20 T10
 Great George St.
Cresswell St. G12 20 T10
Cressy St. G51 33 R12
Crest Av. G13 18 P8
Crestlea Av., Pais. PA2 46 K16
Creswell Ter. (Udd.) G71 57 GG16
 Kylepark Dr.
Crichton Ct. G45 64 X19
Crichton Pl. G21 22 X10
 Crichton St.
Crichton St. G21 22 X10
Crieff Ct. G3 35 U12
 North St.
Criffell Gdns. G32 55 CC14
Criffell Rd. G32 55 CC14
Crimea St. G2 35 V12
Crinan Gdns. (Bishop.) G64 11 Y7
Crinan Rd. (Bishop.) G64 11 Y7
Crinan St. G31 37 Y12
Cripps Av., Clyde. G81 5 M7
Croft Rd. (Camb.) G72 66 BB17
Croft Wynd (Udd.) G71 69 HH17
Croftbank Av. (Both.) G71 69 HH19
Croftbank Cres. (Both.) G71 69 HH19
Croftbank Cres. (Udd.) G71 69 GG17
Croftbank St. G21 22 X10
Croftbank St. (Udd.) G71 69 GG17
Croftburn Dr. G44 64 W18
Croftcroighn Rd. G33 38 BB11
Croftend Av. G44 64 X17
Croftfoot Cotts. (Gart.) G69 27 HH9
Croftfoot Cres. G45 65 Y18
Croftfoot Dr. G45 64 X18
Croftfoot Quad. G45 64 X18
Croftfoot Rd. G44 64 W18
Croftfoot Rd. G45 64 W18
Croftfoot St. G45 65 Y18
Croftfoot Ter. G45 64 X18
Crofthead St. (Udd.) G71 69 GG17
Crofthill Av. (Udd.) G71 69 GG17
Crofthill Rd. G44 64 W17
Crofthouse Dr. G44 64 X18
Croftmont Av. G44 64 X18
Croftmoraig Av. (Chry.) 15 HH6
 G69
Crofton Av. G44 64 W18
Croftpark Av. G44 64 W18
Croftside Av. G44 64 X18
Croftspar Av. G32 39 CC13
Croftspar Dr. G32 39 CC13
Croftspar Gro. G32 39 CC13
Croftspar Pl. G32 39 CC13
Croftwood (Bishop.) G64 11 Y6
Croftwood Av. G44 64 W18
Cromart Pl. (Chry.) G69 14 FF7
Cromarty Av. G43 63 U17
Cromarty Av. (Bishop.) 11 Z7
 G64
Cromarty Gdns. (Clark.) 63 V19
 G76
Crombie Gdns. (Bail.) G69 56 EE14
Cromdale St. G51 33 R13
Cromer La., Pais. PA3 30 J12
 Abbotsburn Way
Cromer St. G20 21 U9
Cromer Way, Pais. PA3 30 J12
 Mosslands Rd.
Crompton Av. G44 63 V17

Street	Page	Ref
Daly Gdns. (Blan.) G72	69	GG19
Dalziel Dr. G41	50	T14
Dalziel Quad. G41	50	T14
Dalziel Dr.		
Dalziel Rd. G52	32	N12
Damshot Cres. G53	49	Q15
Damshot Rd. G53	49	Q16
Danby Rd. (Bail.) G69	55	DD14
Danes Av. G14	19	Q10
Danes Cres. G14	18	P9
Danes Dr. G14	18	P9
Danes La. N. G14	19	Q10
Upland Rd.		
Danes La. S. G14	19	Q10
Dunglass Av.		
Dargarvel Av. G41	50	S14
Darkwood Cres., Pais. PA3	29	H13
Darkwood Dr., Pais. PA3	29	H13
Darkwood Cres.		
Darleith St. G32	38	AA13
Darley Rd. (Cumb.) G68	70	NN1
Darnaway Av. G33	39	CC11
Darnaway Dr. G33	39	CC11
Darnaway St. G33	39	CC11
Darnick St. G21	23	Y10
Hobden St.		
Darnley Cres. (Bishop.) G64	10	X6
Darnley Gdns. G41	51	U15
Darnley Path (Thorn.) G46	61	R17
Kennisholm Av.		
Darnley Pl. G41	51	U15
Darnley Rd.		
Darnley Rd. G41	51	U15
Darnley Rd. (Barr.) G78	60	N18
Darnley St. G41	51	U15
Darroch Way (Cumb.) G67	71	PP2
Dartford St. G22	21	V10
Darvel Cres., Pais. PA1	47	M14
Darvel St. G53	60	N17
Darwin Pl., Clyde. G81	4	J6
Dava St. G51	34	S12
Davaar Rd., Pais. PA2	46	K16
Davaar Rd., Renf. PA4	31	M11
Davaar St. G40	53	Y14
Daventry Dr. G12	20	S9
David Pl. (Bail.) G69	55	DD14
David Pl., Pais. PA3	31	L12
Killarn Way		
David St. G40	37	Y13
David Way, Pais. PA3	31	L12
Killarn Way		
Davidson Gdns. G14	19	Q10
Westland Dr.		
Davidson Pl. G32	39	CC13
Davidson St. G40	53	Y15
Davidson St., Clyde. G81	18	N8
Davidston Pl. (Kirk.) G66	13	DD6
Davieland Rd. (Giff.) G46	62	S19
Daviot St. G51	33	Q13
Dawes La. N. G14	19	Q10
Upland Rd.		
Dawson Pl. G4	21	V10
Dawson Rd.		
Dawson Rd. G4	21	V10
Dealston Rd. (Barr.) G78	59	L18
Dean Pk. Dr. (Camb.) G72	67	CC18
Dean Pk. Rd., Renf. PA4	32	N11
Dean St., Clyde. G81	5	M7
Deanbrae St. (Udd.) G71	69	GG17
Deanfield Quad. G52	32	N13
Deans Av. (Camb.) G72	67	CC18
Deanside La. G4	36	W12
Rottenrow		
Deanside Rd. G52	32	P12
Deanston Dr. G41	51	U16
Deanwood Av. G44	63	U18
Deanwood Rd. G44	63	U18
Debdale Cotts. G13	19	R9
Whittingehame Dr.		
Dechmont Av. (Camb.) G72	67	CC18
Dechmont Gdns. (Udd.) G71	57	GG15
Dechmont Gdns. (Blan.) G72	68	FF19
Dechmont Pl. (Camb.) G72	67	CC18
Dechmont Rd. (Udd.) G71	57	GG15
Dechmont St. G31	53	Z14
Dechmont Vw. (Udd.) G71	57	HH16
Hamilton Vw.		
Dee Av., Pais. PA2	45	G15
Dee Av., Renf. PA4	18	N10
Dee Dr., Pais. PA2	45	G15
Dee Pl., John. PA5	43	C16
Dee St. G33	37	Z11
Deepdene Rd. (Bears.) G61	7	Q7
Deepdene Rd. (Chry.) G69	15	HH7
Delburn St. G31	53	Z14
Delhi Av., Clyde. G81	4	J6
Delny Pl. G33	39	DD12
Delvin Rd. G44	63	V17
Denbeck St. G32	38	AA13
Denbrae St. G32	38	AA13
Dene Wk. (Bishop.) G64	23	Z8
Denewood Av., Pais. PA2	46	J16
Denham St. G22	21	V10
Denholme Dr. (Giff.) G46	62	T19
Denkenny Sq. G15	6	N6
Denmark St. G22	22	W10
Denmilne Path G34	40	FF12
Denmilne Pl. G34	40	FF12
Denmilne Rd. (Bail.) G69	40	FF12
Denmilne St. G34	40	FF12
Derby St. G3	35	U12
Derby Ter. La. G3	35	U12
Derby St.		
Derwent St. G22	21	V10
Despard Av. G32	55	DD14
Despard Gdns. G32	55	DD14
Deveron Av. (Giff.) G46	62	T19
Deveron Rd. (Bears.) G61	7	Q7
Deveron St. G33	37	Z11
Devol Cres. G53	48	P16
Devon Gdns. G12	20	S10
Hyndland Rd.		
Devon Gdns. (Bishop.) G64	10	X6
Devon Pl. G41	51	V14
Devon St. G5	51	V14
Devondale Av. (Blan.) G72	68	FF19
Devonshire Gdns. G12	20	S10
Devonshire Gdns. La. G12	20	S10
Hyndland Rd.		
Devonshire Ter. G12	20	S10
Devonshire Ter. La. G12	20	S10
Hughenden Rd.		
Dewar Clo. (Udd.) G71	57	HH15
Diana Av. G13	18	P8
Dick St. G20	21	U10
Henderson St.		
Dickens Av., Clyde. G81	4	K6
Dilwara Av. G14	33	R11
Dimity St., John. PA5	43	D15
Dinard Dr. (Giff.) G46	62	T18
Dinart St. G33	37	Z11
Dinduff St. G34	40	FF11
Dingwall St. G3	34	T12
Kelvinhaugh St.		
Dinmont Pl. G41	51	U15
Norham St.		
Dinmont Rd. G41	50	T15
Dinwiddie St. G21	37	Z11
Dipple Pl. G15	6	P7
Dirleton Av. G41	51	U16
Dirleton Dr., Pais. PA2	45	H15
Dirleton Gate (Bears.) G61	7	Q7
Dixon Av. G42	51	V15
Dixon Rd. G42	52	W15
Dixon St. G1	35	V13
Dixon St., Pais. PA1	46	K14
Dobbies Ln. G4	35	V11
Dobbies Ln. Pl. G4	36	W12
Dochart Av., Renf. PA4	32	N11
Dochart St. G33	38	AA11
Dock St., Clyde. G81	17	M8
Dodhill Pl. G13	18	P9
Dodside Gdns. G32	55	CC14
Dodside Pl. G32	55	CC14
Dodside St. G32	55	CC14
Dolan St. (Bail.) G69	40	EE13
Dollar Ter. G20	20	T8
Crosbie St.		
Dolphin Rd. G41	50	T15
Don Av., Renf. PA4	32	N11
Don Dr., Pais. PA2	45	G15
Don Pl., John. PA5	43	C16
Don St. G33	37	Z12
Donald Way (Udd.) G71	57	HH16
Donaldson Dr., Renf. PA4	17	M10
Ferguson St.		
Donaldson Grn. (Udd.) G71	57	HH16
Donaldswood Pk., Pais. PA2	46	J16
Donaldswood Rd., Pais. PA2	46	J16
Doncaster St. G20	21	V10
Doon Cres. (Bears.) G61	7	Q6
Doon Side (Cumb.) G67	71	PP3
Doon St., Clyde. G81	5	M6
Doonfoot Rd. G43	62	T17
Dora St. G40	53	Y14
Dorchester Av. G12	20	S9
Dorchester Ct. G12	20	S9
Dorchester Av.		
Dorchester Pl. G12	20	S9
Dorlin Rd. G33	25	DD9
Dormanside Ct. G53	48	P14
Dormanside Gate G53	48	P14
Dormanside Gro. G53	48	P14
Dormanside Rd. G53	48	P14
Dornal Av. G13	18	N8
Dornford Av. G32	55	CC15
Dornford Rd. G32	55	CC15
Dornie Dr. G32	55	CC16
Dornie Dr. (Thorn.) G46	61	R18
Dornoch Av. (Giff.) G46	62	T19
Dornoch Pl. (Bishop.) G64	11	Z7
Dornoch Pl. (Chry.) G69	14	FF7
Dornoch Rd. (Bears.) G61	7	Q7
Dornoch St. G40	36	X13
Dornoch Way (Cumb.) G68	71	PP1
Dorset Sq. G3	35	U12
Dorset St.		
Dorset St. G3	35	U12
Dosk Av. G13	18	N8
Dosk Pl. G13	18	N8
Dougalston Rd. G23	9	U7
Douglas Av. G32	54	BB15
Douglas Av. (Giff.) G46	62	T19
Douglas Av. (Lenzie) G66	13	CC5
Douglas Av. (Ruther.) G73	65	Z17
Douglas Av. (Elder.), John. PA5	44	E15
Douglas Ct. (Lenzie) G66	13	CC5
Douglas Cres. (Udd.) G71	57	HH16
Douglas Dr. G15	6	N7
Douglas Dr. (Bail.) G69	39	DD13
Douglas Dr. (Both.) G71	69	HH19
Douglas Dr. (Camb.) G72	66	AA17
Douglas Gdns. (Giff.) G46	62	T19
Douglas Gdns. (Bears.) G61	7	R6
Douglas Gdns. (Lenzie) G66	13	CC5
Douglas Gdns. (Udd.) G71	69	GG17
Douglas La. G2	35	V12
West George St.		
Douglas Pk. Cres. (Bears.) G61	8	S5
Douglas Pl. (Bears.) G61	7	R5
Douglas Pl. (Kirk.) G66	13	CC5
Douglas Av.		
Douglas Rd., Renf. PA4	31	L12
Douglas St. G2	35	V12
Douglas St. (Udd.) G71	57	HH16
Douglas St., Pais. PA1	30	J13
Douglas Ter. G41	51	U15
Glencairn Dr.		
Douglas Ter., Pais. PA3	30	K11
Dougray Pl. (Barr.) G78	59	M19
Dougrie Dr. G45	64	W18
Dougrie Pl. G45	64	X18
Dougrie Rd. G45	64	W19
Dougrie St. G45	64	X18
Dougrie Ter. G45	64	W18
Doune Cres. (Bishop.) G64	11	Y6
Doune Gdns. G20	21	U10
Doune Quad. G20	21	U10
Dove St. G53	60	P17
Dovecot G43	50	T16
Shawhill Rd.		
Dovecothall St. (Barr.) G78	59	M18
Dover St. G3	35	U12
Dowanfield Rd. (Cumb.) G67	70	NN3
Dowanhill Pl. G11	34	T11
Old Dumbarton Rd.		
Dowanhill St. G11	34	T11
Dowanhill St. G12	34	T11

Dowanside La. G12	20	T10
Byres Rd.		
Dowanside Rd. G12	20	T10
Dowanvale Ter. G11	34	S11
White St.		
Downcraig Dr. G45	64	W19
Downcraig Gro. G45	64	W19
Downcraig Rd. G45	64	W19
Downcraig Ter. G45	64	W19
Downfield Gdns. (Both.) G71	69	GG19
Downfield St. G32	54	AA14
Downie Clo. (Udd.) G71	57	HH16
Downiebrae Rd. (Ruther.) G73	53	Y15
Downs St. G21	22	X10
Dowrie Cres. G53	48	P15
Dows Pl. G4	21	V10
Possil Rd.		
Drainie St. G34	40	EE12
Westerhouse Rd.		
Drake St. G40	36	X13
Drakemire Av. G45	64	W18
Drakemire Dr. G44	64	W18
Drakemire Dr. G45	64	W18
Dreghorn St. G31	37	Z12
Drem Pl. G11	34	S11
Merkland St.		
Drimnin Rd. G33	25	DD9
Drive Rd. G51	33	R12
Drochil St. G34	40	EE11
Drumbeg Dr. G53	60	P17
Drumbeg Pl. G53	60	P17
Drumbottie Rd. G21	23	Y9
Drumby Cres. (Clark.) G76	62	T19
Drumcavel Rd. (Muir.) G69	26	FF8
Drumchapel Gdns. G15	6	P7
Drumchapel Pl. G15	6	P7
Drumchapel Rd. G15	6	P7
Drumclog Gdns. G33	24	AA9
Drumcross Rd. G53	49	Q15
Drumhead Pl. G32	54	AA15
Drumhead Rd. G32	54	AA15
Drumilaw Rd. (Ruther.) G73	65	Y17
Drumilaw Way (Ruther.) G73	65	Y17
Drumlaken Av. G23	8	T7
Drumlaken Ct. G23	8	T7
Drumlaken St. G23	8	T7
Drumlanrig Av. G34	40	FF11
Drumlanrig Pl. G34	40	FF11
Drumlanrig Quad. G34	40	FF11
Drumlochy Rd. G33	38	BB11
Drummond Av. (Ruther.) G73	52	X16
Drummond Dr., Pais. PA1	47	N14
Drummond Gdns. G13	19	R9
Crow Rd.		
Drummore Rd. G15	6	P5
Drumover Dr. G31	54	AA14
Drumoyne Av. G51	33	R12
Drumoyne Circ. G51	33	R13
Drumoyne Dr. G51	33	R12
Drumoyne Pl. G51	33	R13
Drumoyne Circ.		
Drumoyne Quad. G51	33	R13
Drumoyne Rd. G51	33	R13
Drumoyne Sq. G51	33	R13
Drumpark St. (Thorn.) G46	61	R18
Drumpark St., Coat. ML5	57	HH14
Dunnachie Dr.		
Drumpellier Av. (Bail.) G69	56	EE14
Drumpellier Pl. (Bail.) G69	56	EE14
Drumpellier Rd. (Bail.) G69	56	EE14
Drumpellier St. G33	37	Z11
Drumreoch Dr. G42	52	X16
Drumreoch Pl. G42	52	X16
Drumry Pl. G15	6	N7
Drumry Rd., Clyde. G81	5	L6
Drumry Rd. E. G15	5	M7
Drums Av., Pais. PA3	29	H13
Drums Cres., Pais. PA3	30	J13
Drums Rd. G53	48	P14
Drumsack Av. (Chry.) G69	26	FF8
Drumsargard Rd. (Ruther.) G73	65	Z17
Drumshaw Dr. G32	55	CC16
Drumvale Dr. (Chry.) G69	15	GG7
Drury St. G2	35	V12
Dryad St. (Thorn.) G46	61	R17
Dryborough Av., Pais. PA2	45	H15
Dryburgh Av. (Ruther.) G73	53	Y16
Dryburgh Gdns. G20	21	U10
Dryburgh Rd. (Bears.) G61	7	Q5
Dryburgh Wk. (Mood.) G69	15	HH6
Dryburn Av. G52	32	P13
Drygate G4	36	X12
Drygrange Rd. G33	39	CC11
Drymen Pl. (Lenzie) G66	13	CC6
Drymen Rd. (Bears.) G61	7	Q5
Drymen St. G52	33	R13
Morven St.		
Drymen Wynd (Bears.) G61	7	R6
Drynoch Pl. G22	21	V8
Drysdale St. G14	18	N9
Duart Dr. (Elder.), John. PA5	44	E15
Duart St. G20	20	T8
Dubs Rd. (Barr.) G78	60	N18
Dubton Path G34	40	EE11
Dubton St. G34	40	EE11
Duchall Pl. G14	18	P10
Duchess Pl. (Ruther.) G73	53	Z16
Duchess Rd. (Ruther.) G73	53	Z15
Duchess Way (Bail.) G69	41	GG13
Park Rd.		
Duchray Dr., Pais. PA1	48	N14
Duchray La. G33	37	Z11
Duchray St.		
Duchray St. G33	37	Z11
Dudhope St. G33	39	CC11
Dudley Dr. G12	20	S10
Dudley La. G12	20	S10
Clarence Dr.		
Duffus Pl. G32	55	CC16
Duffus St. G34	40	EE11
Duffus Ter. G32	55	CC16
Duich Gdns. G23	9	U7
Duisdale Rd. G32	55	CC16
Duke St. G4	36	X12
Duke St. G31	36	X12
Duke St., Pais. PA2	46	K15
Duke St. (Linw.), Pais. PA3	28	F13
Dukes Gate (Both.) G71	69	GG18
Dukes Rd. (Bail.) G69	41	GG13
Dukes Rd. (Camb.) G72	65	Z17
Dukes Rd. (Ruther.) G73	65	Z17
Dulnain St. (Camb.) G72	67	DD17
Dulsie Rd. G21	23	Z9
Dumbarton Rd. G11	34	S11
Dumbarton Rd. G14	18	N9
Dumbarton Rd. (Old Kil.) G60	4	J6
Dumbarton Rd., Clyde. G81	4	J6
Dumbarton Rd. (Dunt.), Clyde. G81	4	K5
Dumbreck Av. G41	50	S14
Dumbreck Ct. G41	50	S14
Dumbreck Pl. (Kirk.) G66	13	DD6
Dumbreck Rd. G41	50	S14
Dumbreck Sq. G41	50	S14
Dumbreck Av.		
Dunagoil Rd. G45	64	W19
Dunagoil St. G45	64	X19
Dunagoil Ter. G45	64	X19
Dunalistair Dr. G33	24	BB9
Dunan Pl. G33	39	DD12
Dunard Rd. (Ruther.) G73	53	Y16
Dunard St. G20	21	U10
Dunard Way, Pais. PA3	30	J12
Mosslands Rd.		
Dunaskin St. G11	34	T11
Dunbar Av. (Ruther.) G73	53	Z16
Dunbar Av., John. PA5	43	D16
Dunbar Rd., Pais. PA2	45	H15
Dunbeith Pl. G20	20	T9
Dunblane St. G4	35	V11
Dunbrach Rd. (Cumb.) G68	70	MM2
Duncan Av. G14	19	Q10
Duncan La. G14	19	Q10
Duncan Av.		
Duncan La. N. G14	19	Q10
Ormiston Av.		
Duncan La. S. G14	19	Q10
Duncan Av.		
Duncan St., Clyde. G81	5	L6
Duncansby Rd. G33	39	CC13
Dunchattan Pl. G31	36	X12
Duke St.		
Dunchattan St. G31	36	X12
Dunchurch Rd., Pais. PA1	31	M13
Dunclutha Dr. (Both.) G71	69	HH19
Dunclutha St. G40	53	Y15
Duncombe St. G20	20	T8
Duncombe Vw., Clyde. G81	5	M6
Kirkoswald Dr.		
Duncraig Cres., John. PA5	43	C16
Duncrub Dr. (Bishop.) G64	10	X7
Duncruin St. G20	20	T8
Duncryne Av. G32	55	CC14
Duncryne Gdns. G32	55	DD14
Duncryne Pl. (Bishop.) G64	22	X8
Dundas La. G1	36	W12
Dundas St. G1	36	W12
Dundasvale Ct. G4	35	V11
Maitland St.		
Dundasvale Rd. G4	35	V11
Maitland St.		
Dundee Dr. G52	48	P14
Dundee Path G52	49	Q14
Dundee Dr.		
Dundonald Av., John. PA5	43	C15
Dundonald Rd. G12	20	T10
Dundonald Rd., Pais. PA3	31	L12
Dundrennan Rd. G42	51	U16
Dunearn Pl., Pais. PA2	47	L14
Dunearn St. G4	35	U11
Dunellan St. G52	33	R13
Dungeonhill Rd. G34	40	FF12
Dunglass Av. G14	19	Q10
Dunglass La. G14	19	Q10
Dunglass Av.		
Dunglass La. N. G14	19	Q10
Verona Av.		
Dunglass La. S. G14	19	Q10
Dunglass Av.		
Dungoil Av. (Cumb.) G68	70	LL2
Dungoil Rd. (Lenzie) G66	13	DD6
Dungoyne St. G20	20	T8
Dunira St. G32	54	AA14
Dunivaig St. G33	39	DD12
Dunkeld Av. (Ruther.) G73	53	Y16
Dunkeld Dr. (Bears.) G61	8	S6
Dunkeld Gdns. (Bishop.) G64	11	Y7
Dunkeld La. (Chry.) G69	15	HH7
Burnbrae Av.		
Dunkeld St. G31	53	Z14
Dunkenny Pl. G15	6	N6
Dunkenny Rd. G15	6	N6
Dunkenny Sq. G15	6	N6
Dunlop Cres. (Both.) G71	69	HH19
Dunlop Cres., Renf. PA4	17	M10
Fulbar St.		
Dunlop Gro. (Udd.) G71	57	HH15
Dunlop St. G1	36	W13
Dunlop St. (Camb.) G72	67	DD17
Dunlop St. (Linw.), Pais. PA3	28	F13
Dunlop St., Renf. PA4	17	M10
Fulbar St.		
Dunmore La. G5	35	V13
Norfolk St.		
Dunmore St. G5	35	V13
Dunmore St., Clyde. G81	17	M8
Dunn St. G40	53	Y14
Dunn St., Clyde. G81	4	K6
Dunn St. (Dunt.), Clyde. G81	4	K5
Dunn St., Pais. PA1	47	L14
Dunnachie Dr., Coat. ML5	57	HH14
Dunnichen Pl. (Bishop.) G64	11	Z7
Dunning St. G31	53	Z14
Dunolly St. G21	37	Y11
Dunottar St. G33	38	BB11
Dunottar St. (Bishop.) G64	11	Z7
Dunphail Dr. G34	40	FF12
Dunphail Rd. G34	40	FF12
Dunragit St. G31	37	Z12
Dunrobin Av. (Elder.), John. PA5	44	F15
Dunrobin St. G31	37	Y13
Dunrod St. G32	54	BB14
Dunside Dr. G53	60	P17
Dunskaith Pl. G34	40	FF12
Dunskaith St. G34	40	FF12

Dunsmuir St. G51   34   S12
Dunster Gdns. (Bishop.) G64   11   Y6
Dunswin Av., Clyde. G81   4   K6
Dunswin Ct., Clyde. G81   4   K6
Dunswin Av.
Dunsyre Pl. G23   9   U7
Dunsyre St. G33   38   AA12
Duntarvie Cres. G34   40   FF12
Duntarvie Dr. G34   40   EE12
Duntarvie Pl. G34   40   EE12
Duntarvie Quad. G34   40   FF12
Duntarvie Rd. G34   40   EE12
Dunterle Ct. (Barr.) G78   59   M18
Dunterlie Av. G13   18   P9
Duntiglennan Rd., Clyde.   5   L5
   G81
Duntocher Rd. (Bears.) G61   6   P5
Duntocher Rd., Clyde. G81   4   K6
Duntocher Rd. (Dunt.),   5   L5
   Clyde. G81
Duntocher St. G21   22   X10
Northcroft Rd.
Duntreath Av. G13   18   N8
Duntreath Av. G15   18   N8
Duntreath Dr. G15   6   N7
Duntreath Gdns. G15   6   N7
Duntreath Gro. G15   6   N7
Duntroon St. G31   37   Y12
Dunure Dr. (Ruther.) G73   64   X17
Dunure St. G20   20   T8
Dunvegan Av. (Elder.),   44   F15
   John. PA5
Dunvegan Ct. G13   18   P9
Kintillo Dr.
Dunvegan Dr. (Bishop.)   11   Y6
   G64
Dunvegan Quad., Renf.   17   L10
   PA4
Kirklandneuk Rd.
Dunwan Av. G13   18   N8
Dunwan Pl. G13   18   N8
Durban Av., Clyde. G81   4   J6
Durham St. G41   34   T13
Durness Av. (Bears.) G61   8   S5
Durno Path G33   39   DD12
Duror St. G32   38   BB13
Durris Gdns. G32   55   CC14
Durrockstock Cres., Pais.   45   G16
   PA2
Durrockstock Rd., Pais. PA2   45   G16
Durward Av. G41   50   T15
Durward Cres., Pais. PA2   45   G15
Durwood Ct. G41   50   T15
Duthil St. G51   33   Q13
Dyce La. G11   34   S11
Dyers La. G1   36   W13
Turnbull St.
Dyers Wynd, Pais. PA1   30   K13
Gilmour St.
Dyke Pl. G13   18   P8
Dyke Rd. G13   18   N9
Dyke Rd. G14   18   N9
Dyke St. (Bail.) G69   40   FF13
Dykebar Av. G13   18   P9
Dykebar Cres., Pais. PA2   47   L15
Dykefoot Dr. G53   49   Q16
Dykehead La. G33   39   CC12
Dykehead Rd. (Bail.) G69   41   GG13
Dykehead St. G33   39   CC12
Dykemuir Pl. G21   23   Y10
Dykemuir Quad. G21   23   Y10
Dykemuir St.
Dykemuir St. G21   23   Y10

E

Eagle Cres. (Bears.) G61   6   P5
Eagle St. G4   36   W11
Eaglesham Ct. G51   35   U13
Blackburn St.
Eaglesham Pl. G51   35   U13
Earl Haig Rd. G52   32   N12
Earl La. G14   19   Q10
Harland St.
Earl Pl. G14   19   Q10
Earl St. G14   18   P10
Earlbank Av. G14   19   Q10
Earlbank La. N. G14   19   Q10
Dunglass Av.

Earlbank La. S. G14   19   Q10
Verona Av.
Earls Ct. (Mood.) G69   15   GG7
Longdale Rd.
Earls Gate (Both.) G71   69   GG18
Earls Hill (Cumb.) G68   70   LL2
Earlsburn Rd. (Lenzie) G66   13   DD6
Earlspark Av. G43   51   U16
Earn Av. (Bears.) G61   8   S6
Earn Av., Renf. PA4   32   N11
Almond Av.
Earn St. G33   38   AA11
Earnock St. G33   23   Z10
Earnside St. G32   38   BB13
Easdale Dr. G32   54   BB14
East Av., Renf. PA4   17   M10
East Barns St., Clyde. G81   17   M8
East Bath La. G2   35   V12
Sauchiehall St.
East Buchanan St., Pais.   30   K13
   PA1
East Campbell St. G1   36   X13
East Greenlees Av.   67   CC18
   (Camb.) G72
East Greenlees Cres.   66   BB18
   (Camb.) G72
East Greenlees Dr.   66   BB18
   (Camb.) G72
East Greenlees Gro.   66   BB18
   (Camb.) G72
East Greenlees Rd.   66   BB18
   (Camb.) G72
East Hallhill Rd. (Bail.) G69   40   EE13
East Kilbride Expressway   66   BB19
   (Camb.) G72
East Kilbride Rd. (Ruther.)   65   Z17
   G73
East La., Pais. PA1   47   L14
East Reid St. (Ruther.) G73   53   Z16
East Rd. (Kilb.), John. PA10   42   B14
East Springfield Ter.   23   Y8
   (Bishop.) G64
East Thomson St., Clyde.   5   L6
   G81
East Wellington St. G31   37   Z13
East Whitby St. G31   53   Z14
Eastburn Rd. G21   23   Y9
Eastcote Av. G14   19   R10
Eastcroft (Ruther.) G73   53   Y16
Eastcroft Ter. G21   23   Y10
Easter Av. (Udd.) G71   69   GG17
Easter Garngaber Rd.   13   DD5
   (Lenzie) G66
Easter Ms. (Udd.) G71   69   GG17
Church St.
Easter Queenslie Rd. G33   39   DD12
Eastercraigs G31   37   Y12
Easterhill Pl. G32   54   AA14
Easterhill St. G32   54   AA14
Easterhouse Path G34   40   FF12
Easterhouse Pl. G34   40   FF12
Easterhouse Quad. G34   40   FF12
Easterhouse Rd. G34   40   FF12
Easterhouse Rd. (Bail.) G69   40   FF12
Eastfield Av. (Camb.) G72   66   AA17
Eastfield Rd. G21   22   X10
Eastfield Rd. (Cumb.) G68   70   MM2
Eastgate (Gart.) G69   27   HH9
Easthall Pl. G33   39   DD12
Eastmuir St. G32   38   BB13
Eastvale Pl. G3   34   T12
Eastwood Av. G41   50   T16
Eastwood Av. (Giff.) G46   62   T19
Eastwood Ct. (Thorn.) G46   61   R18
Main St.
Eastwood Cres. (Thorn.)   61   R18
   G46
Eastwood Rd. (Chry.) G69   15   GG7
Eastwood Vw. (Camb.) G72   67   DD17
Eastwoodmains Rd. (Giff.)   62   S19
   G46
Eastwoodmains Rd.   62   S19
   (Clark.) G76
Easwald Bk. (Mill.Pk.),   42   B15
   John. PA10
Eccles St. G22   22   X9
Eckford St. G32   54   BB14
Eday St. G22   22   W9
Edderton Pl. G34   40   EE12

Eddleston Pl. (Camb.) G72   67   DD17
Eddlewood Path G33   39   DD12
Eddlewood Pl. G33   39   DD12
Eddlewood Rd. G33   39   DD12
Edelweiss Ter. G11   34   S11
Gardner St.
Eden La. G33   37   Z11
Eden Pk. (Both.) G71   69   GG19
Eden Pl. (Camb.) G72   67   CC17
Eden Pl., Renf. PA4   32   N11
Eden St. G33   37   Z11
Edenwood St. G31   38   AA13
Edgam Dr. G52   33   Q13
Edgefauld Av. G21   22   X10
Edgefauld Dr. G21   22   X10
Edgefauld Pl. G21   22   X9
Balgrayhill Rd.
Edgefauld Rd. G21   22   X10
Edgehill La. G11   20   S10
Marlborough Av.
Edgehill Rd. G11   20   S10
Edgehill Rd. (Bears.) G61   7   R5
Edgemont St. G41   51   U16
Edinbeg Av. G42   52   X16
Edinbeg Pl. G42   52   X16
Edinburgh Rd. G33   37   Z12
Edinburgh Rd. (Bail.) G69   39   DD12
Edington Gdns. (Chry.) G69   15   GG6
Edington St. G4   35   V11
Edison St. G52   32   N12
Edmiston Dr. G51   33   R13
Edmiston Dr. (Linw.), Pais.   28   E13
   PA3
Edmiston St. G31   53   Z14
Edmondstone Ct., Clyde.   17   M8
   G81
Yokerburn Ter.
Edrom Path G32   38   AA13
Edrom St.
Edrom St. G32   38   AA13
Edward Av., Renf. PA4   18   N10
Edward St. G3   34   T12
Lumsden St.
Edward St. (Bail.) G69   41   GG13
Edward St., Clyde. G81   17   M8
Edwin St. G51   34   T13
Edzell Ct. G14   33   Q11
Edzell Dr. (Elder.), John.   44   F15
   PA5
Edzell Gdns. (Bishop.) G64   23   Z8
Edzell Pl. G14   33   Q11
Edzell St. G14   33   Q11
Egidia Av. (Giff.) G46   62   S19
Egilsay Cres. G22   22   W8
Egilsay Pl. G22   22   W8
Egilsay St. G22   22   W8
Egilsay Ter. G22   22   W8
Eglinton Ct. G5   35   V13
Eglinton Dr. (Giff.) G46   62   T19
Eglinton La. G5   51   V14
Eglinton St.
Eglinton St. G5   51   V14
Eighth St. (Udd.) G71   57   GG15
Eildon Dr. (Barr.) G78   59   M19
Eileen Gdns. (Bishop.) G64   11   Y7
Elba La. G31   37   Z13
Elcho St. G40   36   X13
Elder Gro. (Udd.) G71   57   HH16
Elder St. G51   33   R12
Elderbank (Bears.) G61   7   R6
Elderpark Gdns. G51   33   R12
Elderpark Gro. G51   33   R12
Elderpark St. G51   33   R12
Elderslie St. G3   35   U11
Eldin Pl. (Elder.), John. PA5   44   E15
Eldon Gdns. (Bishop.) G64   10   X7
Eldon St. G3   35   U11
Eldon Ter. G11   34   S11
Caird Dr.
Elgin St. G40   37   Y13
Elibank St. G33   38   BB11
Elie St. G11   34   T11
Elizabeth Cres. (Thorn.)   62   S18
   G46
Elizabeth St. G51   34   T13
Elizabethan Way, Renf. PA4   31   M11
Cockels Ln.
Ellangowan Rd. G41   50   T16
Ellergreen Rd. (Bears.) G61   7   R6

Ellerslie St., John. PA5 44 E14
Ellesmere St. G22 21 V10
Ellinger Ct., Clyde. G81 4 K6
  Scott St.
Elliot Av. (Giff.) G46 62 T19
Elliot Av., Pais. PA2 45 G16
Elliot Dr. (Giff.) G46 62 T18
Elliot La. G3 35 U12
  Elliot St.
Elliot Pl. G3 35 U12
Elliot St. G3 35 U12
Ellisland Av., Clyde. G81 5 M6
Ellisland Cres. (Ruther.) 64 X17
  G73
Ellisland Rd. G43 62 T17
Ellisland Rd. (Cumb.) G67 71 PP3
Ellismuir Fm. Rd. (Bail.) 56 FF14
  G69
Ellismuir Pl. (Bail.) G69 56 FF14
Ellismuir Rd. (Bail.) G69 56 FF14
Elliston Av. G53 61 Q17
Elliston Cres. G53 61 Q17
Elliston Dr. G53 61 Q17
Elliston Pl. G53 61 Q17
  Ravenscraig Dr.
Ellon Dr. (Linw.), Pais. PA3 28 E13
Elm Av. (Lenzie) G66 13 CC5
Elm Av., Renf. PA4 17 M10
Elm Bk. (Bishop.) G64 11 Y7
Elm Dr., John. PA5 43 D16
Elm Gdns. (Bears.) G61 7 R5
Elm La. E. G14 19 Q10
  Elm St.
Elm La. W. G14 19 Q10
  Elm St.
Elm Rd. (Ruther.) G73 65 Y18
Elm Rd., Clyde. G81 5 L5
Elm Rd., Pais. PA4 47 L15
Elm St. G14 19 Q10
Elm Wk. (Bears.) G61 7 R5
Elmbank Av. (Udd.) G71 57 HH16
Elmbank Cres. G2 35 V12
  Elmbank St.
Elmbank La. G3 35 U12
  North St.
Elmbank St. G2 35 V12
Elmbank St. La. G2 35 V12
  Elmbank St.
Elmfoot St. G5 52 W15
Elmira Rd. (Muir.) G69 26 FF8
Elmore Av. G44 63 V17
Elmore La. G44 63 V17
Elmslie Ct. (Bail.) G69 56 EE14
Elmvale Row G21 22 X10
Elmvale Row E. G21 22 X10
  Elmvale Row
Elmvale Row W. G21 22 X10
  Elmvale Row
Elmvale St. G21 22 X9
Elmwood Av. G11 19 R10
Elmwood Ct. (Both.) G71 69 HH19
  Blantyre Mill Rd.
Elmwood Gdns. G11 19 R10
  Randolph Rd.
Elmwood Gdns. (Kirk.) 12 BB5
  G66
Elmwood La. G11 19 R10
  Elmwood Av.
Elmwood Ter. G11 19 R10
  Crow Rd.
Elphin St. G23 8 T7
  Invershiel Rd.
Elphinstone Pl. G51 34 T12
Elrig Rd. G44 63 V17
Elspeth Gdns. (Bishop.) 11 Y7
  G64
Eltham St. G22 21 V10
Elvan Ct. G32 38 AA13
  Edrom St.
Elvan St. G32 38 AA13
Embo Dr. G13 18 P9
Emerson Rd. (Bishop.) G64 11 Y7
Emerson St. G20 21 V9
Emily Pl. G31 36 X13
Endfield Av. G12 20 S9
Endrick Bk. (Bishop.) G64 11 Y6
Endrick Dr. (Bears.) G61 7 R6
Endrick Dr., Pais. PA1 31 L13
Endrick St. G21 22 W10

Endsleigh Gdns. G11 20 S10
  Partickhill Rd.
Ensay St. G22 22 W8
Enterkin St. G32 54 AA14
Ericht Rd. G43 62 T17
Eriska Av. G14 18 P9
Erradale St. G22 21 V8
Erriboll Pl. G22 21 V8
Erriboll St. G22 21 V8
Errogie St. G34 40 EE12
Errol Gdns. G5 52 W14
Erskine Av. G41 50 S14
Erskine Sq. G52 32 N12
Erskine Vw., Clyde. G81 5 L6
  Singer St.
Erskinefauld Rd. (Linw.), 28 E13
  Pais. PA3
Ervie St. G34 40 FF12
Esk Av., Renf. PA4 32 N11
Esk Dr., Pais. PA2 45 G15
Esk St. G14 18 N9
Esk Way, Pais. PA2 45 G15
Eskbank St. G32 38 BB13
Eskdale Dr. (Ruther.) G73 53 Z16
Eskdale Rd. (Bears.) G61 7 Q7
Eskdale St. G42 51 V15
Esmond St. G3 34 T11
Espedair St., Pais. PA2 46 K14
Essenside Av. G15 7 Q7
Essex Dr. G14 19 R10
Essex La. G14 19 R10
Esslemont Av. G14 18 P9
Estate Quad. G32 55 CC16
Estate Rd. G32 55 CC16
Etive Av. (Bears.) G61 8 S6
Etive Ct., Clyde. G81 5 M5
Etive Cres. (Bishop.) G64 11 Y7
Etive Dr. (Giff.) G46 62 T19
Etive St. G32 38 BB13
Eton Gdns. G12 35 U11
  Oakfield Av.
Eton La. G12 35 U11
  Great George St.
Eton Pl. G12 35 U11
  Oakfield Av.
Eton Ter. G12 35 U11
  Oakfield Av.
Ettrick Av., Renf. PA4 32 N11
Ettrick Ct. (Camb.) G72 67 DD18
  Gateside Av.
Ettrick Cres. (Ruther.) G73 53 Z16
Ettrick Oval, Pais. PA2 45 G16
Ettrick Pl. G43 50 T16
Ettrick Ter., John. PA5 43 C16
Ettrick Way, Renf. PA4 32 N11
Evan Cres. (Giff.) G46 62 T19
Evan Dr. (Giff.) G46 62 T19
Evanton Dr. (Thorn.) G46 61 R18
Evanton Pl. (Thorn.) G46 61 R18
  Evanton Dr.
Everard Ct. G21 22 X8
Everard Dr. G21 22 X8
Everard Pl. G21 22 X8
Everard Quad. G21 22 X8
Everglades, The (Chry.) 26 EE8
  G69
Eversley St. G32 54 BB14
Everton Rd. G53 49 Q15
Ewart Pl. G3 34 T12
  Kelvinhaugh St.
Ewing Pl. G31 37 Z13
Ewing St. (Ruther.) G73 53 Y16
Ewing St. (Kilb.), John. 42 B14
  PA10
Exchange Pl. G1 36 W12
  Buchanan St.
Exeter Dr. G11 34 S11
Exeter La. G11 34 S11
  Exeter Dr.
Exhibition Way G3 35 U12
Eynort St. G22 21 V8

F

Fagan Ct. (Blan.) G72 69 GG19
Faifley Rd., Clyde. G81 5 L5
Fairbairn Cres. (Thorn.) G46 62 S19
Fairbairn Path G40 53 Y14
  Ruby St.

Fairbairn St. G40 53 Y14
  Dalmarnock Rd.
Fairburn St. G32 54 AA14
Fairfax Av. G44 64 W17
Fairfield Gdns. G51 33 R12
Fairfield Pl. G51 33 R12
Fairfield Pl. (Both.) G71 69 HH19
Fairfield St. G51 33 R12
Fairhaven Dr. G23 20 T8
Fairhill Av. G53 49 Q16
Fairholm St. G32 54 AA14
Fairley St. G51 34 S13
Fairlie Pk. Dr. G11 34 S11
Fairway Av., Pais. PA2 46 J16
Fairways (Bears.) G61 6 P5
Fairways Vw., Clyde. G81 5 M5
Fairyknowe Gdns. (Both.) 69 HH19
  G71
Falcon Cres., Pais. PA3 29 H13
Falcon Rd., John. PA5 43 C16
Falcon Ter. G20 20 T8
Falcon Ter. La. G20 20 T8
Falfield St. G5 51 V14
Falkland Cres. (Bishop.) 23 Z8
  G64
Falkland La. G12 20 S10
  Clarence Dr.
Falkland Mans. G12 20 S10
  Clarence Dr.
Falkland St. G12 20 S10
Falloch Rd. G42 51 V16
Falloch Rd. (Bears.) G61 7 Q7
Fallside Rd. (Both.) G71 69 HH19
Falside Av., Pais. PA2 46 K15
Falside Rd. G32 54 BB14
Falside Rd., Pais. PA2 46 J15
Fara St. G23 21 U8
Farie St. (Ruther.) G73 53 Y16
Farm Ct. (Both.) G71 69 HH18
Farm La. (Udd.) G71 69 HH17
  Myers Cres.
Farm Pk. (Lenzie) G66 13 CC6
Farm Rd. G41 50 S14
Farm Rd. (Blan.) G72 68 FF19
Farm Rd. (Dalmuir), Clyde. 4 J6
  G81
Farm Rd. (Dunt.), Clyde. 5 L5
  G81
Farme Cross (Ruther.) G73 53 Y15
Farmeloan Rd. (Ruther.) 53 Y16
  G73
Farmington Av. G32 39 CC13
Farmington Gdns. G32 39 CC13
Farmington Gate G32 39 CC13
Farmington Gro. G32 39 CC13
Farne Dr. G44 63 V18
Farnell St. G4 35 V11
Farrier Ct., John. PA5 43 D14
Faskally Av. (Bishop.) G64 10 X6
Faskin Cres. G53 48 N16
Faskin Pl. G53 48 N16
Faskin Rd. G53 48 N16
Fasque Pl. G15 6 N6
Fastnet St. G33 38 BB12
Fauldhouse St. G5 52 W14
Faulds (Bail.) G69 40 FF13
Faulds Gdns. (Bail.) G69 40 FF13
Fauldshead Rd., Renf. PA4 17 M10
Fauldspark Cres. (Bail.) G69 40 FF13
Fauldswood Cres., Pais. 45 H15
  PA2
Fauldswood Dr., Pais. PA2 45 H15
Fearnmore Rd. G20 20 T8
Felton Pl. G13 18 N8
Fendoch St. G32 54 BB14
Fenella St. G32 38 BB13
Fennsbank Av. (Ruther.) 65 Z18
  G73
Fenwick Dr. (Barr.) G78 59 M19
Fenwick Pl. (Giff.) G46 62 S19
Fenwick Rd. (Giff.) G46 62 T18
Fereneze Av. (Barr.) G78 59 L18
Fereneze Av., Renf. PA4 31 L12
Fereneze Cres. G13 18 P8
Fereneze Dr., Pais. PA2 46 J16
Fereneze Rd. (Barr.) G78 58 J19
Fergus Av., Pais. PA3 29 H13
  Westburn Av.
Fergus Ct. G20 21 U10

111

Foxbar Rd., Pais. PA2 45 G16
Foxes Gro. (Lenzie) G66 13 DD5
Foxglove Pl. G53 60 P18
Foxhills Pl. G23 9 U7
Foxley St. G32 55 CC15
Foyers Ct. G13 18 P9
Kirkton Av.
Foyers Ter. G21 23 Y10
Francis St. G5 51 V14
Frankfield Rd. G33 25 DD9
Frankfield St. G33 37 Z11
Frankfort St. G41 51 U15
Franklin St. G40 52 X14
Fraser Av. (Ruther.) G73 53 Z16
Fraser Av., John. PA5 44 E15
Fraser St. (Camb.) G72 66 AA17
Fraserbank St. G21 22 W10
Keppochhill Rd.
Frazer St. G40 37 Y13
Freeland Ct. G53 60 P17
Freeland Dr. G53 60 P17
Freeland Dr. (Inch.), Renf. 16 J9
PA4
Freelands Ct. (Old Kil.) G60 4 J5
Freelands Pl. (Old Kil.) G60 4 J6
Freelands Rd. (Old Kil.) G60 4 J5
French St. G40 52 X14
French St., Clyde. G81 4 K6
French St., Renf. PA4 31 L11
Freuchie St. G34 40 EE12
Friar Av. (Bishop.) G64 11 Y6
Friars Ct. Rd. (Chry.) G69 14 EE7
Friars Pl. G13 19 Q8
Friarscourt Av. G13 7 Q7
Friarscourt La. G13 19 Q8
Arrowsmith Av.
Friarton Rd. G43 63 U17
Friendship Way, Renf. PA4 31 M11
Fruin Pl. G22 22 W10
Fruin Rd. G15 6 N7
Fruin St. G22 22 W10
Fulbar Av., Renf. PA4 17 M10
Fulbar Ct., Renf. PA4 17 M10
Fulbar Av.
Fulbar Cres., Pais. PA2 45 G15
Fulbar Gdns., Pais. PA2 45 G15
Peacock Dr.
Fulbar La., Renf. PA4 17 M10
Fulbar Rd. G51 33 Q12
Fulbar Rd., Pais. PA2 45 G15
Fulbar St., Renf. PA4 17 M10
Fullarton Av. G32 54 BB15
Fullarton La. G32 54 BB15
Fullarton Rd. G32 54 AA16
Fullarton Rd. (Cumb.) G68 70 NN1
Fullerton St., Pais. PA3 30 J12
Fullerton Ter., Pais. PA3 30 K12
Fulmar Ct. (Bishop.) G64 22 X8
Fulmar Pl., John. PA5 43 C16
Fulton Cres. (Kilb.), John. 42 B14
PA10
Fulton St. G13 19 Q8
Fulwood Av. G13 18 N8
Fulwood Av. (Linw.), Pais. 28 E13
PA3
Fulwood Pl. G13 18 N8
Fyvie Av. G43 62 S17

G

Gadie Av., Renf. PA4 32 N11
Gadie St. G33 37 Z12
Gadloch Av. (Kirk.) G66 13 CC7
Gadloch Gdns. (Kirk.) G66 13 CC6
Gadloch St. G22 22 W9
Gadlock Vw. (Kirk.) G66 13 CC7
Gadsburn Ct. G21 23 Z9
Wallacewell Quad.
Gadshill St. G21 36 X11
Gailes Pk. (Both.) G71 69 GG19
Gailes Rd. (Cumb.) G68 70 NN1
Gailes St. G40 53 Y14
Gairbraid Av. G20 20 T9
Gairbraid Ct. G20 20 T9
Gairbraid Pl. G20 20 T9
Gairbraid Ter. (Bail.) G69 41 HH13
Gairn St. G11 34 S11
Castlebank St.
Gala Av., Renf. PA4 32 N11

Gala St. G33 38 AA11
Galbraith Av. G51 33 R12
Burghead Dr.
Galbraith St. G51 33 Q12
Moss Rd.
Galdenoch St. G33 38 BB11
Gallacher Av., Pais. PA2 45 H15
Gallan Av. G23 9 U7
Galloway Dr. (Ruther.) G73 65 Y18
Galloway St. G21 22 X9
Gallowflat St. (Ruther.) G73 53 Y16
Reid St.
Gallowgate G1 36 W13
Gallowgate G4 36 W13
Gallowgate G31 37 Y13
Gallowgate G40 37 Y13
Gallowhill Av. (Lenzie) G66 13 CC5
Gallowhill Gro. (Kirk.) G66 13 CC5
Gallowhill Rd. (Kirk.) G66 13 CC5
Gallowhill Rd., Pais. PA3 30 K13
Galston St. G53 60 N17
Gamrie Dr. G53 48 P16
Gamrie Gdns. G53 48 P16
Gamrie Rd. G53 48 P16
Gannochy Dr. (Bishop.) G64 11 Z7
Gantock Cres. G33 38 BB12
Gardenside Av. G32 54 BB16
Gardenside Av. (Udd.) G71 69 GG17
Gardenside Cres. G32 54 BB16
Gardenside Gro. G32 54 BB16
Gardenside Pl. G32 54 BB16
Gardenside St. (Udd.) G71 69 GG17
Gardner Gro. (Udd.) G71 57 HH16
Gardner La. (Bail.) G69 56 FF14
Church St.
Gardner St. G11 34 S11
Gardyne St. G34 40 EE11
Garfield St. G31 37 Y13
Garforth Rd. (Bail.) G69 55 DD14
Gargrave Av. (Bail.) G69 55 DD14
Garion Dr. G13 18 P9
Talbot Dr.
Garlieston Rd. G33 39 DD13
Garmouth Ct. G51 33 R12
Garmouth St.
Garmouth Gdns. G51 33 R12
Garmouth St. G51 33 R12
Garnet La. G3 35 V11
Garnet St.
Garnet St. G3 35 V11
Garnethill St. G3 35 V11
Garngaber Av. (Lenzie) G66 13 CC5
Garngaber Ct. (Kirk.) G66 13 DD5
Woodilee Rd.
Garnie Av., Ersk. PA8 4 J7
Garnie Cres., Ersk. PA8 4 J7
Garnie La., Ersk. PA8 4 J7
Garnie Oval, Ersk. PA8 4 J7
Garnie Pl., Ersk. PA8 4 J7
Garnieland Rd., Ersk. PA8 4 J7
Garnkirk La. G33 25 DD9
Garnkirk St. G21 36 X11
Garnock St. G21 36 X11
Garrell Way (Cumb.) G67 70 NN3
Garrioch Cres. G20 20 T9
Garrioch Dr. G20 20 T9
Garrioch Gate G20 20 T9
Garrioch Quad. G20 20 T9
Garrioch Rd. G20 20 T10
Garriochmill Rd. G20 21 U10
Raeberry St.
Garriochmill Way G20 21 U10
Woodside Rd.
Garrowhill Dr. (Bail.) G69 55 DD14
Garry Av. (Bears.) G61 8 S7
Garry Dr., Pais. PA2 45 H15
Garry St. G44 51 V16
Garscadden Rd. G15 6 P7
Garscadden Rd. S. G13 18 P8
Garscadden Vw., Clyde. G81 5 M6
Kirkoswald Dr.
Garscube Cross G4 35 V11
Garscube Mill (Bears.) G61 8 S7
Maryhill Rd.
Garscube Rd. G4 21 V10
Garscube Rd. G20 21 V10
Gartartan Rd., Pais. PA1 32 N13
Gartcarron Hill (Cumb.) G68 70 MM2
Dunbrach Rd.

Gartconnell Dr. (Bears.) G61 7 R5
Gartconnell Gdns. (Bears.) 7 R5
G61
Gartconnell Rd. (Bears.) 7 R5
G61
Gartcosh Rd. (Gart.) G69 41 HH12
Gartcraig Path G33 38 AA11
Gartcraig Pl.
Gartcraig Pl. G33 38 AA11
Gartcraig Rd. G33 38 AA12
Gartferry Av. (Chry.) G69 15 GG7
Gartferry Rd. (Mood.) G69 15 GG7
Gartferry St. G21 23 Y10
Garth St. G1 36 W12
Garthamlock Rd. G33 39 DD11
Garthland Dr. G31 37 Y12
Garthland La., Pais. PA1 30 K13
Gartliston Ter. (Bail.) G69 41 HH13
Gartloch Cotts. (Gart.) G69 27 GG10
Gartloch Cotts. (Muir.) G69 26 EE9
Gartloch Rd. G33 38 AA11
Gartloch Rd. G34 39 CC11
Gartloch Rd. (Gart.) G69 26 EE10
Gartly St. G44 63 U18
Clarkston Rd.
Gartmore Gdns. (Udd.) G71 57 GG16
Gartmore La. (Chry.) G69 15 HH7
Gartmore Rd., Pais. PA1 47 L14
Gartmore Ter. (Camb.) G72 66 AA18
Gartness St. G31 37 Y12
Gartocher Dr. G32 39 CC13
Gartocher Rd. G32 39 CC13
Gartochmill Rd. G20 21 U10
Gartons Rd. G21 23 Z10
Gartshore Rd. (Kirk.) G66 15 GG5
Gartshore Rd. (Chry.) G69 15 GG5
Garturk St. G42 51 V15
Garvald Ct. G40 53 Y14
Baltic St.
Garvald St. G40 53 Y14
Garve Av. G44 63 V18
Garvel Cres. G33 39 DD13
Garvel Rd. G33 39 DD13
Garvock Dr. G43 62 S17
Gas St., John. PA5 44 E14
Gask Pl. G13 18 N8
Gaskin Path G33 25 DD9
Clayhouse Rd.
Gatehouse St. G32 38 BB13
Gateside Av. (Camb.) G72 67 CC17
Gateside Cres. (Barr.) G78 59 L19
Gateside Pl. (Kilb.), John. 42 B14
PA10
Gateside Rd. (Barr.) G78 59 L19
Gateside St. G31 37 Y13
Gauldry Av. G52 49 Q14
Gauze St., Pais. PA1 30 K13
Gavins Rd., Clyde. G81 5 L5
Gavinton St. G44 63 U18
Gear Ter. G40 53 Y15
Geary St. G23 8 T7
Torrin Rd.
Geddes Rd. G21 23 Z8
Gelston St. G32 54 BB14
General Terminus Quay 35 U13
G51
Generals Gate (Udd.) G71 69 GG17
Cobblerigg Way
Gentle Row, Clyde. G81 4 K5
George Av., Clyde. G81 5 M6
Robert Burns Av.
George Cres., Clyde. G81 5 M6
George Gray St. (Ruther.) 53 Z16
G73
George La., Pais. PA1 46 K14
George St.
George Mann Ter. 65 Y17
(Ruther.) G73
George Pl., Pais. PA1 46 K14
George Reith Av. G12 19 R9
George Sq. G2 36 W12
George St. G1 36 W12
George St. (Bail.) G69 56 EE14
George St. (Barr.) G78 59 L18
George St., John. PA5 43 D14
George St., Pais. PA1 46 J14
Gertrude Pl. (Barr.) G78 59 L19
Gibb St. G21 36 X11
Royston Rd.

Gibson Cres., John. PA5 43 D15
Gibson Rd., Renf. PA4 31 L11
Gibson St. G12 34 T11
Gibson St. G40 36 X13
Giffnock Pk. Av. (Giff.) G46 62 T18
Gifford Dr. G52 32 P13
Gifford Wynd, Pais. PA2 45 G15
Gilbert St. G12 34 T12
Gilbertfield Pl. G33 38 BB11
Gilbertfield Rd. (Camb.) 67 CC18
  G72
Gilbertfield St. G33 38 BB11
Gilfillan Way, Pais. PA2 45 G16
Gilhill St. G20 20 T8
Gilia St. (Camb.) G72 66 AA17
Gillies La. (Bail.) G69 56 FF14
  Bredisholm Rd.
Gilmerton St. G32 54 BB14
Gilmour Av., Clyde. G81 5 L5
Gilmour Cres. (Ruther.) 52 X16
  G73
Gilmour Pl. G5 52 W14
Gilmour St., Clyde. G81 5 M6
Gilmour St., Pais. PA1 30 K13
Girthon St. G32 55 CC14
Girvan St. G33 37 Z11
Gladney Av. G13 18 N8
Gladsmuir Rd. G52 32 P13
Gladstone Av. (Barr.) G78 59 L19
Gladstone Av., John. PA5 43 C16
Gladstone St. G4 35 V11
Glaive Rd. G13 7 Q7
Glamis Av. (Elder.), John. 44 E15
  PA5
Glamis Gdns. (Bishop.) G64 11 Y6
Glamis Pl. G31 53 Z14
  Glamis Rd.
Glamis Rd. G31 53 Z14
Glanderston Av. (Barr.) 60 N19
  G78
Glanderston Dr. G13 18 P8
Glaselune St. G34 40 FF12
  Lochdochart Rd.
Glasgow Airport (Abbots.), 30 J11
  Pais. PA3
Glasgow Bri. G1 35 V13
Glasgow Bri. G5 35 V13
Glasgow Grn. G1 36 W13
Glasgow Grn. G40 36 W13
Glasgow Rd. G53 60 N18
Glasgow Rd. (Cumb.) G67 70 MM4
Glasgow Rd. (Cumb.V.) 71 PP2
  G67
Glasgow Rd. (Bail.) G69 55 DD14
Glasgow Rd. (Udd.) G71 56 FF16
Glasgow Rd. (Blan.) G72 68 FF19
Glasgow Rd. (Camb.) G72 54 AA16
Glasgow Rd. (Turnlaw) G72 66 AA19
Glasgow Rd. (Ruther.) G73 52 X15
Glasgow Rd. (Barr.) G78 59 M18
Glasgow Rd., Clyde. G81 17 L8
Glasgow Rd. (Hardgate), 5 L5
  Clyde. G81
Glasgow Rd., Pais. PA1 31 L13
Glasgow Rd., Renf. PA4 18 N10
Glasgow St. G12 21 U10
Glassel Rd. G34 40 FF11
Glasserton Pl. G43 63 U17
Glasserton Rd. G43 63 U17
Glassford St. G1 36 W12
Glebe, The (Both.) G71 69 HH19
Glebe Av. (Both.) G71 69 HH19
  Green St.
Glebe Ct. G4 36 W12
Glebe Hollow (Both.) G71 69 HH19
  Glebe Wynd
Glebe Pl. (Camb.) G72 66 BB17
Glebe Pl. (Ruther.) G73 52 X16
Glebe St. G4 36 W11
Glebe St., Renf. PA4 17 M10
Glebe Wynd (Both.) G71 69 HH19
Gleddoch Rd. G52 32 N13
Glen Affric Av. G53 61 Q18
Glen Affric Dr. G53 61 Q18
Glen Affric Pl. G53 61 Q18
Glen Alby Pl. G53 61 Q18
Glen Av. G32 38 BB13
Glen Av. (Chry.) G69 15 GG7
Glen Clunie Av. G53 61 Q18

Glen Clunie Dr. G53 61 Q18
Glen Clunie Pl. G53 61 Q18
Glen Cona Dr. G53 61 Q17
Glen Cres. G13 18 N8
Glen Douglas Dr. (Cumb.) 70 MM2
  G68
Glen Esk Cres. G53 61 Q18
Glen Esk Dr. G53 61 Q18
Glen Etive Pl. (Ruther.) G73 66 AA19
Glen Fyne Rd. (Cumb.) G68 70 LL2
Glen Gdns. (Elder.), John. 44 F14
  PA5
Glen La., Pais. PA3 30 K13
Glen Lednock Dr. (Cumb.) 70 MM2
  G68
Glen Livet Pl. G53 61 Q18
Glen Loy Pl. G53 61 Q18
Glen Mallie Dr. G53 61 Q18
Glen Markie Dr. G53 61 Q18
Glen Moriston Rd. G53 61 Q18
Glen Nevis Pl. (Ruther.) G73 65 Z19
Glen Ogle St. G32 55 CC14
Glen Orchy Dr. G53 61 Q18
Glen Orchy Pl. G53 61 Q18
Glen Pk. Av. (Thorn.) G46 61 R19
Glen Rd. G32 38 BB12
Glen Sax Dr., Renf. PA4 32 N11
Glen St. (Camb.) G72 67 CC18
Glen St. (Barr.) G78 59 M18
Glen St., Pais. PA3 30 J13
Glen Vw. (Cumb.) G67 71 QQ2
Glenacre Cres. (Udd.) G71 57 GG16
Glenacre Dr. G45 64 W18
Glenacre Quad. G45 64 W18
Glenacre Rd. (Cumb.) G67 70 NN4
Glenacre St. G45 64 W18
Glenacre Ter. G45 64 W18
Glenallan Way, Pais. PA2 45 G16
Glenalmond Rd. (Ruther.) 65 Z18
  G73
Glenalmond St. G32 54 BB14
Glenapp Av., Pais. PA2 47 L15
Glenapp Pl. (Mood.) G69 15 GG6
  Whithorn Cres.
Glenapp Rd., Pais. PA2 47 L15
Glenapp St. G41 51 U14
Glenarklet Dr., Pais. PA2 47 L15
Glenartney Row (Chry.) 14 FF7
  G69
Glenashdale Way, Pais. 47 L15
  PA2
  Glenbrittle Dr.
Glenavon Av. (Ruther.) G73 65 Z18
Glenavon Rd. G20 20 T8
  Thornton St.
Glenavon Ter. G11 34 S11
  Crow Rd.
Glenbank Av. (Lenzie) G66 13 CC6
Glenbank Dr. (Thorn.) G46 61 R19
Glenbank Rd. (Lenzie) G66 13 CC6
Glenbarr St. G21 36 X11
Glenbervie Cres. (Cumb.) 70 NN2
  G68
Glenbervie Pl. G23 8 T7
Glenbrittle Dr., Pais. PA2 47 L15
Glenbrittle Way, Pais. PA2 47 L15
Glenbuck Av. G33 24 AA9
Glenbuck Dr. G33 24 AA9
Glenburn Av. (Bail.) G69 40 FF13
Glenburn Av. (Chry.) G69 15 GG7
Glenburn Av. (Camb.) G72 65 Z17
Glenburn Cres., Pais. PA2 46 J16
Glenburn Gdns. (Bishop.) 10 X7
  G64
Glenburn La. G20 21 U8
  Thornton St.
Glenburn Rd. (Giff.) G46 62 S19
Glenburn Rd. (Bears.) G61 7 Q5
Glenburn Rd., Pais. PA2 45 H16
Glenburn St. G20 21 U8
Glenburnie Pl. G34 40 EE12
Glencairn Dr. G41 50 T15
Glencairn Dr. (Chry.) G69 15 GG7
Glencairn Dr. (Ruther.) G73 52 X16
Glencairn Gdns. G41 51 U15
  Glencairn Dr.
Glencairn La. G41 51 U15
  Shields Rd.
Glencairn Rd. (Cumb.) G67 71 QQ3

Glencairn Rd., Pais. PA3 31 L12
Glencally Av., Pais. PA2 47 L15
Glencart Gro. (Mill.Pk.), 43 C15
  John. PA10
  Milliken Pk. Rd.
Glenclora Dr., Pais. PA2 47 L15
Glencloy St. G20 20 T8
Glencoats Cres., Pais. PA3 29 H13
Glencoats Dr., Pais. PA3 29 H13
Glencoe Pl. G13 19 R8
Glencoe Rd. (Ruther.) G73 65 Z18
Glencoe St. G13 19 R8
Glencorse Rd., Pais. PA2 46 J15
Glencorse St. G32 38 AA12
Glencroft Av. (Udd.) G71 57 GG16
Glencroft Rd. G44 64 W17
Glencryan Rd. (Cumb.) G67 71 PP4
Glendale Cres. (Bishop.) 23 Z8
  G64
Glendale Dr. (Bishop.) G64 23 Z8
Glendale Pl. G31 37 Y13
  Glendale St.
Glendale Pl. (Bishop.) G64 23 Z8
Glendale St. G31 37 Y13
Glendaruel Av. (Bears.) G61 8 S6
Glendaruel Rd. (Ruther.) 66 AA19
  G73
Glendarvel Gdns. G22 22 W10
Glendee Gdns., Renf. PA4 31 M11
Glendee Rd., Renf. PA4 31 M11
Glendenning Rd. G13 7 R7
Glendevon Pl., Clyde. G81 4 K6
Glendevon Sq. G33 38 BB11
Glendore St. G14 33 R11
Glendower Way, Pais. PA2 45 G16
  Spencer Dr.
Glenduffhill Rd. (Bail.) G69 39 DD13
Gleneagles Av. (Cumb.) 71 PP1
  G67
Gleneagles Cotts. G14 19 Q10
  Dumbarton Rd.
Gleneagles Dr. (Bishop.) 11 Y6
  G64
Gleneagles Gdns. (Bishop.) 11 Y6
  G64
Gleneagles La. N. G14 19 Q10
  Dunglass Av.
Gleneagles La. S. G14 19 Q10
  Harland St.
Gleneagles Pk. (Both.) G71 69 GG19
Gleneagles Ter. G14 19 Q10
  Dumbarton Rd.
Glenelg Quad. G34 40 FF11
Glenfarg Cres. (Bears.) G61 8 S6
Glenfarg Rd. (Ruther.) G73 65 Y18
Glenfarg St. G20 35 V11
Glenfield Cres., Pais. PA2 58 J17
Glenfield Rd., Pais. PA2 46 J16
Glenfinnan Dr. G20 20 T9
Glenfinnan Dr. (Bears.) G61 8 T6
Glenfinnan Pl. G20 20 T9
Glenfinnan Rd. G20 20 T9
Glenfruin Dr., Pais. PA2 47 L15
Glengarry Dr. G52 33 Q13
Glengavel Cres. G33 24 AA9
Glengyre St. G34 40 FF11
Glenhead Cres. G22 22 W9
Glenhead Rd. (Lenzie) G66 13 CC6
Glenhead Rd., Clyde. G81 5 L5
Glenhead St. G22 22 W9
Glenholme, Pais. PA2 45 H15
Glenhove Rd. (Cumb.) G67 71 PP3
Gleniffer Av. G13 18 P9
Gleniffer Cres. (Elder.), 44 F15
  John. PA5
Gleniffer Dr. (Barr.) G78 59 L17
Gleniffer Rd., Pais. PA2 45 H16
Gleniffer Rd., Renf. PA4 31 L11
Gleniffer Vw., Clyde. G81 5 M6
  Kirkoswald Dr.
Glenisa Av. (Chry.) G69 15 HH6
Glenisla St. G31 53 Z14
Glenkirk Dr. G15 6 P7
Glenlee Cres. G52 48 N14
Glenlora Dr. G53 48 P16
Glenlora Ter. G53 48 P16
Glenluce Dr. G32 55 CC14
Glenluce Gdns. (Mood.) G69 15 HH6
  Brady Cres.

114

Glenlui Av. (Ruther.) G73 65 Y17
Glenlyon Pl. (Ruther.) G73 65 Z18
Glenmalloch Pl. (Elder.), 44 F14
John. PA5
Glenmanor Av. (Chry.) G69 15 GG7
Glenmavis St. G4 35 V11
Maitland St.
Glenmore Av. G42 52 X16
Glenmuir Dr. G53 60 P17
Glenpark Rd. G31 37 Y13
Glenpark St. G31 37 Y13
Glenpark Ter. (Camb.) G72 54 AA16
Glenpatrick Bldgs. (Elder.), 44 F15
John. PA5
Glenpatrick Rd. (Elder.), 44 F15
John. PA5
Glenraith Rd. G33 24 BB10
Glenraith Sq. G33 24 BB10
Glenraith Wk. G33 25 CC10
Glenshee St. G31 53 Z14
Glenshiel Av., Pais. PA2 47 L15
Glenshire Av., Pais. PA2 47 L15
Glenside Av. G53 48 P15
Glenside Dr. (Ruther.) G73 65 Z17
Glenspean Pl. G43 62 T17
Glenspean St.
Glenspean St. G43 62 T17
Glentanar Pl. G22 21 V8
Glentanar Rd. G22 21 V8
Glentarbert Rd. (Ruther.) 65 Z18
G73
Glentrool Gdns. G22 22 W10
Glenturret St. G32 54 BB14
Glentyan Av. (Kilb.), John. 42 B14
PA10
Glentyan Dr. G53 60 P17
Glentyan Ter. G53 48 P16
Glenview Cres. (Chry.) G69 15 HH6
Glenview Pl. (Blan.) G72 68 FF19
Glenville Av. (Giff.) G46 62 S18
Glenwood Ct. (Kirk.) G66 12 BB5
Glenwood Dr. (Thorn.) G46 61 R19
Glenwood Gdns. (Kirk.) G66 12 BB5
Glenwood Pl. (Kirk.) G66 12 BB5
Glenwood Rd. (Kirk.) G66 12 BB5
Gloucester Av. (Ruther.) 65 Z17
G73
Gloucester St. G5 35 V13
Gockston Rd., Pais. PA3 30 J12
Gogar Pl. G33 38 AA12
Gogar St. G33 38 AA12
Goldberry Av. G14 18 P9
Goldie Rd. (Udd.) G71 69 HH18
Golf Ct. G44 63 U19
Golf Dr. G15 6 N7
Golf Dr., Pais. PA1 47 M14
Golf Rd. (Ruther.) G73 65 Y18
Golf Vw. (Bears.) G61 6 P5
Golf Vw., Clyde. G81 4 K6
Golfhill Dr. G31 37 Y12
Golfhill La. G31 37 Y12
Whitehill St.
Golfhill Ter. G31 36 X12
Firpark St.
Golspie St. G51 34 S12
Goosedubbs G1 36 W13
Stockwell St.
Gopher Av. (Udd.) G71 57 HH16
Gorbals Cross G5 36 W13
Gorbals La. G5 35 V13
Oxford St.
Gorbals St. G5 35 V13
Gordon Av. G44 63 U19
Gordon Av. (Bail.) G69 39 DD13
Gordon Dr. G44 63 U18
Gordon La. G1 35 V12
Gordon St.
Gordon Rd. G44 63 U19
Gordon St. G1 35 V12
Gordon St., Pais. PA1 46 K14
Gordon Ter. (Blan.) G72 68 FF19
Gorebridge St. G32 38 AA12
Gorget Av. G13 7 Q7
Gorget Pl. G13 7 Q7
Gorget Quad. G13 6 P7
Gorget Av.
Gorse Dr. (Barr.) G78 59 L18
Gorse Pl. (Udd.) G71 57 HH16
Gorsewood (Bishop.) G64 10 X7

Gorstan Pl. G20 20 T9
Wyndford Rd.
Gorstan St. G23 20 T8
Gosford La. G14 18 P10
Dumbarton Rd.
Goudie St., Pais. PA3 30 J12
Gough St. G33 37 Z12
Gourlay Path G21 22 W10
Endrick St.
Gourlay St. G21 22 X10
Crichton St.
Gourock St. G5 51 V14
Govan Cross G51 34 S12
Govan Rd. G51 33 R12
Govanhill St. G42 51 V15
Gowan Brae (Kirk.) G66 13 CC5
Marguerite Av.
Gowanbank Gdns., John. 43 D15
PA5
Floors St.
Gowanlea Av. G15 6 P7
Gowanlea Dr. (Giff.) G46 62 T18
Gowanlea St. (Udd.) G71 57 HH16
Gower La. G51 34 T13
North Gower St.
Gower St. G41 50 T14
Gower Ter. G41 34 T13
Goyle Av. G15 7 Q6
Grace Av. (Bail.) G69 41 GG13
Grace St. G3 35 U12
Graffham Av. (Giff.) G46 62 T18
Grafton Pl. G1 36 W12
Graham Av. (Camb.) G72 67 CC17
Graham Av., Clyde. G81 5 L6
Graham Sq. G31 36 X13
Graham St. (Barr.) G78 59 L18
Graham St., John. PA5 43 D15
Graham Ter. (Bishop.) G64 23 Y8
Grahamston Ct., Pais. PA2 47 M16
Grahamston Cres., Pais. 47 M16
PA2
Grahamston Pk. (Barr.) 59 L17
G78
Grahamston Pl., Pais. PA2 47 M16
Grahamston Rd.
Grahamston Rd. (Barr.) G78 59 L17
Grahamston Rd., Pais. PA2 47 M16
Grainger Rd. (Bishop.) G64 11 Z7
Grampian Av., Pais. PA2 46 J16
Grampian Cres. G32 54 BB14
Grampian Pl. G32 54 BB14
Grampian St. G32 54 BB14
Grampian Way (Barr.) G78 59 M19
Gran St., Clyde. G81 18 N8
Granby La. G12 20 T10
Great George St.
Granby Pl. G12 20 T10
Great George St.
Grandtully Dr. G12 20 T9
Grange (Both.) G71 69 HH19
Blairston Av.
Grange Rd. G42 51 V16
Grange Rd. (Bears.) G61 7 R5
Grangeneuk Gdns. (Cumb.) 70 MM3
G68
Grant St. G3 35 U11
Grantlea Gro. G32 55 CC14
Grantlea Ter. G32 55 CC14
Grantley Gdns. G41 50 T16
Grantley St. G41 50 T16
Granton St. G5 52 X15
Granville St. G3 35 U12
Granville St., Clyde. G81 5 L6
Gray Dr. (Bears.) G61 7 R6
Gray St. G3 34 T11
Great Dovehill G1 36 W13
Great George La. G12 20 T10
Great George St.
Great George St. G12 20 T10
Great Hamilton St., Pais. 46 K15
PA2
Great Kelvin La. G12 21 U10
Glasgow St.
Great Western Rd. G4 20 S9
Great Western Rd. G12 20 T10
Great Western Rd. G13 6 P7
Great Western Rd. G15 6 P7
Great Western Rd., Clyde. 4 J5
G81

Great Western Ter. G12 20 T10
Green, The G40 36 X13
Green Lo. Ter. G40 52 X14
Greenhead St.
Green Pk. (Both.) G71 69 HH19
Green St.
Green Rd. (Ruther.) G73 53 Y16
Green Rd., Pais. PA2 45 G14
Green St. G40 36 X13
Green St. (Both.) G71 69 HH19
Green St., Clyde. G81 5 L6
Greenan Av. G42 52 X16
Greenbank Dr., Pais. PA2 46 J16
Greenbank Rd. (Cumb.) 70 MM3
G68
Greenbank St. (Ruther.) 53 Y16
G73
Greendyke St. G1 36 W13
Greenend Av., John. PA5 43 C15
Greenend Pl. G32 39 CC12
Greenfarm Rd. (Linw.), 28 E13
Pais. PA3
Greenfaulds Cres. (Cumb.) 71 PP4
G67
Greenfaulds Rd. (Cumb.) 70 NN4
G67
Greenfield Av. G32 38 BB12
Greenfield Pl. G32 38 BB13
Budhill Av.
Greenfield Rd. G32 39 CC13
Greenfield St. G51 33 R12
Greengairs Av. G51 33 Q12
Greenhead Rd. (Bears.) G61 7 R6
Greenhead Rd. (Inch.), 16 J8
Renf. PA4
Greenhead St. G40 52 X14
Greenhill (Bishop.) G64 11 Y7
Greenhill Av. (Giff.) G46 62 S19
Greenhill Av. (Gart.) G69 27 GG8
Greenhill Ct. (Ruther.) G73 53 Y16
Greenhill Cres. (Elder.), 44 F15
John. PA5
Greenhill Cres. (Linw.), 28 E13
Pais. PA3
Greenhill Dr. (Linw.), Pais. 28 F13
PA3
Greenhill Rd. (Ruther.) G73 53 Y16
Greenhill Rd., Pais. PA3 30 J13
Greenhill St. (Ruther.) G73 53 Y16
Greenholm Av. (Udd.) G71 57 GG16
Greenholme St. G44 63 V17
Greenknowe Rd. G43 62 S17
Greenlaw Av., Pais. PA1 31 L13
Greenlaw Cres., Pais. PA1 31 L13
Greenlaw Dr., Pais. PA1 31 L13
Greenlaw Rd. G14 17 M9
Greenlaw Ter., Pais. PA1 31 L13
Greenlaw Av.
Greenlea Rd. (Chry.) G69 26 EE8
Greenlea St. G13 19 R9
Greenlees Gdns. (Camb.) 66 AA18
G72
Greenlees Pk. (Camb.) G72 66 BB18
Greenlees Rd. (Camb.) G72 66 BB17
Greenloan Av. G51 33 Q12
Greenmount G22 21 V8
Greenock Av. G44 63 V17
Greenock Rd., Pais. PA3 30 J12
Greenock Rd. (Inch.), Renf. 16 J9
PA4
Greenrig (Udd.) G71 69 GG17
Greenrig St. G33 23 Z10
Greenrig St. (Udd.) G71 69 GG17
Greenrigg Rd. (Cumb.) G67 71 PP3
Greenshields Rd. (Bail.) 40 EE13
G69
Greenside Cres. G33 24 AA10
Greenside St. G33 24 AA10
Greentree Dr. (Bail.) G69 55 DD14
Greenview St. G43 50 T16
Greenways Av., Pais. PA2 45 H15
Greenways Ct., Pais. PA2 45 H15
Greenwell Pl. G51 34 S12
Greenwell St. G51 34 S12
Govan Rd.
Greenwood Av. (Chry.) G69 15 GG7
Greenwood Av. (Camb.) 67 DD17
G72
Greenwood Dr. (Bears.) G61 8 S6

Street	Page	Grid
Greenwood Quad., Clyde. G81	5	M7
Greer Quad., Clyde. G81	5	L6
Grenville Dr. (Camb.) G72	66	AA18
Gretna St. G40	53	Y14
Greyfriars St. G32	38	AA12
Greystone Av. (Ruther.) G73	65	Z17
Greywood St. G13	19	R8
Grierson La. G33	37	Z12
Lomax St.		
Grierson St. G33	37	Z12
Grieve Rd. (Cumb.) G67	71	PP2
Griqua Ter. (Both.) G71	69	HH19
Grogary Rd. G15	6	P6
Springside Pl.		
Grosvenor Cres. G12	20	T10
Observatory Rd.		
Grosvenor Cres. La. G12	20	T10
Byres Rd.		
Grosvenor La. G12	20	T10
Byres Rd.		
Grosvenor Mans. G12	20	T10
Observatory Rd.		
Grosvenor Ter. G12	20	T10
Grove, The (Kilb.), John. PA10	42	B14
Grove Pk. (Lenzie) G66	13	CC6
Groveburn Av. (Thorn.) G46	62	S18
Grovepark Ct. G20	35	V11
Grovepark Gdns. G20	35	V11
Grovepark Pl. G20	21	V10
Grovepark St. G20	21	V10
Groves, The (Bishop.) G64	23	Z8
Woodhill Rd.		
Grudie St. G34	40	EE12
Gryffe Av., Renf. PA4	17	L9
Gryffe Cres., Pais. PA2	45	G15
Gryffe St. G44	63	V17
Guildford St. G33	39	CC11
Gullane Cres. (Cumb.) G68	70	NN1
Gullane St. G11	34	S11
Purdon St.		
Guthrie Dr. (Udd.) G71	57	HH15
Guthrie St. G20	20	T9

H

Street	Page	Grid
Haberlea Av. G53	61	Q18
Haberlea Gdns. G53	61	Q19
Haddow Gro. (Udd.) G71	57	HH16
Hagg Cres., John. PA5	43	D14
Hagg Pl., John. PA5	43	D14
Hagg Rd., John. PA5	43	D15
Haggs Rd. G41	50	T15
Haggs Wd. Av. G41	50	S15
Haghill Rd. G31	37	Z12
Haig Dr. (Bail.) G69	55	DD14
Haig St. G21	23	Y10
Hailes Av. G32	39	CC13
Haining, The, Renf. PA4	31	M11
Haining Rd., Renf. PA4	17	M10
Hairmyres St. G42	51	V15
Govanhill St.		
Hairst St., Renf. PA4	17	M10
Halbeath Av. G15	6	N6
Halbert St. G41	51	U15
Haldane La. G14	19	Q10
Haldane St.		
Haldane St. G14	19	Q10
Halgreen Av. G15	5	M6
Halifax Way, Renf. PA4	31	M11
Britannia Way		
Hall St., Clyde. G81	5	L7
Hallbrae St. G33	38	AA11
Halley Dr. G13	18	N8
Halley Pl. G13	18	N9
Halley Sq. G13	18	N8
Halley St. G13	18	N8
Hallforest St. G33	38	BB11
Gartloch Rd.		
Hallhill Cres. G33	39	DD13
Hallhill Rd. G32	38	BB13
Hallhill Rd. G33	39	DD13
Hallhill Rd., John. PA5	43	C16
Halliburton Cres. G34	40	EE12
Ware Rd.		
Hallidale Cres., Renf. PA4	32	N11
Hallrule Dr. G52	33	Q13
Hallside Av. (Camb.) G72	67	DD17
Hallside Cres. (Camb.) G72	67	DD17
Hallside Dr. (Camb.) G72	67	DD17
Hallside Rd. (Camb.) G72	67	DD18
Hallside St. G5	52	W14
Hallydown Dr. G13	19	Q9
Halton Gdns. (Bail.) G69	55	DD14
Hamilton Av. G41	50	S14
Hamilton Cres. (Camb.) G72	67	CC18
Hamilton Cres., Renf. PA4	17	M9
Hamilton Dr. G12	21	U10
Hamilton Dr. (Giff.) G46	62	T19
Hamilton Dr. (Both.) G71	69	HH19
Hamilton Dr. (Camb.) G72	66	BB17
Hamilton Pk. Av. G12	21	U10
Hamilton Rd. G32	55	DD15
Hamilton Rd. (Both.) G71	69	HH19
Hamilton Rd. (Camb.) G72	66	BB17
Hamilton Rd. (Ruther.) G73	53	Y16
Hamilton St. G42	52	W15
Hamilton St., Clyde. G81	17	M8
Hamilton St., Pais. PA3	30	K13
Hamilton Ter., Clyde. G81	17	M8
Hamilton Vw. (Udd.) G71	57	HH16
Hamiltonhill Cres. G22	21	V10
Hamiltonhill Rd.		
Hamiltonhill Rd. G22	21	V10
Hampden Dr. G42	51	V16
Cathcart Rd.		
Hampden La. G42	51	V16
Cathcart Rd.		
Hampden Ter. G42	51	V16
Cathcart Rd.		
Hampden Way, Renf. PA4	31	M11
Lewis Av.		
Hangingshaw Pl. G42	52	W16
Hanover Clo. G42	51	V16
Battlefield Gdns.		
Hanover Ct., Pais. PA1	31	L13
Kelburne Gdns.		
Hanover Gdns., Pais. PA1	46	J14
Broomlands St.		
Hanover St. G1	36	W12
Hanson St. G31	36	X12
Hapland Av. G53	49	Q15
Hapland Rd. G53	49	Q15
Harbour La., Pais. PA3	30	K13
Harbour Rd., Pais. PA3	30	K12
Harburn Pl. G23	9	U7
Harbury Pl. G14	18	N9
Harcourt Dr. G31	37	Y12
Roebank St.		
Hardgate Dr. G51	33	Q12
Hardgate Gdns. G51	33	Q12
Hardgate Pl. G51	33	Q12
Hardgate Rd. G51	33	Q12
Hardie Av. (Ruther.) G73	53	Z16
Hardridge Av. G52	49	Q15
Hardridge Rd.		
Hardridge Pl. G52	49	R15
Hardridge Rd. G52	49	Q15
Harefield Dr. G14	18	P9
Harelaw Av. G44	63	U18
Harelaw Av. (Barr.) G78	59	M19
Harelaw Cres., Pais. PA2	46	J16
Harhill St. G51	33	R12
Harland Cotts. G14	33	Q11
South St.		
Harland St. G14	19	Q10
Harlaw Gdns. (Bishop.) G64	11	Z7
Harley St. G51	34	T13
Harmetray St. G22	22	W9
Harmony Ct. G52	34	S12
Helen St.		
Harmony Pl. G51	34	S12
Harmony Row G51	34	S12
Harmony Sq. G51	34	S12
Harmsworth St. G11	33	R11
Harport St. (Thorn.) G46	61	R18
Harriet St. (Ruther.) G73	53	Y16
Harris Rd. G23	9	U7
Harris Rd. (Old Kil.) G60	4	J5
Harrison Dr. G51	34	S13
Harrow Ct. G15	6	N6
Linkwood Dr.		
Harrow Pl. G15	6	N6
Hart St. G31	38	AA13
Hart St. (Linw.), Pais. PA3	28	E13
Hartfield Ter., Pais. PA2	47	L15
Hartlaw Cres. G52	32	P13
Hartree Av. G13	18	N8
Hartstone Pl. G53	48	P16
Hartstone Rd. G53	48	P16
Hartstone Ter. G53	48	P16
Harvey St. G4	36	W11
Harvie St. G51	34	T13
Harwood Gdns. (Mood.) G69	15	HH6
Dryburgh Wk.		
Harwood St. G32	38	AA12
Hastie St. G3	34	T11
Old Dumbarton Rd.		
Hatfield Dr. G12	19	R9
Hathaway Dr. (Giff.) G46	62	S19
Hathaway La. G20	21	U9
Avenuepark St.		
Hathaway St. G20	21	U9
Hathersage Av. (Bail.) G69	40	EE13
Hathersage Dr. (Bail.) G69	40	EE13
Hathersage Gdns. (Bail.) G69	40	EE13
Hatters Row G40	52	X14
Dalmarnock Rd.		
Hatton Dr. G52	48	P14
Hatton Gdns. G52	48	P14
Haugh Rd. G3	34	T12
Haughburn Pl. G53	48	P16
Haughburn Rd. G53	48	P16
Haughburn Ter. G53	49	Q16
Havelock La. G11	34	T11
Dowanhill St.		
Havelock St. G11	34	T11
Hawick Av., Pais. PA2	45	H15
Hawick St. G13	18	N8
Hawkhead Av., Pais. PA2	47	L15
Hawkhead Rd., Pais. PA1	47	L14
Hawkhead Rd., Pais. PA2	47	L14
Hawthorn Av. (Bishop.) G64	23	Y8
Hawthorn Av. (Lenzie) G66	13	CC5
Hawthorn Av., Ersk. PA8	16	K8
Hawthorn Av., John. PA5	44	E15
Hawthorn Cres., Ersk. PA8	4	K7
Hawthorn Quad. G22	22	W9
Hawthorn Rd., Ersk. PA8	16	K8
Hawthorn St. G22	22	W9
Hawthorn St., Clyde. G81	5	L6
Hawthorn Ter. (Udd.) G71	57	HH16
Douglas St.		
Hawthorn Wk. (Bishop.) G64	23	Z8
Letham Dr.		
Hawthorn Wk. (Camb.) G72	65	Z17
Hawthornden Gdns. G23	9	U7
Hay Dr., John. PA5	44	E14
Hayburn Cres. G11	20	S10
Hayburn Gate G11	34	S11
Fortrose St.		
Hayburn La. G11	20	S10
Queensborough Gdns.		
Hayburn St. G11	34	S11
Hayfield St. G5	52	W14
Hayhill Cotts. (Gart.) G69	27	HH9
Hayle Gdns. (Chry.) G69	15	GG6
Haylynn St. G14	33	R11
Haymarket St. G32	38	AA12
Haystack Pl. (Lenzie) G66	13	CC6
Hayston Cres. G22	21	V9
Hayston St. G22	21	V9
Haywood St. G22	21	V9
Hazel Av. G44	63	U18
Clarkston Rd.		
Hazel Av. (Lenzie) G66	13	CC5
Hazel Av., John. PA5	44	E15
Hazel Dene (Bishop.) G64	11	Y7
Hazel Gro. (Kirk.) G66	13	CC5
Hazel Rd. (Cumb.) G67	71	QQ2
Hazel Ter. (Udd.) G71	57	HH16
Douglas St.		
Hazelden Gdns. G44	63	U18
Hazellea Dr. (Giff.) G46	62	T18
Hazelwood Av., Pais. PA2	45	G16
Hazelwood Gdns. (Ruther.) G73	65	Z18
G73		
Hazelwood Rd. G41	50	T14
Hazlitt St. G20	21	V9
Heath Av. (Bishop.) G64	23	Y8
Heath Av. (Lenzie) G66	13	CC6

Holyrood Cres. G20	35	U11
Holyrood Quad. G20	35	U11
Holywell St. G31	37	Y13
Homeston Av. (Both.) G71	69	HH18
Honeybog Rd. G52	32	N13
Hood St., Clyde. G81	5	M7
Hope St. G2	35	V12
Hopefield Av. G12	20	T9
Hopehill Pl. G20	21	V10
Hopehill Rd.		
Hopehill Rd. G20	21	V10
Hopeman Av. (Thorn.) G46	61	R18
Hopeman Dr. (Thorn.) G46	61	R18
Hopeman Path (Thorn.) G46	61	R18
Kennishead Pl.		
Hopeman Rd. (Thorn.) G46	61	R18
Hopeman St. (Thorn.) G46	61	R18
Hopetoun Pl. G23	9	U7
Hopetoun Ter. G21	23	Y10
Foresthall Dr.		
Hornal Rd. (Udd.) G71	69	HH18
Hornbeam Dr., Clyde. G81	5	L6
Hornbeam Rd. (Udd.) G71	57	HH16
Horndean Ct. (Bishop.) G64	11	Y6
Horndean Cres. G33	39	CC11
Horne St. G22	22	X9
Hawthorn St.		
Hornshill Rd. (Stepps) G33	25	DD8
Hornshill St. G21	23	Y10
Horsburgh St. G33	39	CC11
Horse Shoe La. (Bears.) G61	7	R6
Horse Shoe Rd. (Bears.) G61	7	R5
Horselethill Rd. G12	20	T10
Hospital St. G5	51	V14
Hotspur St. G20	21	U10
Houldsworth La. G3	35	U12
Finnieston St.		
Houldsworth St. G3	35	U12
Househillmuir Cres. G53	49	Q16
Househillmuir La. G53	49	Q16
Househillmuir Pl. G53	49	Q16
Househillmuir Rd. G53	60	P17
Househillwood Cres. G53	48	P16
Househillwood Rd. G53	60	P17
Housel Av. G13	18	P8
Houston Pl. G5	35	U13
Houston Pl. (Elder.), John. PA5	44	F15
Houston Sq., John. PA5	43	D14
Houston St. G5	35	U13
Houston St., Renf. PA4	17	M10
Howard St. G1	35	V13
Howard St., Pais. PA1	47	L14
Howat St. G51	34	S12
Howden Dr. (Linw.), Pais. PA3	28	E13
Howford Rd. G52	48	P14
Howgate Av. G15	6	N6
Howieshill Av. (Camb.) G72	66	BB17
Howieshill Rd. (Camb.) G72	66	BB18
Howth Dr. G13	19	R8
Howth Ter. G13	19	R8
Howwood St. G41	35	U13
Hoylake Pk. (Both.) G71	69	GG19
Hoylake Pl. G23	9	U7
Hozier Cres. (Udd.) G71	57	GG16
Hozier St. G40	52	X14
Hubbard Dr. G11	33	R11
Hugh Murray Gro. (Camb.) G72	67	CC17
Hughenden Dr. G12	20	S10
Hughenden Gdns. G12	20	S10
Hughenden La. G12	20	S10
Hughenden Rd. G12	20	S10
Hughenden Ter. G12	20	S10
Hughenden Rd.		
Hugo St. G20	21	U9
Hume Dr. (Both.) G71	69	HH18
Hume Dr. (Udd.) G71	57	GG16
Hume Rd. (Cumb.) G67	71	PP2
Hume St., Clyde. G81	5	L7
Hunter Pl. (Kilb.), John. PA10	42	B15
Hunter Rd. (Ruther.) G73	53	Z15
Hunter St. G4	36	X13
Hunter St., Pais. PA1	30	K13
Hunterfield Dr. (Camb.) G72	66	AA17

Hunterhill Av., Pais. PA2	46	K14
Hunterhill Rd.		
Hunterhill Rd., Pais. PA2	46	K14
Hunters Hill Ct. G21	22	X9
Belmont Rd.		
Huntersfield Rd., John. PA5	43	C15
Huntershill Rd. (Bishop.) G64	22	X8
Huntershill St. G21	22	X9
Huntershill Way (Bishop.) G64	22	X8
Crowhill Rd.		
Huntingdon Rd. G21	36	X11
Huntingdon Sq. G21	36	X11
Huntingdon Rd.		
Huntingtower Rd. (Bail.) G69	56	EE14
Huntley Rd. G52	32	N12
Huntly Av. (Giff.) G46	62	T19
Huntly Dr. (Camb.) G72	66	BB18
Huntly Gdns. G12	20	T10
Huntly Path (Chry.) G69	15	HH7
Burnbrae Av.		
Huntly Rd. G12	20	T10
Huntly Ter., Pais. PA2	47	L15
Hurlet Rd. G53	48	N16
Hurlet Rd., Pais. PA2	47	M16
Hurley Hawkin (Bishop.) G64	23	Z8
Hurlford Av. G13	18	N8
Hutcheson Rd. (Thorn.) G46	62	S19
Hutcheson St. G1	36	W12
Hutchinson Ct. G2	35	V12
Hope St.		
Hutchinson Pl. (Camb.) G72	67	DD18
Hutchison Ct. (Giff.) G46	62	S19
Berryhill Rd.		
Hutchison Dr. (Bears.) G61	8	S7
Hutton Dr. G51	33	R12
Huxley St. G20	21	U9
Hydepark Pl. G21	22	X9
Springburn Rd.		
Hydepark St. G3	35	U12
Hyndal Av. G53	49	Q15
Hyndland Av. G11	34	S11
Hyndland Rd. G12	20	S10
Hyndland St. G11	34	T11
Hyndlee Dr. G52	33	Q13
Hyslop Pl., Clyde. G81	5	L6
Albert Rd.		

I

Iain Dr. (Bears.) G61	7	Q5
Iain Rd. (Bears.) G61	7	Q5
Ibrox St. G51	34	T13
Ibrox Ter. G51	34	S13
Ibrox Ter. La. G51	34	S13
Ibroxholm Av. G51	34	S13
Edmiston Dr.		
Ibroxholm La. G51	34	T13
Paisley Rd. W.		
Ibroxholm Oval G51	34	S13
Ibroxholm Pl. G51	34	S13
Paisley Rd. W.		
Ilay Av. (Bears.) G61	19	R8
Ilay Ct. (Bears.) G61	20	S8
Ilay Rd. (Bears.) G61	20	S8
Inchbrae Rd. G52	49	Q14
Inchcruin Pl. G15	6	N6
Inchfad Pl. G15	6	N6
Inchfad Pl. G15	6	N6
Inchinnan Rd., Pais. PA3	30	K12
Inchinnan Rd., Renf. PA4	17	L10
Inchkeith Pl. G32	38	BB12
Inchlaggan Pl. G15	6	N6
Inchlee St. G14	33	R11
Inchmoan Pl. G15	6	N6
Inchmurrin Dr. (Ruther.) G73	65	Z19
Inchmurrin Gdns. (Ruther.) G73	65	Z19
Inchmurrin Pl. (Ruther.) G73	65	Z19
Inchoch St. G33	39	DD11
Incholm La. G11	33	R11
Byron St.		

Incholm St. G11	33	R11
Byron St.		
Inchrory Pl. G15	6	N6
Incle St., Pais. PA1	30	K13
India Dr. (Inch.), Renf. PA4	16	J9
India St. G2	35	V12
Inga St. G20	21	U8
Ingerbreck Av. (Ruther.) G73	65	Z18
Ingleby Dr. G31	37	Y12
Inglefield St. G42	51	V15
Ingleneuk Av. G33	24	BB9
Ingleside (Lenzie) G66	13	CC5
Inglestone Av. (Thorn.) G46	62	S19
Inglis St. G31	37	Y13
Ingram St. G1	36	W12
Inishail Rd. G33	39	CC11
Inkerman Rd. G52	32	N13
Innerwick Dr. G52	32	P13
Inver Rd. G33	39	DD12
Inveraray Dr. (Bishop.) G64	11	Y6
Invercanny Dr. G15	6	N6
Invercanny Pl. G15	6	P6
Inverclyde Gdns. G11	19	R10
Broomhill Dr.		
Inverclyde Gdns. (Ruther.) G73	66	AA18
Inveresk Cres. G32	38	BB13
Inveresk St. G32	38	BB13
Inverewe Av. (Thorn.) G46	61	Q18
Inverewe Dr. (Thorn.) G46	61	Q19
Inverewe Gdns. (Thorn.) G46	61	Q19
Inverewe Pl. (Thorn.) G46	61	Q18
Invergarry Av. (Thorn.) G46	61	Q19
Invergarry Ct. (Thorn.) G46	61	Q19
Invergarry Dr. (Thorn.) G46	61	Q19
Invergarry Gdns. (Thorn.) G46	61	Q19
Invergarry Gro. (Thorn.) G46	61	Q19
Invergarry Pl. (Thorn.) G46	61	Q19
Invergarry Quad. (Thorn.) G46	61	R19
Invergarry Vw. (Thorn.) G46	61	R19
Inverglas Av., Renf. PA4	32	N11
Morriston Cres.		
Invergordon Av. G43	51	U16
Invergyle Dr. G52	32	P13
Inverkar Dr., Pais. PA2	45	H15
Inverkip St. G5	36	W13
Inverlair Av. G43	63	U17
Inverlair Av. G44	63	U17
Inverleith St. G32	37	Z13
Inverlochy St. G33	39	CC11
Inverness St. G51	33	Q13
Inveroran Dr. (Bears.) G61	8	S6
Invershiel Rd. G23	8	T7
Invershin Dr. G20	20	T9
Wyndford Rd.		
Inverurie St. G21	22	W10
Inzievar Ter. G32	54	BB15
Iona Cres. (Old Kil.) G60	4	J5
Iona Dr. (Old Kil.) G60	4	J5
Iona Dr., Pais. PA2	46	J16
Iona Gdns. (Old Kil.) G60	4	J5
Iona La. (Chry.) G69	15	HH7
Heathfield Av.		
Iona Pl. (Old Kil.) G60	4	J5
Iona Rd. (Ruther.) G73	66	AA18
Iona Rd., Renf. PA4	31	M11
Iona St. G51	34	S12
Iona Way (Stepps) G33	25	CC10
Iris Av. G45	65	Y18
Irongray St. G31	37	Z12
Irvine Dr. (Linw.), Pais. PA3	28	L13
Irvine St. G40	53	Y14
Irving Av., Clyde. G81	5	L5
Stewart Dr.		
Irving Quad., Clyde. G81	5	L5
Stewart Dr.		
Iser La. G41	51	U16
Island Rd. (Cumb.) G67	70	MM4
Islay Av. (Ruther.) G73	66	AA18
Islay Cres. (Old Kil.) G60	4	J5
Islay Cres., Pais. PA2	46	J16
Islay Dr. (Old Kil.) G60	4	J5

Ivanhoe Rd. G13 19 Q8
Ivanhoe Rd. (Cumb.) G67 70 NN4
Ivanhoe Rd., Pais. PA2 45 G15
Ivanhoe Way, Pais. PA2 45 G15
Ivanhoe Rd.
Ivybank Av. (Camb.) G72 67 CC18

J

Jacks Rd. (Udd.) G71 69 HH17
Jagger Gdns. (Bail.) G69 55 DD14
Jamaica St. G1 35 V13
James Dunlop Gdns. 23 Y8
(Bishop.) G64
Graham Ter.
James Gray St. G41 51 U16
James Morrison St. G1 36 W13
St. Andrews Sq.
James Nisbet St. G21 36 X11
James St. G40 52 X14
James Watt La. G2 35 V12
James Watt St.
James Watt St. G2 35 V12
Jamieson Ct. G42 51 V15
Jamieson Path G42 51 V15
Jamieson St.
Jamieson St. G42 51 V15
Janebank Av. (Camb.) G72 67 CC18
Janefield Av., John. PA5 43 D15
Janefield St. G31 37 Y13
Janes Brae (Cumb.) G67 70 NN4
Janetta St., Clyde. G81 5 L6
Jardine St. G20 21 U10
Jardine Ter. (Gart.) G69 27 GG9
Jasgray St. G42 51 U15
Jean Armour Dr., Clyde. 5 M6
G81
Jean Maclean Pl. (Bishop.) 11 Y5
G64
Jedburgh Av. (Ruther.) 53 Y16
G73
Jedburgh Dr., Pais. PA2 45 H15
Jedburgh Gdns. G20 21 U10
Jedworth Av. G15 6 P6
Jedworth Rd. G15 6 P6
Jellicoe St., Clyde. G81 4 K6
Jenny's Well Ct., Pais. PA2 47 L15
Jenny's Well Rd.
Jenny's Well Rd., Pais. PA2 47 L15
Jerviston Rd. G33 39 CC11
Jessie St. G42 52 W15
Jessiman Sq., Renf. PA4 31 L11
Jocelyn Sq. G1 36 W13
John Brown Pl. (Chry.) G69 26 FF8
John Knox La. G4 36 X12
Drygate
John Knox St. G4 36 X12
John Knox St., Clyde. G81 17 M8
John Lang St., John. PA5 44 E14
John St. G1 36 W12
John St. (Barr.) G78 59 L18
John St., Pais. PA1 46 J14
Johnsburn Dr. G53 60 P17
Johnsburn Rd. G53 60 P17
Johnshaven St. G43 50 T16
Shawbridge St.
Johnston Rd. (Gart.) G69 27 HH9
Johnston St., Pais. PA1 46 K14
Gordon St.
Johnstone Av. G52 32 P13
Johnstone Av., Clyde. G81 17 M8
Johnstone Dr. (Camb.) G72 66 BB17
Johnstone Dr. (Ruther.) 53 Y16
G73
Joppa St. G33 38 AA12
Jordan St. G14 33 Q11
Jordanhill Cres. G13 19 Q9
Jordanhill Dr. G13 19 Q9
Jordanhill La. G13 19 R9
Austen Rd.
Jordanvale Av. G14 33 Q11
Jowitt Av., Clyde. G81 5 M7
Jubilee Bk. (Kirk.) G66 13 CC6
Heriot Rd.
Jubilee Path (Bears.) G61 7 R6
Jubilee Ter., John. PA5 43 C15
Julian Av. G12 20 T10
Julian La. G12 20 T10
Julian Av.

Juniper Ct. (Kirk.) G66 12 BB5
Juniper Pl. G32 55 DD14
Juniper Pl., John. PA5 44 E16
Juniper Ter. G32 55 DD14
Jura Av., Renf. PA4 31 M11
Jura Ct. G52 33 R13
Jura Dr. (Old Kil.) G60 4 J5
Jura Rd.
Jura Dr. (Blan.) G72 68 FF18
Jura Gdns. (Old Kil.) G60 4 J5
Jura Rd.
Jura Pl. (Old Kil.) G60 4 J5
Jura Rd.
Jura Rd. (Old Kil.) G60 4 J5
Jura Rd., Pais. PA2 46 J16
Jura St. G52 33 R13

K

Kaim Dr. G53 61 Q17
Kames St. G5 51 V14
Karol Path G4 35 V11
St. Peters St.
Katewell Av. G15 6 N6
Katrine Av. (Bishop.) G64 11 Y7
Katrine Dr., Pais. PA2 45 G15
Katrine Pl. (Camb.) G72 66 BB17
Kay St. G21 22 X10
Kaystone Rd. G15 6 P7
Keal Av. G15 18 P8
Keal Cres. G15 18 P8
Keal Dr. G15 18 P8
Keal Pl. G15 18 P8
Kearn Av. G15 6 P7
Kearn Pl. G15 6 P7
Keats Pk. (Both.) G71 69 HH18
Keir Dr. (Bishop.) G64 10 X7
Keir St. G41 51 U14
Keirhill Rd. (Cumb.) G68 70 MM3
Woodburn Way
Keirs Wk. (Camb.) G72 66 BB17
Keith Av. (Giff.) G46 62 T18
Keith Ct. G11 34 T11
Keith St.
Keith St. G11 34 T11
Kelbourne St. G20 21 U10
Kelburn St. (Barr.) G78 59 L19
Kelburne Dr., Pais. PA1 31 L13
Kelburne Gdns. (Bail.) G69 56 EE14
Kelburne Gdns., Pais. PA1 31 L13
Kelburne Oval, Pais. PA1 31 L13
Kelhead Av. G52 32 N13
Kelhead Dr. G52 32 N13
Kelhead Path G52 32 P13
Kelhead Pl. G52 32 N13
Kellas St. G51 34 S13
Kells Pl. G15 6 N6
Kelso Av. (Ruther.) G73 53 Y16
Kelso Av., Pais. PA2 45 H15
Kelso Gdns. (Mood.) G69 15 GG6
Whithorn Cres.
Kelso Pl. G14 18 N9
Kelso St. G13 18 N9
Kelso St. G14 18 N9
Kelton St. G32 54 BB14
Kelty Pl. G5 35 V13
Bedford St.
Kelty St. G5 51 V14
Eglinton St.
Kelvin Av. G52 32 N11
Kelvin Ct. G12 19 R9
Kelvin Cres. (Bears.) G61 7 R7
Kelvin Dr. G20 20 T10
Kelvin Dr. (Bishop.) G64 11 Y7
Kelvin Dr. (Chry.) G69 15 GG7
Kelvin Dr. (Barr.) G78 59 M19
Kelvin Rd. (Cumb.) G67 71 PP4
Kelvin Rd. (Udd.) G71 57 GG16
Kelvin Way G3 34 T11
Kelvin Way (Both.) G71 69 HH18
Bracken Ter.
Kelvindale Bldgs. G12 20 T9
Kelvindale Rd.
Kelvindale Cotts. G12 20 T9
Kelvindale Rd.
Kelvindale Gdns. G20 20 T9
Kelvindale Glen G12 20 T9
Kelvindale Rd.
Kelvindale Pl. G20 20 T9

Kelvindale Rd. G12 20 T9
Kelvindale Rd. G20 20 T9
Kelvingrove St. G3 35 U12
Kelvingrove Ter. G3 35 U12
Kelvingrove St.
Kelvinhaugh Pl. G3 34 T12
Kelvinhaugh St.
Kelvinhaugh St. G3 34 T12
Kelvinside Av. G20 21 U10
Queen Margaret Dr.
Kelvinside Dr. G20 21 U10
Kelvinside Gdns. G20 21 U10
Kelvinside Gdns. E. G20 21 U10
Kelvinside Gdns. La. G20 21 U10
Kelvinside Gdns.
Kelvinside Ter. S. G20 21 U10
Kelvinside Ter. W. G20 21 U10
Kemp Av., Pais. PA3 31 L11
Kemp St. G21 22 X10
Kempock St. G31 53 Z14
Kempsthorn Cres. G53 48 P15
Kempsthorn Path G53 48 P15
Kempsthorn Rd. G53 48 P15
Kendal Av. G12 20 S9
Kendal Av. (Giff.) G46 62 T18
Kendal Dr. G12 20 S9
Kendal Ter. G12 20 S9
Kendoon Av. G15 6 N6
Kenilworth Av. G41 50 T16
Kenilworth Cres. (Bears.) 7 Q5
G61
Kenilworth Way, Pais. PA2 45 G16
Kenmar Gdns. (Udd.) G71 56 FF16
Kenmore Gdns. (Bears.) 8 S5
G61
Kenmore Rd. (Cumb.) G67 71 PP3
Kenmore St. G32 38 BB13
Kenmuir Av. G32 55 DD14
Kenmuir Rd. G32 55 CC16
Kenmuirhill Rd. G32 55 CC15
Kenmure Av. (Bishop.) G64 10 X7
Kenmure Cres. (Bishop.) 10 X7
G64
Kenmure Dr. (Bishop.) G64 10 X7
Kenmure Gdns. (Bishop.) 10 X7
G64
Kenmure Row G22 9 V7
Kenmure St. G41 51 U14
Kenmure Way (Ruther.) 65 Y18
G73
Kennedar Dr. G51 33 R12
Kennedy Ct. (Giff.) G46 62 T18
Braidholm Cres.
Kennedy St. G4 36 W12
Kennet St. G21 37 Y11
Kennishead Av. (Thorn.) 61 R17
G46
Kennishead Path (Thorn.) 61 R17
G46
Kennishead Pl.
Kennishead Pl. (Thorn.) 61 R17
G46
Kennishead Rd. G43 61 R17
Kennishead Rd. (Thorn.) 61 R17
G46
Kennishead Rd. G53 61 Q18
Kennisholm Av. (Thorn.) 61 R17
G46
Kennisholm Path (Thorn.) 61 R18
G46
Kennisholm Av.
Kennisholm Pl. (Thorn.) 61 R17
G46
Kennoway Dr. G11 33 R11
Kennoway La. G11 33 R11
Thornwood Dr.
Kennyhill Sq. G31 37 Y12
Kensington Dr. (Giff.) G46 62 T19
Kensington Gate G12 20 T10
Kensington Rd. G12 20 T10
Kent Dr. (Ruther.) G73 65 Z17
Kent Rd. G3 35 U12
Kent St. G40 36 X13
Kentallen Rd. G33 39 DD13
Kentigern Ter. (Bishop.) 23 Y8
G64
Keppel Dr. G44 52 X16
Keppoch St. G21 22 W10
Keppochhill Rd. G21 22 X10

Keppochhill Rd. G22	22	W10
Kerfield La. G15	6	N6
Kerfield Pl. G15	6	N6
Kerr Dr. G40	36	X13
Kerr Gdns. (Udd.) G71	57	HH16
Kerr Pl. G40	36	X13
Kerr St. G40	36	X13
Kerr St. (Barr.) G78	59	L19
Kerr St., Pais. PA3	30	J13
Kerrera Pl. G33	39	CC13
Kerrera Rd. G33	39	CC13
Kerry Pl. G15	6	N6
Kerrycroy Av. G42	52	W16
Kerrycroy Pl. G42	52	W16
Kerrycroy Av.		
Kerrycroy St. G42	52	W16
Kerrydale St. G40	53	Y14
Kerrylamont Av. G42	52	X16
Kersland La. G12	20	T10
Kersland St.		
Kersland St. G12	20	T10
Kessington Dr. (Bears.) G61	8	S6
Kessington Rd. (Bears.) G61	8	S6
Kessock Dr. G22	21	V10
Kessock Pl. G22	21	V10
Kestral Ct., Clyde. G81	5	L5
Kestrel Pl., John. PA5	43	C16
Kestrel Rd. G13	19	Q9
Kew Gdns. G12	20	T10
Ruthven St.		
Kew Gdns. (Udd.) G71	57	HH16
Kew La. G12	20	T10
Saltoun St.		
Kew Ter. G12	20	T10
Keyden St. G41	35	U13
Kibbleston Rd. (Kilb.), John. PA10	42	B14
Kidston St. G5	52	W14
Kierhill Rd. (Cumb.) G68	70	MM3
Kilbarchan Rd., John. PA5	43	C15
Kilbarchan Rd. (Mill.Pk.), John. PA10	43	C15
Kilbarchan St. G5	35	V13
Bedford St.		
Kilbeg Ter. (Thorn.) G46	61	Q18
Kilberry St. G21	37	Y11
Kilbirnie St. G5	51	V14
Kilbowie Ct., Clyde. G81	5	L6
Crown Av.		
Kilbowie Rd. (Cumb.) G67	71	PP3
Kilbowie Rd., Clyde. G81	5	L5
Kilbrennan Rd. (Linw.), Pais. PA3	28	E13
Kilbride St. G5	52	W15
Kilbride Vw. (Udd.) G71	57	HH16
Hamilton Vw.		
Kilburn Gro. (Blan.) G72	68	FF19
Kilburn Pl. G13	18	P9
Kilchattan Dr. G44	52	W16
Kilcloy Av. G15	6	P6
Kildale St. (Ruther.) G73	52	X16
Kildale Way (Ruther.) G73	52	X16
Kildary Av. G44	63	V17
Kildary Rd. G44	63	V17
Kildermorie Rd. G34	40	EE12
Kildonan Dr. G11	34	S11
Kildonan Ter. G51	34	S13
Copland Rd.		
Kildrostan St. G41	51	U15
Terregles Av.		
Kildrum Rd. (Cumb.) G67	71	PP2
Kilearn Rd., Pais. PA3	31	L12
Kilearn Way, Pais. PA3	31	L12
Clyde Rd.		
Kilfinan St. G22	21	V8
Kilkerran Dr. G33	24	AA9
Killarn Way, Pais. PA3	31	L12
Killearn Dr., Pais. PA1	48	N14
Killearn St. G22	21	V10
Killermont Av. (Bears.) G61	8	S7
Killermont Ct. (Bears.) G61	8	S6
Killermont Meadows (Both.) G71	69	GG19
Killermont Rd. (Bears.) G61	8	S6
Killermont St. G2	36	W12
Killermont Vw. G20	8	S7
Killiegrew Rd. G41	50	T15
Killin St. G32	54	BB14

Killoch Av., Pais. PA3	29	H13
Killoch Dr. G13	18	P8
Killoch Dr. (Barr.) G78	59	M19
Killoch Rd., Pais. PA3	29	H13
Kilmailing Rd. G44	63	V17
Kilmair Pl. G20	20	T9
Wyndford Rd.		
Kilmaluag Ter. (Thorn.) G46	61	Q18
Kilmany Dr. G32	38	AA13
Kilmany Gdns. G32	38	AA13
St. Mark St.		
Kilmardinny Av. (Bears.) G61	7	R5
Kilmardinny Cres. (Bears.) G61	7	R5
Kilmardinny Dr. (Bears.) G61	7	R5
Kilmardinny Gate (Bears.) G61	7	R5
Kilmardinny Av.		
Kilmardinny Gro. (Bears.) G61	7	R5
Kilmarnock Rd. G41	62	T17
Kilmarnock Rd. G43	62	T17
Kilmartin Pl. (Thorn.) G46	61	R18
Kilmaurs Dr. (Giff.) G46	63	U18
Kilmaurs St. G51	33	R13
Kilmorie Dr. (Ruther.) G73	52	X16
Kilmory Av. (Udd.) G71	57	HH16
Spindlehowe Rd.		
Kilmuir Cres. (Thorn.) G46	61	Q18
Kilmuir Dr. (Thorn.) G46	61	R18
Kilmuir Rd. (Thorn.) G46	61	R18
Kilmuir Rd. (Udd.) G71	57	GG15
Kilmun La. G20	20	T8
Kilmun St.		
Kilmun Pl. G20	20	T8
Kilmun St.		
Kilmun St. G20	20	T8
Kilnside Rd., Pais. PA1	30	K13
Kiloran St. (Thorn.) G46	61	R18
Kilpatrick Av., Pais. PA2	45	H15
Kilpatrick Cres., Pais. PA2	46	J15
Kilpatrick Dr., Renf. PA4	31	L12
Campsie Dr.		
Kilpatrick Way (Udd.) G71	57	HH16
Kiltearn Rd. G33	39	DD12
Kilvaxter Dr. (Thorn.) G46	61	R18
Kilwynet Way, Pais. PA3	31	L12
Kimberley St., Clyde. G81	4	J5
Kinalty Rd. G44	63	V17
Kinarvie Cres. G53	48	N16
Kinarvie Gdns. G53	48	N16
Kinarvie Rd.		
Kinarvie Pl. G53	48	N16
Kinarvie Rd. G53	48	N16
Kinarvie Ter. G53	48	N16
Kinbuck St. G22	22	W10
Kincaid Gdns. (Camb.) G72	66	BB17
Kincardine Cres. (Bishop.) G64	23	Y8
Graham Ter.		
Kincardine Dr. (Bishop.) G64	23	Y8
Kincardine Pl. (Bishop.) G64	23	Z8
Kincardine Sq. G33	39	CC11
Kincath Av. (Ruther.) G73	65	Z18
Kinclaven Av. G15	6	P6
Kincraig St. G51	33	Q13
Kinellan Rd. (Bears.) G61	7	R7
Kinellar Dr. G14	18	P9
Kinfauns Dr. G15	6	N6
Kinfauns Ter. G51	34	S13
Copland Rd.		
King Edward La. G13	19	R9
King Edward Rd.		
King Edward Rd. G13	19	R9
King George V Bri. G1	35	V13
King George V Bri. G5	35	V13
King George V Dock G51	32	P11
King Pl. (Bail.) G69	41	HH13
King St. G1	36	W13
King St. (Ruther.) G73	53	Y16
King St., Clyde. G81	17	M8
King St., Pais. PA1	30	J13
Kingarth La. G42	51	V15
Kingarth St.		

Kingarth St. G42	51	V15
Kingfisher Dr. G13	18	N8
Kinghorn Dr. G44	52	W16
Kinglas Rd. (Bears.) G61	7	Q7
King's Bri. G5	52	W14
King's Bri. G40	52	W14
Kings Cres. (Camb.) G72	66	BB17
Kings Cres. (Elder.), John. PA5	44	F14
Kings Cross G31	36	X12
King's Dr. G40	52	X14
Kings Dr. (Cumb.) G68	70	NN1
Kings Inch Rd., Renf. PA4	17	M9
Kings La. W., Renf. PA4	17	M10
Bell St.		
King's Pk. Av. G44	63	V17
King's Pk. Av. (Ruther.) G73	63	V17
Kings Pk. Rd. G44	51	V16
Kings Pl. G22	21	V8
Kings Rd., John. PA5	44	E15
King's Vw. (Cumb.) G68	70	NN1
Kingsacre Rd. G44	52	W16
Kingsacre Rd. (Ruther.) G73	52	W16
Kingsbarns Dr. G44	51	V16
Kingsborough Gdns. G12	20	S10
Kingsborough Gate G12	20	S10
Prince Albert Rd.		
Kingsborough La. G12	20	S10
Prince Albert Rd.		
Kingsborough La. E. G12	20	S10
Kingsborough Gdns.		
Kingsborough Ter. G12	20	S10
Hyndland Rd.		
Kingsbrae Av. G44	52	W16
Kingsbridge Cres. G44	64	W17
Kingsbridge Dr. G44	64	W17
Kingsbridge Dr. (Ruther.) G73	64	W17
Kingsburgh Dr., Pais. PA1	31	L13
Kingsburn Dr. (Ruther.) G73	65	Y17
Kingsburn Gro. (Ruther.) G73	65	Y17
Kingscliffe Av. G44	64	W17
Kingscourt Av. G44	64	W17
Kingsdale Av. G44	52	W16
Kingsdyke Av. G44	52	W16
Kingsford Av. G44	63	U18
Kingsheath Av. (Ruther.) G73	64	X17
Kingshill Dr. G44	64	W17
Kingshouse Av. G44	64	W17
Kingshurst Av. G44	52	W16
Kingsknowe Dr. (Ruther.) G73	64	X17
Kingsland Cres. G52	32	P13
Kingsland Dr. G52	32	P13
Kingsland La. G52	33	Q13
Berryknowes Rd.		
Kingsley Av. G42	51	V15
Kingsley Ct. (Udd.) G71	57	HH16
Kingslynn Dr. G44	64	W17
Kingslynn La. G44	64	W17
Kingslynn Dr.		
Kingsmuir Dr. (Ruther.) G73	64	X17
Kingston Av. (Udd.) G71	57	HH16
Kingston Bri. G3	35	U13
Kingston Bri. G5	35	U13
Kingston Pl., Clyde. G81	4	J6
Kingston St. G5	35	V13
Kingsway G14	18	P9
Kingsway Ct. G14	18	P9
Kingswood Dr. G44	64	W17
Kingussie Dr. G44	64	W17
Kiniver Dr. G15	6	P7
Kinloch Av. (Camb.) G72	66	BB18
Kinloch Av. (Linw.), Pais. PA3	28	E13
Pentland Av.		
Kinloch Rd., Renf. PA4	31	L11
Kinloch St. G40	53	Z14
Kinmount Av. G44	51	V16
Kinmount La. G44	51	V16
Kinmount Av.		
Kinnaird Cres. (Bears.) G61	8	S6
Kinnaird Dr. (Linw.), Pais. PA3	28	E13
Kinnaird Pl. (Bishop.) G64	23	Y8

121

Liddel Rd. (Cumb.) G67 70 NN3
Liddell St. G32 55 CC15
Liddesdale Av., Pais. PA2 44 F16
Liddesdale Pl. G22 22 W8
 Liddesdale Sq.
Liddesdale Rd. G22 22 W8
Liddesdale Sq. G22 22 W8
Liddesdale Ter. G22 22 X8
Liff Gdns. (Bishop.) G64 23 Z8
Liff Pl. G34 40 FF11
Lightburn Pl. G32 38 BB12
Lightburn Rd. G31 37 Z13
 Duke St.
Lightburn Rd. (Camb.) G72 67 CC18
Lilac Av., Clyde. G81 4 J6
Lilac Cres. (Udd.) G71 57 HH16
Lilac Gdns. (Bishop.) G64 23 Y8
Lillyburn Pl. G15 6 N5
Lily St. G40 53 Y14
Lilybank Av. (Muir.) G69 26 FF8
Lilybank Av. (Camb.) G72 67 CC18
Lilybank Gdns. G12 34 T11
Lilybank Gdns. La. G12 20 T10
 Great George St.
Lilybank La. G12 34 T11
 Lilybank Gdns.
Lilybank Ter. G12 20 T10
 Great George St.
Lilybank Ter. La. G12 20 T10
 Great George St.
Lime Gro. (Lenzie) G66 13 CC5
Lime Gro. (Blan.) G72 68 FF19
Lime La. G14 19 Q10
 Lime St.
Lime St. G14 19 Q10
Limecraigs Cres., Pais. PA2 46 J16
Limecraigs Rd., Pais. PA2 45 H16
Limeside Av. (Ruther.) G73 53 Y16
Limeside Gdns. (Ruther.) 53 Z16
 G73
 Calderwood Rd.
Limetree Av. (Udd.) G71 57 HH16
Limetree Dr., Clyde. G81 5 L6
Limeview Av., Pais. PA2 45 H16
Limeview Cres., Pais. PA2 45 H16
Limeview Rd., Pais. PA2 45 H16
 Limeview Av.
Limeview Way, Pais. PA2 45 H16
 Limeview Av.
Linacre Dr. G32 39 CC13
Linacre Gdns. G32 39 CC13
Linbank Av. G53 49 Q16
Linburn Pl. G52 32 P13
Linburn Rd. G52 32 N12
Linclive Link Rd. (Linw.), 28 F13
 Pais. PA3
Linclive Ter. (Linw.), Pais. 28 F13
 PA3
Lincoln Av. G13 18 P9
Lincoln Av. (Udd.) G71 57 GG15
Lindams (Udd.) G71 69 GG17
Linden Dr., Clyde. G81 5 L5
Linden Pl. G13 19 R8
Linden St. G13 19 R8
Lindores Av. (Ruther.) G73 53 Y16
Lindores St. G42 51 V16
 Somerville Dr.
Lindrick Dr. G23 9 U7
Lindsay Dr. G12 20 S9
Lindsay Pl. G12 20 S9
Lindsay Pl. (Lenzie) G66 13 CC6
Lindsay Pl., John. PA5 44 E14
 Thorn Brae
Lindsaybeg Rd. (Lenzie) G66 13 DD6
Lindsaybeg Rd. (Chry.) G69 14 EE7
Linfern Rd. G12 20 T10
Links Rd. G32 55 CC14
Links Rd. G44 64 W18
Linkwood Av. G15 6 N6
 Kinfauns Dr.
Linkwood Cres. G15 6 N6
Linkwood Dr. G15 6 N6
Linkwood Pl. G15 6 N6
 Kinfauns Dr.
Linlithgow Gdns. G32 39 CC13
Linn Brae, John. PA5 43 D15
Linn Cres., Pais. PA2 46 J16
Linn Dr. G44 63 U18
Linn Pk. G44 63 V18

Linn Pk. Gdns., John. PA5 44 E15
Linnet Av., John. PA5 43 C16
Linnet Pl. G13 18 N8
Linnhe Av. G44 63 V18
Linnhe Av. (Bishop.) G64 11 Y7
Linnhe Dr. (Barr.) G78 59 L17
Linnhe Pl. (Blan.) G72 68 FF19
Linnhead Dr. G53 60 P17
Linnhead Pl. G14 18 P10
Linnpark Av. G44 63 U19
Linnpark Ct. G44 63 U19
Linnwood Ct. G44 63 V17
 Bowling Grn. Rd.
Linside Av., Pais. PA1 47 L14
Lintfield Ln. (Udd.) G71 69 HH17
 Myers Cres.
Linthaugh Rd. G53 48 P15
Linthaugh Ter. G53 49 Q15
 Linthaugh Rd.
Linthouse Bldgs. G51 33 R12
 Holmfauld Rd.
Linthouse Rd. G51 33 R11
Lintlaw (Blan.) G72 68 FF19
Lintlaw Dr. G52 33 Q13
Linton St. G33 38 AA12
Linwell Cres., Pais. PA2 46 J16
Linwood Moss Rd. (Linw.), 28 F13
 Pais. PA3
Linwood Rd., Pais. PA1 28 F13
Linwood Rd. (Linw.), Pais. 28 F13
 PA3
Linwood Ter. G12 21 U10
 Glasgow St.
Lismore Av., Renf. PA4 31 M11
Lismore Dr., Pais. PA2 46 J16
Lismore Gdns. (Mill.Pk.), 43 C15
 John. PA10
 Tandlehill Rd.
Lismore Pl. (Chry.) G69 15 HH6
 Altnacreag Gdns.
Lismore Rd. G12 20 S10
Lister Rd. G52 32 P12
Lister St. G4 36 W11
Lithgow Cres., Pais. PA2 47 L15
Little Dovehill G1 36 W13
Little Holm, Clyde. G81 4 K6
Little St. G3 35 U12
Littlehill St. G21 22 X10
 Edgefauld Rd.
Littleton Dr. G23 8 T7
 Rothes Dr.
Littleton St. G23 8 T7
 Rothes Dr.
Livingstone Av. G52 32 P12
Livingstone Cres. (Blan.) 68 FF19
 G72
Livingstone St. G21 22 W10
 Keppochhill Rd.
Livingstone St., Clyde. G81 5 M7
Lloyd Av. G32 54 BB15
Lloyd St. G31 37 Y12
Lloyd St. (Ruther.) G73 53 Y15
Loanbank Quad. G51 34 S12
Loancroft Av. (Bail.) G69 56 FF14
Loancroft Gdns. (Udd.) G71 69 GG17
Loancroft Pl. (Bail.) G69 56 EE14
Loanend Cotts. (Camb.) G72 67 DD19
Loanfoot Av. G13 18 P8
Loanhead Av. (Linw.), Pais. 28 E13
 PA3
Loanhead Av., Renf. PA4 17 M10
Loanhead La. (Linw.), Pais. 28 E13
 PA3
 Loanhead Rd.
Loanhead Rd. (Linw.), Pais. 28 E13
 PA3
Loanhead St. G32 38 AA12
Lobnitz Av., Renf. PA4 17 M10
Loch Achray St. G32 55 CC14
Loch Katrine St. G32 55 CC14
Loch Laidon St. G32 55 CC14
Loch Rd. (Stepps) G33 25 CC9
Loch Voil St. G32 55 CC14
Lochaber Dr. (Ruther.) G73 65 Z18
Lochaber Rd. (Bears.) G61 8 S7
Lochaline Av., Pais. PA2 45 H15
Lochaline Dr. G44 63 V18
Lochalsh Dr., Pais. PA2 45 G15
Lochalsh Pl. (Blan.) G72 68 EE19

Lochar Cres. G53 49 Q15
Lochard Dr., Pais. PA2 45 H15
Lochay St. G32 55 CC14
Lochbrae Dr. (Ruther.) G73 65 Z18
Lochbridge Rd. G34 40 EE12
Lochbroom Dr., Pais. PA2 45 H15
Lochburn Cres. G20 21 U8
Lochburn Gro. G20 21 U8
 Cadder Rd.
Lochburn Pas. G20 21 U8
Lochburn Rd. G20 20 T9
Lochdochart Path G34 40 FF12
 Lochdochart Rd.
Lochdochart Rd. G34 40 FF12
Lochearn Cres., Pais. PA2 45 H15
Lochearnhead Rd. G33 25 CC9
Lochend Av. (Gart.) G69 27 GG8
Lochend Cres. (Bears.) G61 7 Q6
Lochend Dr. (Bears.) G61 7 Q6
Lochend Rd. G34 40 EE11
Lochend Rd. (Bears.) G61 7 R6
Lochend Rd. (Gart.) G69 27 GG8
Locher Rd. (Kilb.), John. 42 A14
 PA10
Lochfauld Rd. G23 9 V7
Lochfield Cres., Pais. PA2 46 K15
Lochfield Dr., Pais. PA2 47 L15
Lochfield Gdns. G34 40 FF11
Lochfield Rd., Pais. PA2 46 K15
Lochgilp St. G20 20 T8
Lochgoin Av. G15 6 N6
Lochgreen St. G33 24 AA10
Lochhead Av. (Linw.), Pais. 28 E13
 PA3
Lochiel La. (Ruther.) G73 65 Z18
Lochiel Rd. (Thorn.) G46 61 R18
Lochinver Cres., Pais. PA2 45 H15
Lochinver Dr. G44 63 V18
Lochinver Gro. (Camb.) G72 67 CC17
 Andrew Sillars Av.
Lochlea Av., Clyde. G81 5 M6
Lochlea Rd. G43 62 T17
Lochlea Rd. (Cumb.) G67 71 QQ2
Lochlea Rd. (Ruther.) G73 64 X17
Lochleven La. G42 51 V16
 Battlefield Rd.
Lochleven Rd. G42 51 V16
Lochlibo Av. G13 18 N9
Lochlibo Cres. (Barr.) G78 59 L19
Lochlibo Rd. (Barr.) G78 59 L19
Lochlibo Ter. (Barr.) G78 59 L19
Lochmaben Rd. G52 48 N14
Lochmaddy Av. G44 63 V18
Lochside (Bears.) G61 7 R6
 Drymen Rd.
Lochside (Gart.) G69 27 GG9
Lochside St. G41 51 U15
 Minard Rd.
Lochview Cotts. (Gart.) G69 27 GG10
Lochview Cres. G33 24 AA10
Lochview Dr. G33 24 AA10
Lochview Gdns. G33 24 AA10
Lochview Pl. G33 24 AA10
Lochview Rd. (Bears.) G61 7 R6
Lochview Ter. (Gart.) G69 27 GG10
Lochwood Ln. (Mood.) G69 15 HH6
Lochwood St. G33 38 AA11
Lochy Av., Renf. PA4 32 N11
Lochy Gdns. (Bishop.) G64 11 Y7
Lockerbie Av. G43 63 U17
Lockhart Av. (Camb.) G72 67 CC17
Lockhart Dr. (Camb.) G72 67 CC17
Lockhart St. G21 37 Y11
Locksley Av. G13 19 Q8
Locksley Rd., Pais. PA2 45 G15
Logan Dr. (Cumb.) G68 70 MM2
Logan Dr., Pais. PA3 30 J13
Logan St. G5 52 W15
Logan Twr. (Camb.) G72 67 DD18
 Claude Av.
Loganswell Dr. (Thorn.) G46 61 Q19
Loganswell Gdns. (Thorn.) 61 R19
 G46
Loganswell Pl. (Thorn.) G46 61 R19
Loganswell Rd. (Thorn.) 61 R19
 G46
Logie St. G51 34 S12
Lomax St. G33 37 Z12
Lomond Av., Renf. PA4 31 L11

Lomond Ct. (Barr.) G78   59   M19
Lomond Cres., Pais. PA2   46   J16
Lomond Dr. (Both.) G71   69   HH18
Lomond Dr. (Barr.) G78   59   L18
Lomond Gdns. (Elder.),   44   F15
  John. PA5
Lomond Pl. (Stepps) G33   25   CC10
Lomond Rd. (Bears.) G61   7   R7
Lomond Rd. (Bishop.) G64   10   X6
Lomond Rd. (Lenzie) G66   13   CC5
Lomond Rd. (Udd.) G71   57   GG15
Lomond St. G22   21   V9
Lomond Vw., Clyde. G81   5   L6
  Granville St.
London Arc. G1   36   W13
  London Rd.
London La. G1   36   W13
  London Rd.
London Rd. G1   36   W13
London Rd. G31   53   Z14
London Rd. G32   54   BB15
London Rd. G40   52   X14
London St., Renf. PA4   17   M9
Lonend, Pais. PA1   46   K14
Long Row (Bail.) G69   40   FF13
Longay Pl. G22   22   W8
Longay St. G22   22   W8
Longcroft Dr., Renf. PA4   17   M10
Longdale Rd. (Chry.) G69   15   GG7
Longden St., Clyde. G81   17   M8
Longford St. G33   37   Z12
Longlee (Bail.) G69   56   EE14
Longmeadow, John. PA5   43   C15
Longstone Rd. G33   38   BB12
Longwill Ter. (Cumb.) G67   71   PP2
Lonmay Rd. G33   39   CC12
Lonsdale Av. (Giff.) G46   62   T18
Loom St. G40   36   X13
  Stevenson St.
Loom Wk. (Kilb.), John.   42   B14
  PA10
  Shuttle St.
Lora Dr. G52   49   R14
Lord Way (Bail.) G69   41   GG13
  Dukes Rd.
Loretto Pl. G33   38   AA12
Loretto St. G33   38   AA12
Lorne Av. (Chry.) G69   26   FF8
Lorne Cres. (Bishop.) G64   11   Z7
Lorne Dr. (Linw.), Pais. PA3   28   E13
Lorne Rd. G52   32   N12
Lorne St. G51   34   T13
Lorne Ter. (Camb.) G72   66   AA18
Lorraine Gdns. G12   20   T10
  Kensington Rd.
Lorraine Rd. G12   20   T10
Loskin Dr. G22   21   V8
Lossie Cres., Renf. PA4   32   N11
Lossie St. G33   37   Z11
Lothian Cres., Pais. PA2   46   J15
Lothian Gdns. G20   21   U10
Lothian St. G52   32   N12
Loudon Gdns., John. PA5   44   E14
Loudon Rd. G33   24   BB9
Loudon Ter. G12   20   T10
  Observatory Rd.
Lounsdale Av., Pais. PA2   45   H14
Lounsdale Cres., Pais. PA2   45   H15
Lounsdale Dr., Pais. PA2   45   H15
Lounsdale Gro., Pais. PA2   45   H15
Lounsdale Ho., Pais. PA2   45   H15
  Gallacher Rd.
Lounsdale Pl. G14   18   P10
Lounsdale Rd., Pais. PA2   45   H15
Lounsdale Way, Pais. PA2   45   H14
Lourdes Av. G52   49   Q14
Lourdes Ct. G52   49   Q14
  Lourdes Av.
Lovat Pl. (Ruther.) G73   65   Z18
Lovat St. G4   36   W11
Love St., Pais. PA3   30   K13
Low Barholm (Kilb.), John.   42   B15
  PA10
Low Cres., Clyde. G81   18   N8
Low Parksail, Ersk. PA8   16   J8
Low Rd. (Castlehead), Pais.   46   J14
  PA2
Lower Bourtree Dr.   65   Z18
  (Ruther.) G73

Lower English Bldgs. G42   51   V14
Lower Millgate (Udd.) G71   57   GG16
Lowndes La., Pais. PA3   30   K13
  New Sneddon St.
Lowndes St. (Barr.) G78   59   M19
Lowther Ter. G12   20   T10
Loyne Dr., Renf. PA4   32   N11
  Morriston Cres.
Luath St. G51   34   S12
Lubas Av. G42   52   W16
Lubas Pl. G42   52   W16
Lubnaig Rd. G43   63   U17
Luckingsford Av. (Inch.),   16   J8
  Renf. PA4
Luckingsford Dr. (Inch.),   16   J8
  Renf. PA4
Luckingsford Rd. (Inch.),   16   J8
  Renf. PA4
Lucy Brae (Udd.) G71   57   GG16
Ludovic Sq., John. PA5   43   D14
Luffness Gdns. G32   54   BB15
Lugar Dr. G52   49   R14
Lugar Pl. G44   64   X17
Luggiebank Pl. (Bail.) G69   57   HH14
Luing Rd. G52   33   R13
Luma Gdns. G51   33   Q12
Lumloch St. G21   23   Y10
Lumsden La. G3   34   T12
  Lumsden St.
Lumsden St. G3   34   T12
Lunan Dr. (Bishop.) G64   23   Z8
Lunan Pl. G51   33   R12
Luncarty Pl. G32   54   BB14
Luncarty St. G32   54   BB14
Lunderston Dr. G53   48   P16
Lundie Gdns. (Bishop.) G64   23   Z8
Lundie St. G32   54   AA14
Luss Rd. G51   33   R12
Lusset Vw., Clyde. G81   5   L6
  Radnor St.
Lusshill Ter. (Udd.) G71   56   EE15
Lyall Pl. G21   22   W10
  Keppochhill Rd.
Lyall St. G21   22   W10
Lybster Cres. (Ruther.) G73   65   Z18
Lye Brae (Cumb.) G67   71   PP3
Lyle Ter., Pais. PA2   46   K15
Lylesland Ct., Pais. PA2   46   K15
Lymburn St. G3   34   T12
Lyndale Pl. G20   20   T8
Lyndale Rd. G20   20   T8
Lyndhurst Gdns. G20   21   U10
Lyndhurst Gdns. La. G20   21   U10
  Melrose Gdns.
Lyne Cft. (Bishop.) G64   11   Y6
Lyne Dr. G23   9   U7
Lynedoch Cres. G3   35   U11
Lynedoch Cres. La. G3   35   U11
  Woodlands Rd.
Lynedoch Pl. G3   35   U11
Lynedoch St. G3   35   U11
Lynedoch Ter. G3   35   U11
Lynn Gdns. G12   20   T10
  Great George St.
Lynn Wk. (Udd.) G71   69   HH17
  Flax Rd.
Lynnhurst (Udd.) G71   57   GG16
Lynton Av. (Giff.) G46   62   S19
Lyon Rd., Pais. PA2   45   G15
Lyon Rd. (Linw.), Pais. PA3   44   E14
Lyoncross Av. (Barr.) G78   59   M19
Lyoncross Cres. (Barr.) G78   59   M18
Lyoncross Rd. G53   48   P15
Lytham Dr. G23   9   U7
Lytham Meadows (Both.)   69   GG19
  G71

M

Macbeth Pl. G31   53   Z14
  Macbeth St.
Macbeth St. G31   53   Z14
Macdonald St. (Ruther.) G73   53   Y16
  Greenhill Rd.
Macdougal St. G43   50   T16
Macdowall St., John. PA5   43   D14
Macdowall St., Pais. PA3   30   J13
Macduff Pl. G31   53   Z14
Macduff St. G31   53   Z14

Mace Rd. G13   7   Q7
Macfarlane Rd. (Bears.) G61   7   R6
Machrie Dr. G45   64   X18
Machrie Rd. G45   64   X18
Machrie St. G45   64   X18
Mackean St., Pais. PA3   30   J13
Mackechnie St. G51   34   S12
Mackeith St. G40   52   X14
Mackenzie Dr. (Mill.Pk.),   42   B15
  John. PA10
Mackie St. G4   22   W10
  Borron St.
Mackiesmill Rd. (Elder.),   44   F16
  John. PA5
Mackinlay St. G5   51   V14
Maclay Av. (Kilb.), John.   42   B15
  PA10
Maclean St. G51   34   T13
Maclean St., Clyde. G81   18   N8
  Wood Quad.
Maclehose Rd. (Cumb.) G67   71   QQ2
Maclellan St. G41   34   T13
Macmillan Gdns. (Udd.) G71   57   HH16
Madison Av. G44   63   V17
Madison La. G44   63   V17
  Carmunnock Rd.
Madras Pl. G40   52   X14
  Madras St.
Madras St. G40   52   X14
Mafeking St. G51   34   S13
Magdalen Way, Pais. PA2   44   F16
Magnus Cres. G44   63   V18
Mahon Ct. (Mood.) G69   15   GG7
Maida St. G43   50   S16
Maidland Rd. G53   49   Q16
Mailerbeg Gdns. (Chry.)   15   GG6
  G69
Mailing Av. (Bishop.) G64   11   Y7
Main Rd. (Elder.), John. PA5   44   F14
Main Rd. (Millarston), Pais.   44   F14
  PA1
Main Rd. (Castlehead),   46   J14
  Pais. PA2
Main St. G40   52   X14
Main St. (Thorn.) G46   61   R18
Main St. (Cumb.) G67   71   PP1
Main St. (Bail.) G69   56   EE14
Main St. (Chry.) G69   26   FF8
Main St. (Both.) G71   69   HH19
Main St. (Udd.) G71   69   GG17
Main St. (Camb.) G72   66   BB17
Main St. (Ruther.) G73   53   Y16
Main St. (Barr.) G78   59   L19
Mainhead Ter. (Cumb.) G67   71   PP1
  Roadside
Mainhill Av. (Bail.) G69   40   FF13
Mainhill Dr. (Bail.) G69   40   FF13
Mainhill Pl. (Bail.) G69   40   FF13
Mainhill Rd. (Bail.) G69   41   GG13
Mains Av. (Giff.) G46   62   S19
Mains Dr., Ersk. PA8   4   J7
Mains Hill, Ersk. PA8   4   J7
Mains River, Ersk. PA8   4   J7
Mains Wd., Ersk. PA8   4   J7
Mainscroft, Ersk. PA8   4   J7
Mair St. G51   35   U13
Maitland Pl., Renf. PA4   31   L11
Maitland St. G4   35   V11
Malcolm St. G31   37   Z13
Malin Pl. G33   38   AA12
Mallaig Path G51   33   Q12
Mallaig Pl. G51   33   Q12
Mallaig Rd. G51   33   Q12
Mallard Rd., Clyde. G81   5   L5
Malloch Cres. (Elder.),   44   E15
  John. PA5
Malloch St. G20   21   U9
Malta St., Clyde. G81   17   M8
Maltbarns St. G20   21   V10
Malvern Ct. G31   37   Y13
Malvern Way, Pais. PA3   30   J12
Mambeg Dr. G51   33   R12
Mamore Pl. G43   62   T17
Mamore St. G43   62   T17
Manchester Dr. G12   20   S9
Manitoba Pl. G31   37   Y13
  Janefield St.
Mannering Ct. G41   50   T16
  Pollokshaws Rd.

Mannering Rd. G41 50 T16
Mannering Rd., Pais. PA2 45 G16
Mannofield (Bears.) G61 7 Q6
  Chesters Rd.
Manor Rd. G14 19 R10
Manor Rd. G15 6 N7
Manor Rd. (Gart.) G69 27 GG9
Manor Rd., Pais. PA2 45 G15
Manor Way (Ruther.) G73 65 Y18
Manresa Pl. G4 35 V11
  Braid Sq.
Manse Av. (Bears.) G61 7 R5
Manse Av. (Both.) G71 69 HH19
Manse Brae G44 63 V17
Manse Ct. (Barr.) G78 59 M18
Manse Rd. G32 55 CC14
Manse Rd. (Bears.) G61 7 R5
Manse Rd. (Bail.) G69 41 GG13
Manse St., Renf. PA4 17 M10
Mansefield Av. (Camb.) G72 66 BB18
Mansefield Dr. (Udd.) G71 69 GG17
Mansel St. G21 22 X9
Mansewood Rd. G43 62 S17
Mansfield Rd. G52 32 N12
Mansfield St. G11 34 T11
Mansion Ct. (Camb.) G72 66 BB17
Mansion St. G22 22 W9
Mansion St. (Camb.) G72 66 BB17
Mansionhouse Av. G32 55 CC16
Mansionhouse Dr. G32 39 CC13
Mansionhouse Gdns. G41 51 U16
  Mansionhouse Rd.
Mansionhouse Gro. G32 55 DD14
Mansionhouse Rd. G32 55 DD14
Mansionhouse Rd. G41 51 U16
Mansionhouse Rd. G42 51 U16
Mansionhouse Rd., Pais. PA1 31 L13
Maple Dr. (Kirk.) G66 12 BB5
Maple Dr., Clyde. G81 4 K5
Maple Dr., John. PA5 44 E16
Maple Rd. G41 50 S14
Mar Gdns. (Ruther.) G73 65 Z18
March La. G41 51 U15
  Nithsdale Dr.
March St. G41 51 U15
Marchbank Gdns., Pais. PA1 47 M14
Marchfield (Bishop.) G64 10 X6
Marchfield Av., Pais. PA3 30 J12
Marchglen Pl. G51 33 Q12
  Mallaig Rd.
Marchmont Gdns. 10 X6
  (Bishop.) G64
Marchmont Ter. G12 20 T10
  Observatory Rd.
Maree Dr. G52 49 R14
Maree Gdns. (Bishop.) G64 11 Y7
Maree Rd., Pais. PA2 45 H15
Marfield St. G32 38 AA13
Margaret St. G1 36 W12
  Martha St.
Margaretta Bldgs. G44 63 V17
  Clarkston Rd.
Marguerite Av. (Lenzie) G66 13 CC5
Marguerite Dr. (Kirk.) G66 13 CC5
Marguerite Gdns. (Kirk.) 13 CC5
  G66
Marguerite Gdns. (Both.) 69 HH18
  G71
Marguerite Gro. (Kirk.) G66 13 CC5
Marine Cres. G51 35 U13
Marine Gdns. G51 35 U13
  Mavisbank Gdns.
Mariscat Rd. G41 51 U15
Marjory Dr., Pais. PA3 31 L12
Marjory Rd., Renf. PA4 31 L11
Market St. G40 36 X13
Markinch St. G5 35 V13
  West St.
Marlborough Av. G11 19 R10
Marlborough La. N. G11 19 R10
  Marlborough Av.
Marlborough La. S. G11 19 R10
  Marlborough Av.
Marldon La. G11 19 R10
  Marlborough Av.
Marlow St. G41 51 U14
Marlow Ter. G41 35 U13
  Seaward St.

Marmion Pl. (Cumb.) G67 70 NN4
Marmion Rd. (Cumb.) G67 70 NN4
Marmion Rd., Pais. PA2 45 G16
Marmion St. G20 21 U10
Marne St. G31 37 Y12
Marnock Ter., Pais. PA2 47 L15
Marnock Way (Chry.) G69 15 GG7
  Braeside Av.
Marshall's La., Pais. PA1 46 K14
Mart St. G1 36 W13
Martha St. G1 36 W12
Martin Cres. (Bail.) G69 40 FF13
Martin St. G40 52 X14
Martlet Dr., John. PA5 43 C16
Martyr St. G4 36 X12
Martyrs Pl. (Bishop.) G64 23 Y8
Marwick St. G31 37 Y12
Mary Sq. (Bail.) G69 41 GG13
Mary St., John. PA5 44 E14
Mary St., Pais. PA2 46 K15
Maryhill Rd. G20 20 S8
Maryhill Rd. (Bears.) G61 8 S7
Maryland Dr. G52 33 R13
Maryland Gdns. G52 33 R13
Marys La., Renf. PA4 17 M10
Maryston Pl. G33 37 Z11
Maryston St. G33 37 Z11
Maryview Gdns. (Udd.) G71 56 FF15
  Old Edinburgh Rd.
Maryville Av. (Giff.) G46 62 T19
Maryville Vw. (Udd.) G71 56 FF15
Marywood Sq. G41 51 U15
Masonfield Av. (Cumb.) G68 70 MM3
Masterton St. G21 22 W10
Mathieson La. G5 52 W14
  Mathieson St.
Mathieson Rd. (Ruther.) G73 53 Z15
Mathieson St. G5 52 W14
Mathieson St., Pais. PA1 31 L13
Matilda Rd. G41 51 U14
Mauchline St. G5 51 V14
Maukinfauld Ct. G32 54 AA14
Maukinfauld Rd. G32 54 AA14
Mauldslie St. G40 53 Y14
Maule Dr. G11 34 S11
Mavis Bk. (Bishop.) G64 22 X8
Mavisbank Gdns. G51 35 U13
Mavisbank Rd. G51 34 S12
  Govan Rd.
Mavisbank Ter., Pais. PA1 46 K14
Maxton Av. (Barr.) G78 59 L18
Maxton Gro. (Barr.) G78 59 L18
Maxton Ter. (Camb.) G72 66 AA18
Maxwell Av. G41 51 U14
Maxwell Av. (Bears.) G61 7 R7
Maxwell Av. (Bail.) G69 56 EE14
Maxwell Dr. G41 50 T14
Maxwell Dr. (Bail.) G69 40 EE13
Maxwell Gdns. G41 50 T14
Maxwell Gro. G41 50 T14
Maxwell Oval G41 51 U14
Maxwell Pl. G41 51 V14
Maxwell Rd. G41 51 U14
Maxwell Sq. G41 51 U14
Maxwell St. G1 36 W13
Maxwell St. (Bail.) G69 56 EE14
Maxwell St., Clyde. G81 4 K6
Maxwell St., Pais. PA3 30 K13
  Old Sneddon St.
Maxwellton Rd., Pais. PA1 45 H14
Maxwellton St., Pais. PA1 46 J14
Maxwellton Trd. Est., Pais. 45 H14
  PA1
Maxwelton Rd. G33 37 Z11
May Rd., Pais. PA2 46 K16
May Ter. G42 51 V16
  Prospecthill Rd.
May Ter. (Giff.) G46 62 T18
Maybank La. G42 51 V15
  Victoria Rd.
Maybank St. G42 51 V15
Mayberry Cres. G32 39 CC13
Mayberry Gdns. G32 39 CC13
Mayberry Gro. G32 39 CC13
Maybole St. G53 60 N17
Mayfield St. G20 21 U9
McAlpine St. G2 35 V13
McArthur St. G43 50 T16
  Pleasance St.

McArthur St., Clyde. G81 17 M8
McAslin Ct. G4 36 W12
McAslin St. G4 36 X12
McCallum Av. (Ruther.) G73 53 Y16
McClue Av., Renf. PA4 17 L10
McClue Rd., Renf. PA4 17 L10
McCracken Av., Renf. PA4 31 L11
McCreery St., Clyde. G81 17 M8
McCulloch St. G41 51 U14
McDonald Av., John. PA5 43 D15
McDonald Cres., Clyde. G81 17 M8
McEwan St. G31 37 Z13
McFarlane St. G4 36 X13
McFarlane St., Pais. PA3 30 J12
McGhee St., Clyde. G81 5 L6
McGown St., Pais. PA3 30 J13
McGregor Av., Renf. PA4 31 L11
  Porterfield Rd.
McGregor St. G51 33 R13
McGregor St., Clyde. G81 17 M8
McIntosh Ct. G31 36 X12
  McIntosh St.
McIntosh St. G31 36 X12
McIntyre Pl., Pais. PA2 46 K15
McIntyre St. G3 35 U12
McIntyre Ter. (Camb.) G72 66 BB17
McIver St. (Camb.) G72 67 CC17
McKay Cres., John. PA5 44 E15
McKenzie Av., Clyde. G81 5 L6
McKenzie St., Pais. PA3 29 H13
McKerrel St., Pais. PA1 31 L13
McLaren Av., Renf. PA4 31 M11
  Newmains Rd.
McLaren Cres. G20 21 U8
McLaren Gdns. G20 21 U8
McLaurin Cres., John. PA5 43 C15
McLean Pl., Pais. PA3 30 J12
McLean Sq. G51 34 T13
McLennan St. G42 51 V16
McLeod St. G4 36 X12
McNair St. G32 38 BB13
McNeil St. G5 52 W14
McNeill Av., Clyde. G81 6 N7
McPhail St. G40 52 X14
McPhater St. G4 35 V11
  Dunblane St.
McPherson Dr. (Both.) G71 69 HH18
  Wordsworth Way
McPherson St. G1 36 W13
  High St.
McTaggart Rd. (Cumb.) G67 70 NN4
Meadow La., Renf. PA4 17 M9
Meadow Rd. G11 34 S11
Meadow Vw. (Cumb.) G67 71 QQ2
Meadowbank La. (Udd.) 68 FF17
  G71
Meadowburn (Bishop.) G64 11 Y6
Meadowburn Av. (Lenzie) 13 DD5
  G66
Meadowhead Av. (Chry.) 15 GG7
  G69
Meadowpark St. G31 37 Y12
Meadowside Av. (Elder.), 44 F15
  John. PA5
Meadowside Quay G11 33 R11
Meadowside St. G11 34 S11
Meadowside St., Renf. PA4 17 M9
Meadowwell St. G32 38 BB13
Meadside Av. (Kilb.), John. 42 B14
  PA10
Meadside Rd. (Kilb.), John. 42 B14
  PA10
Mears Way (Bishop.) G64 11 Z7
Medlar Rd. (Cumb.) G67 71 QQ3
Medwin St. (Camb.) G72 67 DD17
  Mill Rd.
Medwyn St. G14 19 Q10
Meek Pl. (Camb.) G72 66 BB17
Meetinghouse La., Pais. 30 K13
  PA1
  Moss St.
Megan Gate G40 52 X14
  Megan St.
Megan St. G40 52 X14
Meikle Av., Renf. PA4 31 M11
Meikle Rd. G53 49 Q16
Meiklerig Cres. G53 49 Q15
Meikleriggs Dr., Pais. PA2 45 H15

Name	Page	Grid
Meiklewood Rd. G51	33	Q13
Melbourne Av., Clyde. G81	4	J5
Melbourne Ct. (Giff.) G46	62	T18
Melbourne St. G31	36	X13
Meldon Pl. G51	33	R12
Meldrum Gdns. G41	50	T15
Meldrum St., Clyde. G81	18	N8
Melford Av. (Giff.) G46	62	T19
Melford Way, Pais. PA3	31	L12
Knock Way		
Melfort Av. G41	50	S14
Melfort Av., Clyde. G81	5	L6
Melfort Gdns. (Mill.Pk.),	43	C15
John. PA10		
Milliken Pk. Rd.		
Mellerstain Dr. G14	18	N9
Melness Pl. G51	33	Q12
Mallaig Rd.		
Melrose Av. (Bail.) G69	41	GG13
Melrose Av. (Ruther.) G73	53	Y16
Melrose Av., Pais. PA2	45	H15
Melrose Av. (Linw.), Pais.	28	E13
PA3		
Melrose Ct. (Ruther.) G73	53	Y16
Dunard Rd.		
Melrose Gdns. G20	21	U10
Melrose Gdns. (Udd.) G71	57	GG15
Lincoln Av.		
Melrose Pl. (Blan.) G72	68	FF19
Melrose St. G4	35	V11
Queens Cres.		
Melvaig Pl. G20	20	T9
Melvick Pl. G51	33	Q12
Mallaig Rd.		
Melville Ct. G1	36	W12
Brunswick St.		
Melville Gdns. (Bishop.)	11	Y7
G64		
Melville St. G41	51	U14
Memel St. G21	22	X9
Memus Av. G52	49	Q14
Mennock Dr. (Bishop.) G64	11	Y6
Menock Rd. G44	63	V17
Menteith Av. (Bishop.) G64	11	Y7
Menteith Dr. (Ruther.) G73	65	Z19
Menteith Pl. (Ruther.) G73	65	Z19
Menzies Dr. G21	23	Y9
Menzies Pl. G21	23	Y9
Menzies Rd. G21	23	Y9
Merchant La. G1	36	W13
Clyde St.		
Merchants Clo. (Kilb.),	42	B14
John. PA10		
Church St.		
Merchiston St. G32	38	AA12
Merkland Ct. G11	34	S11
Vine St.		
Merkland St. G11	34	S11
Merksworth Way, Pais. PA3	30	J12
Mosslands Rd.		
Merlewood Av. (Both.) G71	69	HH18
Merlin Way, Pais. PA3	31	L12
Merlinford Av., Renf. PA4	18	N10
Merlinford Cres., Renf. PA4	18	N10
Merlinford Dr., Renf. PA4	18	N10
Merlinford Way, Renf. PA4	18	N10
Merrick Gdns. G51	34	S13
Merrick Ter. (Udd.) G71	57	HH16
Merrick Way (Ruther.) G73	65	Y18
Merryburn Av. (Giff.) G46	62	T17
Merrycrest Av. (Giff.) G46	62	T18
Merrycroft Av. (Giff.) G46	62	T18
Merryland Pl. G51	34	T12
Merryland St. G51	34	S12
Merrylee Cres. (Giff.) G46	62	T17
Merrylee Pk. Av. (Giff.) G46	62	T18
Merrylee Pk. La. (Giff.) G46	62	T18
Merrylee Pk. Ms. (Giff.) G46	62	T18
Merrylee Rd. G43	62	T17
Merrylee Rd. G44	62	T17
Merryton Av. G15	6	P6
Merryton Av. (Giff.) G46	62	T18
Merryton Pl. G15	6	P6
Merryvale Av. (Giff.) G46	62	T18
Merryvale Pl. (Giff.) G46	62	T17
Merton Dr. G52	32	P13
Meryon Gdns. G32	55	CC15
Meryon Rd. G32	55	CC15
Methil St. G14	19	Q10
Methuen Rd., Pais. PA3	31	L11
Methven Av. (Bears.) G61	8	S5
Methven St. G31	53	Z14
Methven St., Clyde. G81	4	K6
Metropole La. G1	35	V13
Howard St.		
Mews La., Pais. PA3	30	K12
Renfrew Rd.		
Micklehouse Oval (Bail.)	40	EE13
G69		
Micklehouse Rd.		
Micklehouse Pl. (Bail.) G69	40	EE13
Micklehouse Rd.		
Micklehouse Rd. (Bail.) G69	40	EE13
Micklehouse Wynd (Bail.)	40	EE13
G69		
Micklehouse Rd.		
Mid Cotts. (Gart.) G69	26	FF10
Midcroft (Bishop.) G64	10	X6
Midcroft Av. G44	64	W17
Middle Pk., Pais. PA2	46	J15
Middlemuir Av. (Kirk.) G66	13	CC5
Middlemuir Rd. (Lenzie)	13	CC5
G66		
Middlerigg Rd. (Cumb.) G68	70	MM3
Middlesex Gdns. G41	35	U13
Middlesex St. G41	35	U13
Middleton Cres., Pais. PA3	30	J13
Middleton Rd., Pais. PA3	28	F13
Middleton St. G51	34	T13
Midland St. G1	35	V13
Midlem Dr. G52	33	Q13
Midlem Oval G52	33	Q13
Midlock St. G51	34	T13
Midlothian Dr. G41	50	T15
Midton Cotts. (Mood.) G69	15	HH7
Midton St. G21	22	X10
Midwharf St. G4	36	W11
Migvie Pl. G20	20	T9
Wyndford Rd.		
Milan St. G41	51	V14
Milford St. G33	38	BB12
Mill Ct. (Ruther.) G73	53	Y16
Mill Cres. G40	52	X14
Mill Pl. (Linw.), Pais. PA3	28	E13
Mill Ri. (Lenzie) G66	13	CC6
Mill Rd. (Both.) G71	69	HH19
Mill Rd. (Camb.) G72	67	CC18
Mill Rd., Clyde. G81	17	M8
Mill St. G40	52	X14
Mill St. (Ruther.) G73	53	Y16
Mill St., Pais. PA1	46	K14
Mill Vennel, Renf. PA4	18	N10
High St.		
Millands Av. (Blan.) G72	68	FF19
Millar St., Pais. PA1	30	K13
Millar Ter. (Ruther.) G73	53	Y15
Millarbank St. G21	22	X10
Millarston Av., Pais. PA1	45	H14
Millarston Dr., Pais. PA1	45	H14
Millbeg Cres. G33	39	DD13
Millbeg Pl. G33	39	DD13
Millbrae Ct. G42	51	U16
Millbrae Rd.		
Millbrae Cres. G42	51	U16
Millbrae Cres., Clyde. G81	17	M8
Millbrae Rd. G42	51	U16
Millbrix Av. G14	18	P9
Millburn Av. (Ruther.) G73	65	Y17
Millburn Av., Clyde. G81	18	N8
Millburn Av., Renf. PA4	18	N10
Millburn Dr., Renf. PA4	17	M10
Millburn Rd., Renf. PA4	17	M10
Millburn St. G21	37	Y11
Millburn Way, Renf. PA4	18	N10
Millcroft Rd. (Cumb.) G67	71	PP3
Millcroft Rd. (Ruther.) G73	52	X15
Miller St. G1	36	W12
Miller St. (Bail.) G69	56	EE14
Miller St., Clyde. G81	5	L7
Miller St., John. PA5 .	44	E14
Millerfield Pl. G40	53	Y14
Millerfield Rd. G40	53	Y14
Millers Pl. (Lenzie) G66	13	CC6
Millersneuk Av. (Lenzie)	13	CC6
G66		
Millersneuk Cres. G33	24	BB9
Millersneuk Dr. (Lenzie) G66	13	CC6
Millerston St. G31	37	Y10
Millford Dr. (Linw.), Pais.	28	E13
PA3		
Millgate (Udd.) G71	57	GG16
Millgate Av. (Udd.) G71	57	GG16
Millholm Rd. G44	63	V18
Millhouse Cres. G20	20	T8
Millhouse Dr. G20	20	T8
Millichen Rd. G23	8	T5
Milliken Dr. (Mill.Pk.),	43	C15
John. PA10		
Milliken Pk. Rd. (Mill.Pk.),	43	C15
John. PA10		
Milliken Rd. (Mill.Pk.),	43	C15
John. PA10		
Millpond Dr. G40	36	X13
Millport Av. G44	52	W16
Millroad Dr. G40	36	X13
Millroad Gdns. G40	36	X13
Millroad St. G40	36	X13
Millview (Barr.) G78	59	M18
Millview Pl. G53	60	P18
Millwood St. G41	51	U16
Milnbank St. G31	37	Y12
Milncroft Rd. G33	38	BB11
Milner La. G13	19	R9
Southbrae Dr.		
Milner Rd. G13	19	R9
Milngavie Rd. (Bears.) G61	7	R6
Milnpark Gdns. G41	35	U13
Milnpark St. G41	35	U13
Milovaig St. G23	8	T7
Milrig Rd. (Ruther.) G73	52	X16
Milton Av. (Camb.) G72	66	AA17
Milton Douglas Rd., Clyde.	5	L5
G81		
Milton Dr. (Bishop.) G64	22	X8
Milton Gdns. (Udd.) G71	57	GG16
Milton Mains Rd., Clyde.	5	L5
G81		
Milton St. G4	35	V11
Milverton Av. (Bears.) G61	7	Q5
Milverton Rd. (Giff.) G46	62	S19
Minard Rd. G41	51	U15
Minard Way (Udd.) G71	57	HH16
Newton Dr.		
Minerva St. G3	35	U12
Minerva Way G3	35	U12
Mingarry La. G20	20	T10
Clouston St.		
Mingarry St. G20	21	U10
Mingulay Cres. G22	22	W8
Mingulay Pl. G22	22	X8
Mingulay St. G22	22	W8
Minister Wk. (Bail.) G69	41	GG13
Dukes Rd.		
Minmoir Rd. G53	48	N16
Minstrel Rd. G13	7	Q7
Minto Av. (Ruther.) G73	65	Z18
Minto Cres. G52	33	R13
Minto St. G52	33	R13
Mireton St. G22	21	V9
Mirrlees Dr. G12	20	T10
Mirrlees La. G12	20	T10
Redlands Rd.		
Mitchell Av. (Camb.) G72	67	DD17
Mitchell Av., Renf. PA4	31	L11
Mitchell Dr. (Ruther.) G73	65	Y17
Mitchell La. G1	35	V12
Buchanan St.		
Mitchell Rd. (Cumb.) G67	71	PP3
Mitchell St. G1	35	V12
Mitchell St., Coat. ML5	57	HH14
Mitchellhill Rd. G45	64	X19
Mitchison Rd. (Cumb.) G67	71	PP2
Mitre Ct. G11	19	R10
Mitre Rd.		
Mitre La. G14	19	R10
Mitre La. W. G14	19	R10
Mitre La.		
Mitre Rd. G11	19	R10
Mitre Rd. G14	19	R10
Moat Av. G13	19	Q8
Mochrum Rd. G43	63	U17
Moffat Pl. (Blan.) G72	68	FF19
Moffat St. G5	52	W14
Mogarth Av., Pais. PA2	45	H16
Amochrie Rd.		
Moidart Av., Renf. PA4	17	L10
Moidart Ct. (Barr.) G78	59	L18

Moidart Cres. G52 33 R13
Moidart Rd.
Moidart Pl. G52 33 R13
Moidart Rd.
Moidart Rd. G52 33 R13
Moir La. G1 36 W13
Moir St.
Moir St. G1 36 W13
Molendinar St. G1 36 W13
Mollinsburn St. G21 22 X10
Monach Rd. G33 39 CC12
Monachie Gdns. (Bishop.) 11 Z7
G64
Muirhead Way
Monar Dr. G22 21 V10
Monar Pl. G22 21 V10
Monar St. G22 21 V10
Monart Pl. G20 21 U10
Caithness St.
Moncrieff Av. (Lenzie) G66 13 CC5
Moncrieff Gdns. (Kirk.) G66 13 CC5
Moncrieff Av.
Moncrieff Pl. G20 35 V11
North Woodside Rd.
Moncrieff St. G4 35 V11
Braid Sq.
Moncur St. G40 36 X13
Moness Dr. G52 49 R14
Monifieth Av. G52 49 Q14
Monikie Gdns. (Bishop.) 11 Z7
G64
Muirhead Way
Monkcastle Dr. (Camb.) G72 66 BB17
Monkland Av. (Kirk.) G66 13 CC5
Monkland Vw. (Udd.) G71 57 HH15
Lincoln Av.
Monkland Vw. Cres. (Bail.) 41 HH13
G69
Monksbridge Av. G13 7 Q7
Monkscroft Av. G11 20 S10
Monkscroft Ct. G11 34 S11
Monkscroft Gdns. G11 20 S10
Monkscroft Av.
Monkton Dr. G15 6 P7
Monmouth Av. G12 20 S9
Monreith Av. (Bears.) G61 7 Q7
Monreith Rd. G43 62 T17
Monreith Rd. E. G44 63 V17
Monroe Dr. (Udd.) G71 57 GG15
Monroe Pl. (Udd.) G71 57 GG15
Montague La. G12 20 S10
Montague St. G4 35 U11
Montague Ter. G12 20 S10
Hyndland Rd.
Montclair Pl. (Linw.), Pais. 28 E13
PA3
Monteith Dr. (Clark.) G76 63 V19
Monteith Pl. G40 36 X13
Monteith Row G40 36 X13
Monteith Row La. G40 36 X13
Monteith Pl.
Montford Av. G44 52 W16
Montford Av. (Ruther.) G73 52 W16
Montgomerie Gdns. G14 19 Q10
Lennox Av.
Montgomery Av., Pais. PA3 31 L12
Montgomery Dr. (Giff.) G46 62 T19
Montgomery Dr. (Kilb.), 42 B14
John. PA10
Meadside Av.
Montgomery La. G42 51 V16
Somerville St.
Montgomery Rd., Pais. PA3 31 L12
Montgomery St. G40 52 X14
London Rd.
Montgomery St. (Camb.) 67 DD17
G72
Mill Rd.
Montrave St. G52 49 Q14
Montrave St. (Ruther.) G73 53 Z15
Montreal Ho., Clyde. G81 4 J5
Perth Cres.
Montron Dr. G15 6 P7
Moraine Av.
Montrose Av. G32 54 BB15
Montrose Av. G52 32 N12
Montrose Gdns. (Blan.) G72 68 FF19
Montrose Pl. (Linw.), Pais. 28 E13
PA3

Montrose Rd., Pais. PA2 45 G16
Montrose St. G1 36 W12
Montrose St. G4 36 W12
Montrose St., Clyde. G81 5 L7
Montrose Ter. (Bishop.) G64 23 Z8
Monymusk Gdns. (Bishop.) 11 Z7
G64
Monymusk Pl. G15 6 N5
Moodies Ct. G1 36 W13
Osborne St.
Moodiesburn St. G33 37 Z11
Moorburn Av. (Giff.) G46 62 S18
Moore Dr. (Bears.) G61 7 R6
Moore St. G31 37 Y13
Gallowgate
Moorehouse Av., Pais. PA2 45 H15
Moorfoot (Bishop.) G64 11 Z7
Moorfoot Av. (Thorn.) G46 62 S18
Moorfoot Av., Pais. PA2 46 J15
Moorfoot St. G32 38 AA13
Moorhouse Av. G13 18 N9
Moorhouse St. (Barr.) G78 59 M19
Moorings, The, Pais. PA2 45 H14
Moorpark Av. G52 32 N13
Moorpark Av. (Muir.) G69 26 FF8
Cumbernauld Rd.
Moorpark Dr. G52 32 P13
Moorpark Pl. G52 32 N13
Moorpark Sq., Renf. PA4 31 L11
Morag Av. (Blan.) G72 68 FF19
Moraine Av. G15 6 P7
Moraine Circ. G15 6 P7
Moraine Dr. G15 6 P7
Moraine Pl. G15 6 P7
Moraine Dr.
Morar Av., Clyde. G81 5 L6
Morar Ct. (Cumb.) G67 70 LL4
Morar Ct., Clyde. G81 5 L6
Morar Cres. (Bishop.) G64 10 X7
Morar Cres., Clyde. G81 5 L6
Morar Dr. (Bears.) G61 8 S6
Morar Dr. (Cumb.) G67 70 LL4
Morar Dr. (Ruther.) G73 65 Y18
Morar Dr., Clyde. G81 5 L6
Morar Dr., Pais. PA2 45 G15
Morar Dr. (Linw.), Pais. PA3 28 E13
Morar Pl., Clyde. G81 5 L6
Morar Pl., Renf. PA4 17 L10
Morar Rd. G52 33 R13
Morar Rd., Clyde. G81 5 L6
Morar Ter. (Udd.) G71 57 HH16
Morar Ter. (Ruther.) G73 65 Z18
Moravia Av. (Both.) G71 69 HH18
Moray Gdns. (Cumb.) G68 71 PP1
Moray Gdns. (Udd.) G71 57 GG16
Moray Gate (Both.) G71 69 GG18
Moray Pl. G41 51 U15
Moray Pl. (Bishop.) G64 11 Z7
Moray Pl. (Linw.), Pais. PA3 28 E13
Mordaunt St. G40 53 Y14
Moredun Cres. G32 39 CC12
Moredun Dr., Pais. PA2 45 H15
Moredun Rd., Pais. PA2 45 H15
Moredun St. G32 39 CC12
Morefield Rd. G51 33 Q12
Morgan Ms. G42 51 V14
Morina Gdns. G53 61 Q19
Morion Rd. G13 19 Q8
Morley St. G42 51 V16
Morna Pl. G14 33 R11
Victoria Pk. Dr. S.
Morningside St. G33 37 Z12
Morrin Path G21 22 X10
Crichton St.
Morrin Sq. G4 36 X12
Collins St.
Morrin St. G21 22 X10
Morris Pl. G40 36 X13
Morrison Quad., Clyde. G81 6 N7
Morrison St. G5 35 V13
Morrison St., Clyde. G81 4 K5
Morrisons Ct. G2 35 V12
Argyle St.
Morriston Cres., Renf. PA4 32 N11
Morriston Pk. Dr. (Camb.) 54 BB16
G72
Morriston St. (Camb.) G72 66 BB17
Mortimer St. G20 21 U10
Hotspur St.

Morton Gdns. G41 50 T15
Morven Av. (Bishop.) G64 11 Z7
Morven Av. (Blan.) G72 68 FF19
Morven Av., Pais. PA2 46 J16
Morven Dr. (Linw.), Pais. 28 E13
PA3
Morven Gdns. (Udd.) G71 57 GG16
Morven Rd. (Bears.) G61 7 R5
Morven Rd. (Camb.) G72 66 AA18
Morven St. G52 33 R13
Mosesfield St. G21 22 X9
Mosesfield Ter. G21 22 X9
Balgrayhill Rd.
Moss Av. (Linw.), Pais. PA3 28 E13
Moss Dr. (Barr.) G78 59 L17
Moss Heights Av. G52 33 Q13
Moss Knowe (Cumb.) G67 71 QQ3
Moss Path (Bail.) G69 55 DD14
Castle St.
Moss Rd. G51 33 Q12
Moss Rd. (Kirk.) G66 13 CC5
Moss Rd. (Cumb.) G67 71 QQ2
Moss Rd. (Muir.) G69 26 FF8
Moss St., Pais. PA1 30 K13
Moss-side Rd. G41 50 T15
Mossbank Av. G33 24 AA10
Mossbank Dr. G33 24 AA10
Mosscastle Rd. G33 39 CC11
Mossend La. G33 39 CC12
Mossend Rd., Pais. PA3 30 J12
Mosslands Rd.
Mossend St. G33 39 CC12
Mossgiel Av. (Ruther.) G73 65 Y17
Mossgiel Dr., Clyde. G81 5 M6
Mossgiel Gdns. (Udd.) G71 57 GG16
Mossgiel Pl. (Ruther.) G73 65 Y17
Mossgiel Rd. G43 62 T17
Mossgiel Rd. (Cumb.) G67 71 PP3
Mossgiel Ter. (Blan.) G72 68 FF19
Mossland Rd. G52 32 N12
Mosslands Rd., Pais. PA3 30 J12
Mossneuk Dr., Pais. PA2 46 J16
Mosspark Av. G52 49 R14
Mosspark Boul. G52 49 R14
Mosspark Dr. G52 49 Q14
Mosspark La. G52 49 R15
Mosspark Dr.
Mosspark Oval G52 49 R14
Mosspark Sq. G52 49 R14
Mossvale Cres. G33 39 CC11
Mossvale La., Pais. PA3 30 J13
Mossvale Path G33 25 CC10
Mossvale Rd. G33 24 BB10
Mossvale Sq. G33 39 CC11
Mossvale St., Pais. PA3 30 J12
Mossvale Ter. (Chry.) G69 15 HH6
Mossvale Wk. G33 39 CC11
Mossvale Way G33 39 CC11
Mossview Cotts. (Muir.) 26 FF9
G69
Mossview Quad. G52 33 Q13
Mossview Rd. G33 25 DD9
Mote Hill Rd., Pais. PA3 31 L13
Moulin Circ. G52 48 P14
Moulin Pl. G52 48 P14
Moulin Rd. G52 48 P14
Moulin Ter. G52 48 P14
Mount Annan Dr. G44 51 V16
Mount Harriet Av. (Stepps) 25 DD9
G33
Mount Harriet Dr. (Stepps) 25 CC9
G33
Mount St. G20 21 U10
Mount Stuart St. G41 51 U16
Mount Vernon Av. G32 55 DD14
Mountainblue St. G31 37 Y13
Mountblow Ho., Clyde. G81 4 J5
Melbourne Av.
Mountblow Rd., Clyde. G81 4 K5
Mountgarrie Path G51 33 Q12
Mountgarrie Rd.
Mountgarrie Rd. G51 33 Q12
Mowbray Av. (Gart.) G69 27 GG9
Mowcraigs Ct., Clyde. G81 17 M8
Yokerburn Ter.
Moy St. G11 34 T11
Church St.
Moyne Rd. G53 48 P15
Muckcroft Rd. (Chry.) G69 14 EE6

Newlands Rd. (Udd.) G71	57	GG16
Newlandsfield Rd. G43	50	T16
Newluce Dr. G32	55	CC14
Newmains Rd., Renf. PA4	31	L11
Newmill Rd. G21	23	Z9
Newnham Rd., Pais. PA1	48	N14
Newpark Cres. (Camb.) G72	54	BB16
Newshot Ct., Clyde. G81	17	M8
Clydeholm Ter.		
Newshot Dr., Ersk. PA8	4	J7
Newstead Gdns. G23	9	U7
Newton Av. (Camb.) G72	67	CC17
Newton Av. (Barr.) G78	59	M19
Newton Av. (Elder.), John.	45	G14
PA5		
Newton Brae (Camb.) G72	67	DD17
Newton Dr. (Udd.) G71	57	HH16
Newton Dr. (Elder.), John.	45	G14
PA5		
Newton Fm. Rd. (Camb.)	55	DD16
G72		
Newton Pl. G3	35	U11
Newton Rd. (Lenzie) G66	13	DD6
Newton Sta. Rd. (Camb.)	67	DD17
G72		
Newton St. G2	35	V12
Newton St., Pais. PA1	46	J14
Newton Ter. G3	35	U12
Sauchiehall St.		
Newton Ter. La. G3	35	U11
Elderslie St.		
Newtongrange Av. G32	54	BB15
Newtongrange Gdns. G32	54	BB15
Newtyle Pl. (Bishop.) G64	11	Z7
Newtyle Rd., Pais. PA1	47	L14
Nicholas St. G1	36	W12
Nicholson Ct. (Stepps) G33	25	CC9
Nicholson La. G5	35	V13
Nicholson St.		
Nicholson St. G5	35	V13
Niddrie Rd. G42	51	U15
Niddrie Sq. G42	51	U15
Niddry St., Pais. PA3	30	K13
Nigel Gdns. G41	50	T15
Nigg Pl. G34	40	EE12
Nightingale Pl., John. PA5	43	C16
Nimmo Dr. G51	33	R12
Nisbet St. G31	37	Z13
Nith Av., Pais. PA2	45	G15
Nith Dr., Renf. PA4	32	N11
Nith Pl., John. PA5	43	C16
Nith St. G33	37	Z11
Nithsdale Cres. (Bears.) G61	7	Q5
Nithsdale Dr. G41	51	U15
Nithsdale Pl. G41	51	U14
Nithsdale Rd.		
Nithsdale Rd. G41	50	S14
Nithsdale St. G41	51	U15
Nitshill Rd. (Thorn.) G46	61	Q18
Nitshill Rd. G53	60	N17
Niven St. G20	20	T9
Noldrum Av. G32	55	CC16
Noldrum Gdns. G32	55	CC16
Norbreck Dr. (Giff.) G46	62	T18
Norby Rd. G11	19	R10
Norfield Dr. G44	51	V16
Norfolk Ct. G5	35	V13
Norfolk Cres. (Bishop.) G64	10	X6
Norfolk La. G5	35	V13
Norfolk St.		
Norfolk St. G5	35	V13
Norham St. G41	51	U15
Norman St. G40	52	X14
Norse La. N. G14	19	Q10
Ormiston Av.		
Norse La. S. G14	19	Q10
Verona Av.		
Norse Rd. G14	19	Q10
North Av. (Camb.) G72	66	AA17
North Av., Clyde. G81	5	L7
North Bk. Pl., Clyde. G81	17	M8
North Bk. St.		
North Bk. St., Clyde. G81	17	M8
North Berwick Av. (Cumb.)	70	NN1
G68		
North Berwick Gdns.	70	NN1
(Cumb.) G68		
North Berwick Av.		
North Brae Pl. G13	18	P8

North British Rd. (Udd.) G71	69	GG17
North Canal Bk. G4	36	W11
North Canal Bk. St. G4	36	W11
North Carbrain Rd.	70	NN4
(Cumb.) G67		
North Claremont St. G3	35	U11
North Corsebar Av., Pais.	46	J15
PA2		
North Ct. La. G1	36	W12
Buchanan St.		
North Cft. St., Pais. PA3	30	K13
North Deanpark Av. (Both.)	69	HH18
G71		
North Douglas St., Clyde.	17	M8
G81		
North Dr. G1	36	W13
North Dr. (Linw.), Pais.	28	E13
PA3		
North Elgin St., Clyde. G81	17	M8
North Erskine Pk. (Bears.)	7	Q5
G61		
North Frederick St. G1	36	W12
North Gardner St. G11	20	S10
North Gower St. G51	34	T13
North Gra. Rd. (Bears.) G61	7	R5
North Greenhill Rd., Pais.	30	J12
PA3		
North Hanover Pl. G4	36	W11
North Hanover St. G1	36	W12
North Iverton Pk. Rd.,	44	E14
John. PA5		
North La. (Linw.), Pais. PA3	28	F13
Napier St.		
North Lo. Rd., Renf. PA4	17	M10
North Moraine La. G15	7	Q7
Moraine Av.		
North Pk. Av. (Thorn.) G46	61	R18
North Pk. Av. (Barr.) G78	59	L18
North Pl. G3	35	U12
North St.		
North Portland St. G1	36	W12
North Queen St. G2	36	W12
George Sq.		
North Rd., John. PA5	43	D15
North Spiers Wf. G4	35	V11
North St. G3	35	U12
North St., Clyde. G81	5	L7
Dumbarton Rd.		
North St., Pais. PA3	30	K13
North Vw. (Bears.) G61	7	Q7
North Wallace St. G4	36	W11
North Way (Blan.) G72	68	FF19
North Woodside Rd. G20	21	U10
Northampton Dr. G12	20	S9
Northampton La. G12	20	S9
Northampton Dr.		
Northbank Av. (Camb.) G72	67	CC17
Northbank St. (Camb.) G72	67	CC17
Grahamston Rd.		
Northcroft Rd. G21	22	X10
Northcroft Rd. (Chry.) G69	15	GG7
Northgate Quad. G21	23	Z8
Northgate Rd. G21	23	Z8
Northinch St. G14	33	Q11
Northland Av. G14	19	Q9
Northland Dr. G14	19	Q9
Northland Gdns. G14	19	Q9
Northland La. G14	19	Q10
Upland Rd.		
Northmuir Rd. G15	6	P6
Northpark St. G20	21	U10
Northpark Ter. G12	21	U10
Hamilton Dr.		
Northumberland St. G20	21	U10
Norval St. G11	34	S11
Norwich Dr. G12	20	S9
Norwood (Bears.) G61	7	R6
Norwood Dr. (Giff.) G46	62	S19
Norwood Ter. G12	35	U11
Southpark Av.		
Norwood Ter. (Udd.) G71	57	HH16
Nottingham Av. G12	20	S9
Nottingham La. G12	20	S9
Northampton Dr.		
Novar Dr. G12	20	S10
Novar Gdns. (Bishop.) G64	10	X7
Numrow Ct., Clyde. G81	4	K5
Nuneaton St. G40	53	Y14
Nurseries Rd. (Bail.) G69	39	DD13
Nursery La. G41	51	U15

Nursery St. G41	51	U15
Pollokshaws Rd.		
Nursery St. La. G41	51	U15
Nithsdale Dr.		
Nutberry Ct. G42	51	V15

O

Oak Cres. (Bail.) G69	56	EE14
Oak Dr. (Kirk.) G66	12	BB5
Oak Dr. (Camb.) G72	67	CC18
Oak Pk. (Bishop.) G64	11	Y7
Oak Rd., Clyde. G81	4	K5
Oak Rd., Pais. PA2	47	L15
Oak St. G2	35	V12
Cadogan St.		
Oakbank Dr. (Barr.) G78	60	N19
Oakbank La. G20	21	V10
Oakbank Ter. G20	21	V10
Oakdene Av. (Udd.) G71	57	HH16
Oakfield Av. G12	35	U11
Oakfield La. G12	35	U11
Gibson St.		
Oakfield Ter. G12	35	U11
Oakfield Av.		
Oakhill Av. (Bail.) G69	55	DD14
Oakley Dr. G44	63	U18
Oakley Ter. G31	36	X12
Oaks, The, John. PA5	43	D15
Oakshaw Sch. Brae, Pais.	30	J13
PA1		
Oakshaw St. E., Pais. PA1	30	K13
Oakshaw St. W., Pais. PA1	30	J13
Oakshawhead, Pais. PA1	30	J13
Oakwood Av., Pais. PA2	45	H15
Oatfield St. G21	23	Y10
Oban Ct. G20	21	U10
Oban Dr. G20	21	U10
Oban La. G20	21	U10
Oban Dr.		
Observatory La. G12	20	T10
Observatory Rd.		
Observatory Rd. G12	20	T10
Ochil Dr. (Barr.) G78	59	M19
Ochil Dr., Pais. PA2	46	K16
Ochil Pl. G32	54	BB14
Ochil Rd. (Bishop.) G64	11	Z7
Ochil Rd., Renf. PA4	31	L11
Ochil St. G32	54	BB14
Ochil Vw. (Udd.) G71	57	HH16
Ochiltree Av. G13	19	R8
Ogilvie Pl. G31	54	AA14
Ogilvie St. G31	53	Z14
Old Bothwell Rd. (Both.)	69	HH19
G71		
Old Castle Rd. G44	63	V17
Old Cotts., Pais. PA2	47	M16
Old Dalmarnock Rd. G40	52	X14
Old Dalnottar Rd. (Old Kil.)	4	J5
G60		
Old Dumbarton Rd. G3	34	T11
Old Edinburgh Rd. (Udd.)	57	GG15
G71		
Old Gartcosh Rd. (Gart.)	27	GG9
G69		
Old Glasgow Rd. (Udd.) G71	56	FF16
Old Govan Rd., Renf. PA4	18	N10
Old Greenock Rd. (Inch.),	16	J8
Renf. PA4		
Old Manse Rd. G32	39	CC13
Old Mill Rd. (Both.) G71	69	HH19
* Old Mill Rd. (Udd.) G71	69	GG17
Old Mill Rd. (Camb.) G72	67	CC17
Old Mill Rd., Clyde. G81	5	L5
Old Mill Rd., Pais. PA2	45	H14
Old Renfrew Rd., Renf. PA4	32	P11
Old Rd. (Elder.), John. PA5	44	E14
Old Roundknowe Rd.	56	FF15
(Udd.) G71		
Old Rutherglen Rd. G5	52	W14
Old Shettleston Rd. G32	38	AA13
Old Sneddon St., Pais. PA3	30	K13
Old St., Clyde. G81	4	K5
Old Wd. Rd. (Bail.) G69	56	EE14
Old Wynd G1	36	W13
Oldhall Rd., Pais. PA1	47	M14
Olifard Av. (Both.) G71	69	HH18
Oliphant Cres., Pais. PA2	45	G16

Street	Page	Ref
Queen Elizabeth Sq. G5	52	W14
Queen Margaret Ct. G20	21	U10
Queen Margaret Cres. G12	21	U10
Hamilton Dr.		
Queen Margaret Dr. G12	20	T10
Queen Margaret Dr. G20	21	U10
Queen Margaret Rd. G20	21	U10
Queen Mary Av. G42	51	V15
Queen Mary Av., Clyde. G81	5	M7
Queen Mary St. G40	52	X14
Queen Sq. G41	51	U15
Queen St. G1	36	W12
Queen St. (Ruther.) G73	53	Y16
Queen St., Pais. PA1	46	J14
Queen St., Renf. PA4	17	M10
Queen Victoria Dr. G13	19	Q10
Queen Victoria Dr. G14	19	Q10
Queen Victoria Gate G13	19	Q9
Queenbank Av. (Gart.) G69	27	GG8
Queens Av. (Camb.) G72	66	BB17
Queens Cres. G4	35	V11
Queens Cres. (Bail.) G69	41	GG13
Queens Cross G20	21	U10
Queens Dr. G42	51	U15
Queens Dr. (Cumb.) G68	70	NN1
Queens Dr. La. G42	51	V15
Queens Gdns. G12	20	T10
Victoria Cres. Rd.		
Queens Pk. Av. G42	51	V15
Queens Pl. G12	20	T10
Queens Rd. (Elder.), John. PA5	44	F15
Queensborough Gdns. G12	20	S10
Queensby Av. (Bail.) G69	40	EE13
Queensby Rd.		
Queensby Dr. (Bail.) G69	40	EE13
Queensby Rd.		
Queensby Pl. (Bail.) G69	40	EE13
Queensby Rd.		
Queensby Rd. (Bail.) G69	40	EE13
Queensferry St. G5	52	X15
Rosebery Av.		
Queenshill St. G21	22	X10
Queensland Ct. G52	33	Q13
Queensland Dr. G52	33	Q13
Queensland Gdns. G52	33	Q13
Queensland La. E. G52	32	P13
Kingsland Dr.		
Queensland La. W. G52	33	Q13
Queensland Dr.		
Queenslie Ind. Est. G33	39	CC12
Queenslie St. G33	37	Z11
Quendale Dr. G32	54	AA14
Quentin St. G41	51	U15
Quinton Gdns. (Bail.) G69	40	EE13

R

Street	Page	Ref
Raasay Dr., Pais. PA2	46	J16
Raasay Pl. G22	22	W8
Raasay St. G22	22	W8
Rachan St. G34	40	FF11
Radnor St. G3	35	U12
Argyle St.		
Radnor St., Clyde. G81	5	L6
Raeberry St. G20	21	U10
Raeswood Dr. G53	48	N16
Raeswood Gdns. G53	48	N16
Raeswood Pl. G53	48	N16
Raeswood Rd. G53	48	N16
Raglan St. G4	35	V11
Raith Av. G44	64	W18
Raithburn Av. G45	64	W18
Raithburn Rd. G45	64	W18
Ralston Av. G52	48	N14
Ralston Av., Pais. PA1	48	N14
Ralston Ct. G52	48	N14
Ralston Dr. G52	48	N14
Ralston Path G52	48	N14
Ralston Dr.		
Ralston Pl. G52	48	N14
Ralston Rd. (Bears.) G61	7	R5
Ralston Rd. (Barr.) G78	59	M19
Ralston St., Pais. PA1	47	L14
Seedhill Rd.		
Ram St. G32	38	AA13
Rampart Av. G13	18	P8
Ramsay Av., John. PA5	43	D15
Ramsay Cres. (Mill.Pk.), John. PA10	42	B15
Ramsay Pl., John. PA5	43	D15
Ramsay St., Clyde. G81	4	K6
Ranald Gdns. (Ruther.) G73	65	Z18
Randolph Av. (Clark.) G76	63	U19
Randolph Dr. (Clark.) G76	63	U19
Randolph Gdns. (Clark.) G76	63	U19
Randolph Rd. G11	19	R10
Randolph Ter. (Camb.) G72	66	BB17
Hamilton Rd.		
Ranfurley Rd. G52	32	N13
Rankine Pl., John. PA5	43	D14
Rankine St., John. PA5	43	D14
Rankines La., Renf. PA4	17	M10
Manse St.		
Rannoch Av. (Bishop.) G64	11	Y7
Rannoch Dr. (Bears.) G61	8	S7
Rannoch Dr., Renf. PA4	17	M10
Rannoch Gdns. (Bishop.) G64	11	Y7
Rannoch Pl., Pais. PA2	47	L14
Rannoch Rd. (Udd.) G71	57	GG15
Rannoch Rd., John. PA5	43	D15
Rannoch St. G44	63	V17
Raploch Av. G14	18	P10
Raploch La. G14	18	P10
Raploch Av.		
Ratford St. G51	34	S12
Rathlin St. G51	34	S12
Ratho Dr. G21	22	X9
Rattray St. G32	54	AA14
Ravel Row G31	37	Z13
Ravel Wynd (Udd.) G71	57	HH16
Ravelston Rd. (Bears.) G61	7	R7
Ravelston St. G32	37	Z13
Ravens Ct. (Bishop.) G64	22	X8
Lennox Cres.		
Ravenscliffe Dr. (Giff.) G46	62	S18
Ravenscraig Av., Pais. PA2	46	J15
Ravenscraig Dr. G53	60	P17
Ravenscraig Ter. G53	61	Q17
Ravenshall Rd. G41	50	T16
Ravenstone Rd. (Giff.) G46	62	T18
Ravenswood Av., Pais. PA2	45	G16
Ravenswood Dr. G41	50	T15
Ravenswood Rd. (Bail.) G69	40	FF13
Rayne Pl. G15	6	P6
Red Rd. G21	23	Y10
Red Rd. Ct. G21	23	Y10
Redan St. G40	36	X13
Redcastle Sq. G33	39	CC11
Redford St. G33	37	Z12
Redgate Pl. G14	18	P10
Redhill Rd. (Cumb.) G68	70	MM2
Redhurst Cres., Pais. PA2	45	H16
Redhurst La., Pais. PA2	45	H16
Redhurst Way, Pais. PA2	45	H16
Redlands La. G12	20	T10
Kirklee Rd.		
Redlands Rd. G12	20	T10
Redlands Ter. G12	20	T10
Redlands Ter. La. G12	20	T10
Julian Av.		
Redlawood Pl. (Camb.) G72	68	EE17
Redlawood Rd.		
Redlawood Rd. (Camb.) G72	68	EE17
Redmoss St. G22	21	V9
Rednock St. G22	22	W10
Redpath Dr. G52	32	P13
Redwood Dr. G21	23	Y10
Foresthall Dr.		
Redwood Pl. (Kirk.) G66	12	BB5
Redwood Rd. (Cumb.) G67	71	QQ3
Reelick Av. G13	18	N8
Reelick Quad. G13	18	N8
Reen Pl. (Both.) G71	69	HH18
Regent Moray St. G3	34	T11
Regent Pk. Sq. G41	51	U15
Regent Pk. Ter. G41	51	U15
Pollokshaws Rd.		
Regent Pl., Clyde. G81	4	K6
Regent Sq. (Lenzie) G66	13	CC6
Regent St., Clyde. G81	4	K6
Regent St., Pais. PA1	31	L13
Regents Gate (Both.) G71	69	GG18
Regwood St. G41	50	T16
Reid Av. (Bears.) G61	8	S5
Reid Av. (Linw.), Pais. PA3	28	E13
Reid Pl. G40	52	X14
Muslin St.		
Reid St. G40	52	X14
Reid St. (Ruther.) G73	53	Y16
Reidhouse St. G21	22	X10
Muir St.		
Reidvale St. G31	36	X13
Renfield St. G2	35	V12
Renfield St., Renf. PA4	17	M10
Renfrew Ct. G2	35	V12
Renfrew St.		
Renfrew La. G2	35	V12
Renfield St.		
Renfrew Rd. G51	32	P11
Renfrew Rd., Pais. PA3	30	K13
Renfrew Rd., Renf. PA4	32	P11
Renfrew St. G2	35	V11
Renfrew St. G3	35	V11
Rennies Rd. (Inch.), Renf. PA4	16	J8
Renshaw Dr. G52	32	P13
Renshaw Rd. (Elder.), John. PA5	44	F15
Renton St. G4	36	W11
Renwick St. G41	35	U13
Scotland St.		
Residdl Rd. (Stepps) G33	25	DD9
Reston Dr. G52	32	P13
Reuther Av. (Ruther.) G73	53	Y16
Revoch Dr. G13	18	P8
Rhannan Rd. G44	63	V17
Rhannan Ter. G44	63	V17
Rhindhouse Pl. (Bail.) G69	40	FF13
Rhindhouse Rd. (Bail.) G69	40	FF13
Swinton Av.		
Rhindmuir Av. (Bail.) G69	40	FF13
Rhindmuir Cres. (Bail.) G69	40	FF13
Rhindmuir Dr. (Bail.) G69	40	FF13
Rhindmuir Gro. (Bail.) G69	40	FF13
Rhindmuir Rd. (Bail.) G69	40	FF13
Rhindmuir Vw. (Bail.) G69	40	FF13
Rhindmuir Wynd (Bail.) G69	40	FF13
Rhindmuir Cres.		
Rhinds St., Coat. ML5	57	HH14
Rhinsdale Cres. (Bail.) G69	40	FF13
Rhumhor Gdns., John. PA10	42	B15
Rhymer St. G21	36	X11
Rhymie Rd. G32	55	CC14
Rhynie Dr. G51	34	S13
Riccarton St. G42	52	W15
Riccartsbar Av., Pais. PA2	46	J14
Richard St. G2	35	V12
Cadogan St.		
Richard St., Renf. PA4	17	M10
Richmond Ct. (Ruther.) G73	53	Z16
Richmond Dr. (Bishop.) G64	11	Y6
Richmond Dr. (Camb.) G72	66	AA17
Richmond Dr. (Ruther.) G73	53	Z16
Richmond Dr. (Linw.), Pais. PA3	28	E12
Richmond Gdns. (Chry.) G69	14	EE7
Richmond Gro. (Ruther.) G73	53	Z16
Richmond Pl. (Ruther.) G73	53	Z16
Richmond St. G1	36	W12
Richmond St., Clyde. G81	5	M7
Riddell St., Clyde. G81	5	M6
Riddon Av. G13	18	N8
Riddon Av., Clyde. G81	18	N8
Riddon Pl. G13	18	N8
Riddrie Cres. G33	38	AA12
Riddrie Knowes G33	38	AA12
Riddrie Ter. G33	23	Z10
Provanmill Rd.		
Riddrievale Ct. G33	38	AA11
Riddrievale St. G33	38	AA11
Rigby St. G32	37	Z13
Rigghead Av. (Cumb.) G67	71	PP1
Riggside Rd. G33	39	CC11
Riglands Way, Renf. PA4	17	M10
Riglaw Pl. G13	18	P8
Rigmuir Rd. G51	33	Q13
Rimsdale St. G40	37	Y13
Ringford St. G22	22	X10
Ripon Dr. G12	20	S9
Risk St. G40	36	X13

Street	No.	Grid
Risk St., Clyde. G81	4	K6
Ristol Rd. G13	19	Q9
Anniesland Rd.		
Ritchie Cres. (Elder.), John. PA5	44	F14
Ritchie Pk., John. PA5	44	E14
Ritchie St. G5	51	V14
River Rd. G32	54	BB16
River Rd. G41	51	U16
Mansionhouse Rd.		
Riverbank St. G43	50	T16
Riverford Rd. G43	50	T16
Riverford Rd. (Ruther.) G73	53	Z15
Riversdale Cotts. G14	18	N9
Dumbarton Rd.		
Riversdale La. G14	18	P10
Dumbarton Rd.		
Riverside Ct. G44	63	V19
Riverside Pk. G44	63	V19
Linnpark Av.		
Riverside Pl. (Camb.) G72	67	DD17
Riverside Rd. G43	51	U16
Riverview Av. G5	35	V13
West St.		
Riverview Dr. G5	35	V13
Riverview Gdns. G5	35	V13
Riverview Pl. G5	35	V13
Roaden Av., Pais. PA2	45	G16
Roaden Rd., Pais. PA2	45	G16
Roadside (Cumb.) G67	71	PP1
Robb St. G21	22	X10
Robert Burns Av., Clyde. G81	5	M6
Robert St. G51	34	S12
Robert Templeton Dr. (Camb.) G72	67	CC17
Roberton Av. G41	50	T15
Roberts St., Clyde. G81	4	K6
Robertson La. G2	35	V12
Robertson St.		
Robertson St. G2	35	V12
Robertson St. (Barr.) G78	59	L18
Robertson Ter. (Bail.) G69	40	FF13
Edinburgh Rd.		
Robin Way G32	55	CC16
Robroyston Av. G33	24	AA10
Robroyston Rd. G33	24	AA9
Robroyston Rd. (Bishop.) G64	12	AA7
Roblees Cres. (Giff.) G46	62	S18
Roblees Dr. (Giff.) G46	62	S18
Roblees Rd. (Thorn.) G46	62	S19
Robson Gro. G42	51	V15
Rock Dr. (Kilb.), John. PA10	42	B15
Rock St. G4	21	V10
Rockall Dr. G44	64	W18
Rockbank Pl. G40	37	Y13
Broad St.		
Rockbank Pl., Clyde. G81	5	L5
Glasgow Rd.		
Rockbank St. G40	37	Y13
Rockcliffe St. G40	52	X14
Rockfield Pl. G21	23	Z9
Rockfield Rd. G21	23	Z9
Rockmount Av. (Thorn.) G46	62	S18
Rockmount Av. (Barr.) G78	59	M19
Rockwell Av., Pais. PA2	46	J16
Rodger Dr. (Ruther.) G73	65	Y17
Rodger Pl. (Ruther.) G73	65	Y17
Rodil Av. G44	64	W18
Rodney St. G4	35	V11
Roebank Dr. (Barr.) G78	59	M19
Roebank St. G31	37	Y12
Roffey Pk. Rd., Pais. PA1	31	M13
Rogart St. G40	36	X13
Orr St.		
Rogerfield Rd. (Bail.) G69	40	FF12
Great Western Rd.		
Rokeby Ter. G12	20	T10
Great Western Rd.		
Roman Av. G15	6	P7
Roman Av. (Bears.) G61	7	R5
Roman Ct. (Bears.) G61	7	R5
Roman Dr. (Bears.) G61	7	R5
Roman Gdns. (Bears.) G61	7	R5
Roman Rd. (Bears.) G61	7	R5
Roman Rd., Clyde. G81	5	L5
Romney Av. G44	64	W17
Rona St. G21	37	Y11
Rona Ter. (Camb.) G72	66	AA18
Ronaldsay Dr. (Bishop.) G64	11	Z7
Ronaldsay Pl. (Cumb.) G67	70	MM4
Ronaldsay St. G22	22	W8
Ronay St. G22	22	W8
Rooksdell Av., Pais. PA2	46	J15
Ropework La. G1	36	W13
Clyde St.		
Rose Cotts. G13	19	R9
Crow Rd.		
Rose Dale (Bishop.) G64	23	Y8
Rose Knowe Rd. G42	52	X15
Rose St. G3	35	V12
Rosebank Av. (Blan.) G72	69	GG19
Rosebank Dr. (Camb.) G72	67	CC18
Rosebank Ter. (Bail.) G69	57	GG14
Rosebery Pl., Clyde. G81	5	L7
Miller St.		
Rosebery St. G5	52	X15
Rosedale Av., Pais. PA2	44	F16
Rosedale Dr. (Bail.) G69	56	EE14
Rosedale Gdns. G20	20	T8
Rosefield Gdns. (Udd.) G71	57	GG16
Roselea Gdns. G13	19	R8
Roselea Pl. (Blan.) G72	68	FF19
Rosemont Meadows (Both.) G71	69	GG19
Rosemount (Cumb.) G68	70	NN1
Rosemount Cres. G21	37	Y11
Rosemount St. G21	36	X11
Rosemount Ter. G51	35	U13
Paisley Rd. W.		
Rosevale Rd. (Bears.) G61	7	R6
Rosevale St. G11	34	S11
Rosewood Av., Pais. PA2	45	H15
Rosewood St. G13	19	R8
Roslea Dr. G31	37	Y12
Roslyn Dr. (Bail.) G69	41	GG13
Rosneath St. G51	34	S12
Ross Av., Renf. PA4	31	L11
Ross Hall Pl., Renf. PA4	17	M10
Ross St. G40	36	W13
Ross St., Pais. PA1	47	L14
Rossendale Rd. G41	50	T16
Rossendale Rd. G43	50	T16
Rosshall Av., Pais. PA1	47	M14
Rosshill Av. G52	32	N13
Rosshill Rd. G52	32	N13
Rossie Cres. (Bishop.) G64	23	Z8
Rosslea Dr. (Giff.) G46	62	T19
Rosslyn Av. (Ruther.) G73	53	Y16
Rosslyn Rd. (Bears.) G61	6	P5
Rosslyn Ter. G12	20	T10
Rostan Rd. G43	62	T17
Rosyth Rd. G5	52	X15
Rosyth St. G5	52	X15
Rotherwick Dr., Pais. PA1	48	N14
Rotherwood Av. G13	7	Q7
Rotherwood Av., Pais. PA2	45	G16
Rotherwood La. G13	7	Q7
Rotherwood Av.		
Rotherwood Pl. G13	19	Q8
Rothes Dr. G23	8	T7
Rothes Pl. G23	8	T7
Rottenrow G4	36	W12
Rottenrow E. G4	36	W12
Roual Ter., Pais. PA1	31	L13
Greenlaw Av.		
Rouken Glen Pk. (Thorn.) G46	61	R19
Rouken Glen Rd. (Thorn.) G46	61	R19
Roukenburn St. (Thorn.) G46	61	R18
Roundhill Dr. (Elder.), John. PA5	45	G14
Rowallan Gdns. G11	20	S10
Rowallan La. G11	20	S10
Churchill Dr.		
Rowallan La. E. G11	20	S10
Churchill Dr.		
Rowallan Rd. (Thorn.) G46	61	R19
Rowallan Ter. G33	24	BB10
Rowan Av., Renf. PA4	17	M10
Rowan Cres. (Lenzie) G66	13	CC5
Rowan Dr., Clyde. G81	4	K6
Rowan Gdns. G41	50	S14
Rowan Gdns. (Both.) G71	69	HH18
Rowan Gate, Pais. PA2	46	K15
Rowan Pl. (Camb.) G72	67	CC17
Caledonian Circuit		
Rowan Rd. G41	50	S14
Rowan Rd. (Cumb.) G67	71	QQ2
Rowan St., Pais. PA2	46	K15
Rowand Av. (Giff.) G46	62	T19
Rowandale Av. (Bail.) G69	56	EE14
Rowanlea Av., Pais. PA2	44	F16
Rowanlea Dr. (Giff.) G46	62	T18
Rowanpark Dr. (Barr.) G78	59	L17
Rowans, The (Bishop.) G64	10	X7
Rowans Gdns. (Both.) G71	69	HH18
Rowantree Av. (Ruther.) G73	65	Y17
Rowantree Gdns. (Ruther.) G73	65	Y17
Rowantree Pl., John. PA5	43	D15
Rowantree Rd.		
Rowantree Rd., John. PA5	43	D15
Rowchester St. G40	37	Y13
Rowena Av. G13	7	Q7
Roxburgh La. G12	20	T10
Saltoun St.		
Roxburgh Rd., Pais. PA2	44	F16
Roxburgh St. G12	20	T10
Roy St. G21	22	W10
Royal Bk. Pl. G1	36	W12
Buchanan St.		
Royal Cres. G3	35	U11
Royal Cres. G42	51	V15
Royal Ex. Bldgs. G1	36	W12
Royal Ex. Sq.		
Royal Ex. Ct. G1	36	W12
Queen St.		
Royal Ex. Sq. G1	36	W12
Royal Inch Cres., Renf. PA4	17	M9
Royal Ter. G3	35	U11
Royal Ter. G42	51	V15
Queens Dr.		
Royal Ter. La. G3	35	U11
North Claremont St.		
Royston Rd. G21	36	X11
Royston Rd. G33	24	AA10
Royston Sq. G21	36	X11
Roystonhill G21	36	X11
Rozelle Av. G15	6	P6
Rubislaw Dr. (Bears.) G61	7	R6
Ruby St. G40	53	Y14
Ruchazie Pl. G33	38	AA13
Ruchazie Rd. G32	38	AA13
Ruchazie Rd. G33	38	AA13
Ruchill Pl. G20	21	U9
Ruchill St. G20	21	U9
Ruel St. G44	51	V16
Rufflees Av. (Barr.) G78	59	M18
Rugby Av. G13	18	P8
Rullion Pl. G33	38	AA12
Rumford St. G40	52	X14
Rupert St. G4	35	U11
Rushyhill St. G21	23	Y10
Cockmuir St.		
Ruskin Pl. G12	20	T10
Ruskin Sq. (Bishop.) G64	11	Y7
Ruskin Ter. G12	21	U10
Ruskin Ter. (Ruther.) G73	53	Y15
Russell Cres. (Bail.) G69	56	FF14
Russell St. (Bears.) G61	7	R5
Russell Gdns. (Udd.) G71	57	HH16
Kingston Av.		
Russell St. G11	34	S11
Vine St.		
Russell St., John. PA5	44	E14
Russell St., Pais. PA3	30	J12
Rutherford Av. (Kirk.) G66	14	EE5
Chryston Rd.		
Rutherford La. G2	35	V12
Hope St.		
Rutherglen Bri. G40	52	X14
Rutherglen Bri. G42	52	X14
Rutherglen Rd. G5	52	W14
Rutherglen Rd. (Ruther.) G73	52	W14
Ruthven Av. (Giff.) G46	62	T19
Ruthven La. G12	20	T10
Byres Rd.		
Ruthven Pl. (Bishop.) G64	23	Z8
Ruthven St. G12	20	T10
Rutland Cres. G51	35	U13

Schaw Dr. (Bears.) G61	7	R5	Shamrock St. G4	35	V11	Siemens Pl. G21	37	Y11
Schaw Rd., Pais. PA3	31	L13	Shandon St. G51	34	T12	Siemens St. G21	37	Y11
Schipka Pas. G1	36	W13	*Govan Rd.*			Sievewright St. (Ruther.)	53	Z15
Gallowgate			Shandwick St. G34	40	EE12	G73		
School Av. (Camb.) G72	66	BB17	Shanks Av. (Barr.) G78	59	M19	*Hunter Rd.*		
School Rd. (Stepps) G33	25	DD9	Shanks Cres., John. PA5	43	C15	Silk St., Pais. PA1	30	K13
School Rd., Pais. PA1	32	N13	Shanks St. G20	21	U9	Silkin Av., Clyde. G81	5	M7
School Wynd, Pais. PA1	30	K13	Shannon St. G20	21	U9	Silverburn St. G33	38	AA12
Scioncroft Av. (Ruther.) G73	53	Z16	Shapinsay St. G22	22	W8	Silverdale St. G31	53	Z14
Scone St. G21	22	W10	Sharrocks St. G51	34	T13	Silverfir St. G5	52	W14
Sconser St. G23	9	U7	*Clifford St.*			Silvergrove St. G40	36	X13
Scorton Gdns. (Bail.) G69	55	DD14	Shaw Pl. (Linw.), Pais. PA3	28	E13	Silverwells (Both.) G71	69	HH19
Scotland St. G5	35	U13	Shaw St. G51	34	S12	Silverwells Cres. (Both.)	69	HH19
Scotland St. W. G41	34	T13	Shawbridge St. G43	50	T16	G71		
Scotsblair Av. (Kirk.) G66	13	CC5	Shawfield Dr. G5	52	X15	Simons Cres., Renf. PA4	17	M9
Scotsburn Rd. G21	23	Z10	Shawfield Rd. G5	52	X15	Simpson Ct. (Udd.) G71	69	GG17
Scotstoun Mill Rd. G11	34	T11	Shawhill Rd. G41	50	T16	Simpson Ct., Clyde. G81	5	L7
Partick Bri. St.			Shawhill Rd. G43	50	T16	Simpson St. G20	21	U10
Scotstoun Pl. G14	19	Q10	Shawholm Cres. G43	50	S16	Simshill Rd. G44	63	V18
Scotstoun St.			Shawlands Arc. G41	51	U16	Sinclair Av. (Bears.) G61	7	R5
Scotstoun St. G14	19	Q10	Shawlands Sq. G41	51	U16	Sinclair Dr. G42	51	U16
Scott Av., John. PA5	43	D16	Shawmoss Rd. G41	50	T15	Sinclair Gdns. (Bishop.) G64	23	Y8
Scott Dr. (Bears.) G61	7	Q5	Shawpark St. G20	21	U9	Sinclair St., Clyde. G81	17	M8
Scott Rd. G52	32	N12	Shearer La. G5	35	U13	Singer Rd., Clyde. G81	4	K6
Scott St. G3	35	V11	Shearer Pl. G51	35	U13	Singer St., Clyde. G81	5	L6
Scott St. (Bail.) G69	56	EE14	Sheddons Pl. G32	38	AA13	Sir Michael Pl., Pais. PA1	46	J14
Scott St., Clyde. G81	4	K6	Sheepburn Rd. (Udd.) G71	57	GG16	Sixth Av., Renf. PA4	31	M11
Scotts Rd., Pais. PA2	47	M14	Sheila St. G33	24	AA10	Sixth St. (Udd.) G71	57	GG15
Seafar Rd. (Cumb.) G67	70	NN4	Sheldrake Pl., John. PA5	43	C16	Skaethorn Rd. G20	20	S8
Seafield Dr. (Ruther.) G73	65	Z18	Shelley Ct. G12	20	S9	Skaterig La. G13	19	R9
Seaforth Cres. (Barr.) G78	59	L18	*Shelley Rd.*			Skaterigg Dr. G13	19	R9
Seaforth La. (Chry.) G69	15	HH7	Shelley Dr. (Both.) G71	69	HH18	Skaterigg Gdns. G13	19	R9
Burnbrae Av.			Shelley Dr., Clyde. G81	5	L6	Skaterigg Rd. G13	19	R9
Seaforth Rd. G52	32	P12	Shelley Rd. G12	19	R9	*Crow Rd.*		
Seaforth Rd., Clyde. G81	5	L7	Sheppard St. G21	22	X10	Skelbo Path G34	40	FF11
Seaforth Rd. N. G52	32	P12	*Cowlairs Rd.*			*Auchingill Rd.*		
Seaforth Rd. S. G52	32	P12	Sherbrooke Av. G41	50	T14	Skelbo Pl. G34	40	FF11
Seagrove St. G32	37	Z13	Sherbrooke Dr. G41	50	T14	Skene Rd. G51	34	S13
Seamill Path G53	60	N17	Sherbrooke Gdns. G41	50	T14	Skerray Quad. G22	22	W8
Seamill Pl. G53	60	N17	Sherburn Gdns. (Bail.) G69	55	DD14	Skerray St. G22	22	W8
Seamill St. G53	60	N17	Sheriff Pk. Av. (Ruther.) G73	53	Y16	Skerryvore Pl. G33	38	BB12
Seamore St. G20	35	U11	Sherwood Av. (Udd.) G71	69	HH17	Skerryvore Rd. G33	38	BB12
Seath Rd. (Ruther.) G73	53	Y15	Sherwood Av., Pais. PA1	31	L13	Skibo Dr. (Thorn.) G46	61	R18
Seath St. G42	52	W15	Sherwood Dr. (Thorn.) G46	62	S18	Skibo La. (Thorn.) G46	61	R18
Seaward La. G41	35	U13	Sherwood Pl. G15	6	P6	Skipness Dr. G51	33	R12
Seaward St.			Shetland Dr. G44	64	W18	Skirsa Ct. G23	21	V8
Seaward St. G41	35	U13	Shettleston Rd. G31	37	Z13	Skirsa Pl. G23	21	U8
Second Av. (Stepps) G33	24	BB9	Shettleston Rd. G32	38	AA13	Skirsa Sq. G23	21	U8
Second Av. G44	63	V17	Shettleston Sheddings G31	38	AA13	Skirsa St. G23	21	U8
Second Av. (Bears.) G61	8	S6	*Shettleston Rd.*			Skirving St. G41	51	U16
Second Av. (Kirk.) G66	13	CC7	Shiel Ct. (Barr.) G78	59	L17	Skye Av., Renf. PA4	31	M11
Second Av. (Udd.) G71	57	GG15	Shiel Rd. (Bishop.) G64	11	Y7	Skye Ct. (Cumb.) G67	70	MM4
Second Av., Clyde. G81	5	L6	Shieldaig Dr. (Ruther.) G73	65	Y18	Skye Cres. (Old Kil.) G60	4	J5
Second Av., Renf. PA4	31	M11	Shieldaig Rd. G22	21	V8	Skye Cres., Pais. PA2	46	J16
Second Gdns. G41	50	S14	Shieldbridge Gdns. G23	9	U7	Skye Dr. (Old Kil.) G60	4	J5
Second St. (Udd.) G71	57	GG16	Shieldburn Rd. G51	33	Q12	Skye Dr. (Cumb.) G67	70	MM4
Seedhill, Pais. PA1	46	K14	Shieldhall Gdns. G51	33	Q12	Skye Gdns. (Bears.) G61	6	P5
Seedhill Rd., Pais. PA1	46	K14	Shieldhall Rd. G51	32	P12	Skye Pl. (Cumb.) G67	70	MM4
Seggielea La. G13	19	Q9	Shields Rd. G41	35	U13	Skye Rd. (Cumb.) G67	70	MM4
Helensburgh Dr.			Shilford Av. G13	18	P8	Skye Rd. (Ruther.) G73	65	Z18
Seggielea Rd. G13	19	Q9	Shillay St. G22	22	X8	Skye St. G20	20	T8
Seil Dr. G44	64	W18	Shilton Dr. G53	60	P17	*Bantaskin St.*		
Selborne Pl. G13	19	R9	Shinwell Av., Clyde. G81	5	M7	Slakiewood Av. (Gart.) G69	27	GG8
Selborne Rd.			Shipbank La. G1	36	W13	Slatefield St. G31	37	Y13
Selborne Pl. La. G13	19	R9	*Clyde St.*			Sleads St. G41	35	U13
Selborne Rd.			Shiskine Dr. G20	20	T8	Sloy St. G22	22	W10
Selborne Rd. G13	19	R9	Shiskine Pl. G20	20	T8	Smeaton St. G20	21	U9
Selby Gdns. G32	39	DD13	*Shiskine St.*			Smith Cres., Clyde. G81	5	L5
Selkirk Av. G52	49	Q14	Shiskine St. G20	20	T8	Smith St. G14	33	R11
Selkirk Av., Pais. PA2	45	H15	Shore St. G40	52	X15	Smith Ter. (Ruther.) G73	53	Y15
Selkirk Dr. (Ruther.) G73	53	Z16	Shortbridge St. G20	21	U9	Smithhills St., Pais. PA1	30	K13
Sella Rd. (Bishop.) G64	11	Z7	*Shanks St.*			Smiths La., Pais. PA3	30	K13
Selvieland Rd. G52	32	N13	Shortroods Av., Pais. PA3	30	J12	Smithy Ends (Cumb.) G67	71	PP1
Semple Pl. (Linw.), Pais.	28	E12	Shortroods Cres., Pais. PA3	30	J12	Smithycroft Rd. G33	38	AA11
PA3			Shortroods Rd., Pais. PA3	30	J12	Snaefell Av. (Ruther.) G73	65	Z18
Seton Ter. G31	36	X12	Shotts St. G33	39	CC12	Snaefell Cres. (Ruther.) G73	65	Z17
Settle Gdns. (Bail.) G69	55	DD14	Shuna Pl. G20	21	U9	Snuff Mill Rd. G44	63	V17
Seven Sisters (Kirk.) G66	13	DD5	Shuna St. G20	21	U9	Society St. G31	37	Y13
Seventh Av. (Udd.) G71	57	GG16	Shuttle La. G1	36	W12	Soho St. G40	37	Y13
Seyton Av. (Giff.) G46	62	T19	*George St.*			Sollas Pl. G13	18	N8
Shaftesbury St. G3	35	U12	Shuttle St. G1	36	W12	Solway Pl. (Chry.) G69	26	FF8
Shaftesbury St., Clyde. G81	4	K7	Shuttle St. (Kilb.), John.	42	A14	Solway Rd. (Bishop.) G64	11	Z7
Shafton Pl. G13	19	R8	PA10			Solway St. G40	52	X15
Shafton Rd. G13	19	R8	Shuttle St., Pais. PA1	46	K14	Somerford Rd. (Bears.) G61	7	R7
Shakespeare Av., Clyde.	4	K6	Sidland Rd. G21	23	Z9	Somerled Av., Pais. PA3	30	K11
G81			Sidlaw Av. (Barr.) G78	59	M19	Somerset Pl. G3	35	U11
Shakespeare St. G20	21	U9	*Ochil Dr.*			Somerset Pl. Meuse G3	35	U11
Shamrock Cotts. G13	19	R9	Sidlaw Rd. (Bears.) G61	6	P5	*Elderslie St.*		
Crow Rd.			Sielga Pl. G34	40	EE12	Somervell St. (Camb.) G72	66	AA17

Name	Page	Grid
Somerville Dr. G42	51	V16
Somerville St., Clyde. G81	5	L7
Sorby St. G31	37	Z13
Sorn St. G40	53	Y14
South Annandale St. G42	51	V15
South Av., Clyde. G81	5	L7
South Av., Pais. PA2	46	K16
South Av., Renf. PA4	17	M10
South Bk. St., Clyde. G81	17	M8
South Brook St., Clyde. G81	4	K6
South Campbell St., Pais. PA2	46	K14
South Carbrain Rd. (Cumb.) G67	71	PP4
South Chester St. G32	38	BB13
South Cotts. G14 *Curle St.*	33	R11
South Cft. St., Pais. PA1 *Lawn St.*	30	K13
South Crosshill Rd. (Bishop.) G64	11	Y7
South Deanpark Av. (Both.) G71	69	HH19
South Douglas St., Clyde. G81	17	M8
South Dr. (Linw.), Pais. PA3	28	E13
South Elgin Pl., Clyde. G81 *South Elgin St.*	17	M8
South Elgin St., Clyde. G81	17	M8
South Erskine Pk. (Bears.) G61	7	Q5
South Ex. Ct. G1 *Queen St.*	36	W12
South Frederick St. G1	36	W12
South Hill Av. (Ruther.) G73	65	Z17
South Moraine La. G15 *Moraine Av.*	7	Q7
South Muirhead Rd. (Cumb.) G67	71	PP3
South Pk. Av. (Barr.) G78	59	M19
South Pk. Dr., Pais. PA2	46	K15
South Portland St. G5	35	V13
South Scott St. (Bail.) G69	56	EE14
South Spiers Wf. G4	35	V11
South St. G11	33	Q11
South St. G14	18	P10
South Vesalius St. G32	38	BB13
South Vw. (Kirk.) G66 *Gadloch Av.*	13	CC7
South Vw. (Blan.) G72	68	FF19
South Vw., Clyde. G81	4	K6
South Wardpark Ct. (Cumb.) G67	71	QQ1
South Wardpark Pl. (Cumb.) G67	71	QQ1
South William St., John. PA5	43	D15
South Woodside Rd. G4	35	U11
South Woodside Rd. G20	21	U10
Southampton Dr. G12	20	S9
Southbank St. G31 *Sorby St.*	37	Z13
Southbar Av. G13	18	P8
Southbrae Dr. G13	19	Q9
Southbrae La. G13 *Milner Rd.*	19	R9
Southcroft Rd. (Ruther.) G73	52	X15
Southcroft St. G51	34	S12
Southdeen Av. G15	6	P6
Southdeen Rd. G15	6	P6
Southend Rd., Clyde. G81	5	L5
Southern Av. (Ruther.) G73	65	Y17
Southerness Dr. (Cumb.) G68 *Dornoch Way*	71	PP1
Southesk Av. (Bishop.) G64	10	X7
Southesk Gdns. (Bishop.) G64	10	X6
Southfield Av., Pais. PA2	46	K16
Southfield Cres. G53	49	Q16
Southfield Rd. (Cumb.) G68	70	MM3
Southinch Av. G14	18	N9
Southinch La. G14 *Tweedvale Av.*	18	N9
Southlea Av. (Thorn.) G46	62	S18
Southloch St. G21	22	X10
Southmuir Pl. G20	20	T9
Southpark Av. G12	34	T11
Southpark La. G12 *Glasgow St.*	21	U10
Southpark Ter. G12 *Southpark Av.*	35	U11
Southview Ct. (Bishop.) G64	22	X8
Southview Dr. (Bears.) G61	7	Q5
Southview Pl. (Gart.) G69	27	GG9
Southview Ter. (Bishop.) G64	22	X8
Southwold Rd., Pais. PA1	32	N13
Southwood Dr. G44	64	W17
Spateston Rd., John. PA5	43	C16
Spean St. G44	51	V16
Speirs Rd., John. PA5	44	E14
Speirshall Clo. G14	18	N9
Speirshall Ter. G14	18	N9
Spence St. G20	20	T8
Spencer Dr., Pais. PA2	44	F16
Spencer St. G13	19	R8
Spencer St., Clyde. G81	5	L6
Spey Av., Pais. PA2	45	G15
Spey Dr., Renf. PA4 *Almond Av.*	32	N11
Spey Pl., John. PA5	43	C16
Spey Rd. (Bears.) G61	7	Q7
Spey St. G33	38	AA12
Spiers Gro. (Thorn.) G46	61	R18
Spiers Pl. (Linw.), Pais. PA3	28	E12
Spiers Rd. (Bears.) G61	8	S6
Spiersbridge Av. (Thorn.) G46	61	R18
Spiersbridge La. (Thorn.) G46	61	R18
Spiersbridge Rd. (Thorn.) G46	61	R19
Spiersbridge Ter. (Thorn.) G46	61	R18
Spiersfield Gdns., Pais. PA2	46	J14
Spindlehowe Rd. (Udd.) G71	69	GG17
Spinners Gdns., Pais. PA2	45	H14
Spinners Row, John. PA5	43	C15
Spittal Rd. (Ruther.) G73	64	X18
Spittal Ter. (Camb.) G72	68	EE19
Spoutmouth G1	36	W13
Spring La. G5 *Lawmoor St.*	52	W14
Springbank Rd., Pais. PA3	30	J12
Springbank St. G20	21	U10
Springbank Ter., Pais. PA3	30	J12
Springboig Av. G32	39	CC13
Springboig Rd. G32	39	CC12
Springburn Rd. G21	22	X9
Springburn Rd. (Bishop.) G64	22	X9
Springburn Way G21	22	X10
Springcroft Av. (Bail.) G69	40	EE13
Springcroft Cres. (Bail.) G69	40	EE13
Springcroft Gdns. (Bail.) G69	40	FF13
Springcroft Gro. (Bail.) G69	40	EE13
Springcroft Rd. (Bail.) G69	40	EE13
Springcroft Wynd (Bail.) G69	40	EE13
Springfield Av. (Bishop.) G64	23	Y8
Springfield Av. (Udd.) G71	69	GG17
Springfield Av., Pais. PA1	47	M14
Springfield Ct. G1 *Buchanan St.*	36	W12
Springfield Cres. (Bishop.) G64	23	Y8
Springfield Cres. (Udd.) G71	69	GG17
Springfield Dr. (Barr.) G78	60	N19
Springfield Pk., John. PA5	44	E15
Springfield Pk. Rd. (Ruther.) G73	65	Z17
Springfield Quay G5	35	U13
Springfield Rd. G31	53	Z14
Springfield Rd. G40	53	Y14
Springfield Rd. (Bishop.) G64	11	Y7
Springfield Rd. (Cumb.) G67	71	PP2
Springfield Sq. (Bishop.) G64	23	Y8
Springhill Gdns. G41	51	U15
Springhill Rd. (Bail.) G69	39	DD13
Springhill Rd. (Barr.) G78	59	L19
Springkell Av. G41	50	T14
Springkell Dr. G41	50	S14
Springkell Gdns. G41	50	T15
Springkell Gate G41	50	T15
Springside Pl. G15	6	P6
Springvale Ter. G21 *Hillkirk Pl.*	22	X10
Spruce Av., John. PA5	44	E15
Spruce Dr. (Kirk.) G66	12	BB5
Spruce Rd. (Cumb.) G67	71	QQ2
Spruce St. G22	22	W9
Spynie Pl. (Bishop.) G64	11	Z7
Squire St. G14	33	R11
Staffa Av., Renf. PA4	31	M11
Staffa Dr., Pais. PA2	46	K16
Staffa Rd. (Camb.) G72	66	AA18
Staffa St. G31	37	Y12
Staffa Ter. (Camb.) G72	66	AA18
Staffin Dr. G23	8	T7
Staffin St. G23	9	U7
Stafford St. G4	36	W11
Stag St. G51	34	T12
Stair St. G20	21	U10
Stamford St. G31	37	Y13
Stamford St. G40	37	Y13
Stamperland Gdns. (Clark.) G76	63	U19
Stanalane St. (Thorn.) G46	61	R18
Standburn Rd. G21	23	Z8
Stanely Av., Pais. PA2	45	H15
Stanely Ct., Pais. PA2	45	H16
Stanely Cres., Pais. PA2	45	H16
Stanely Dr., Pais. PA2	46	J15
Stanely Rd., Pais. PA2	46	J15
Stanford St., Clyde. G81	5	M7
Stanhope Dr. (Ruther.) G73	65	Z17
Stanley Dr. (Bishop.) G64	11	Y6
Stanley Pl. (Blan.) G72	68	FF19
Stanley St. G41	35	U13
Stanley St. La. G41 *Milnpark St.*	35	U13
Stanmore Rd. G42	51	V16
Stark Av., Clyde. G81	4	K5
Startpoint St. G33	38	BB12
Station Cres., Renf. PA4	17	M10
Station Rd. G20	20	T8
Station Rd. (Millerston) G33	24	BB9
Station Rd. (Stepps) G33	25	CC9
Station Rd. (Giff.) G46 *Fenwick Rd.*	62	T18
Station Rd. (Bears.) G61	7	Q6
Station Rd. (Bail.) G69	56	FF14
Station Rd. (Muir.) G69	26	FF9
Station Rd. (Both.) G71	69	HH19
Station Rd. (Udd.) G71	69	GG17
Station Rd. (Blan.) G72	69	GG19
Station Rd. (Kilb.), John. PA10	42	B15
Station Rd., Pais. PA1	45	H14
Station Rd., Renf. PA4	17	M10
Station Way (Udd.) G71 *Mansefield Dr.*	69	HH17
Station Wynd (Kilb.), John. PA10	42	B15
Steel St. G1	36	W13
Steeple St. (Kilb.), John. PA10	42	B14
Stenhouse Av. (Muir.) G69 *Station Rd.*	26	FF8
Stenton St. G32	38	AA12
Stepford Path G33 *Stepford Rd.*	40	EE12
Stepford Pl. G33	39	DD12
Stepford Rd. G33	39	DD12
Stephen Cres. (Bail.) G69	39	DD13
Stephenson St. G52	32	N12
Stepps Rd. G33	39	CC11
Stepps Rd. (Kirk.) G66	13	DD7
Steppshill Ter. G33	25	CC9
Stevenson St. G40	36	X13
Stevenson St., Clyde. G81	4	K6
Stevenson St., Pais. PA2	46	K14
Stewart Av., Renf. PA4	31	L11
Stewart Ct. (Barr.) G78 *Stewart St.*	59	M18
Stewart Dr. (Bail.) G69 *Coatbridge Rd.*	41	HH13
Stewart Dr., Clyde. G81	5	L5
Stewart Pl. (Barr.) G78	59	L18
Stewart Rd., Pais. PA2	46	K16
Stewart St. G4	35	V11

Stewart St. (Barr.) G78 59 M18
Stewart St., Clyde. G81 4 K6
Stewarton Dr. (Camb.) G72 66 AA17
Stewarton Rd. (Thorn.) G46 61 R19
Stewartville St. G11 34 S11
Stirling Av. (Bears.) G61 7 R7
Stirling Dr. (Bears.) G61 7 Q5
Stirling Dr. (Bishop.) G64 10 X6
Stirling Dr. (Ruther.) G73 65 Y17
Stirling Dr., John. PA5 43 C15
Stirling Fauld Pl. G5 35 V13
Stirling Gdns. (Bishop.) G64 10 X6
Stirling Rd. G4 36 W12
Stirling St. (Cumb.) G67 71 PP2
Stirling Way, Renf. PA4 31 M11
 York Way
Stirrat St. G20 20 T9
Stirrat St., Pais. PA3 29 H12
Stobcross Rd. G3 35 U12
Stobcross St. G3 35 U12
Stobhill Rd. G21 22 X8
Stobs Dr. (Barr.) G78 59 L17
Stobs Pl. G34 40 FF11
Stock Av., Pais. PA2 46 K14
Stock St., Pais. PA2 46 K15
Stockholm Cres., Pais. PA2 46 K14
Stockwell Pl. G1 36 W13
Stockwell St. G1 36 W13
Stoddard Sq. (Elder.), 44 F14
 John. PA5
 Glenpatrick Rd.
Stonedyke Gro. G15 6 P7
Stonefield Av. G12 20 T9
Stonefield Av., Pais. PA2 46 K15
Stonefield Cres., Pais. PA2 46 K15
Stonefield Dr., Pais. PA2 46 K15
Stonefield Gdns., Pais. PA2 46 K15
Stonefield Grn., Pais. PA2 46 K15
Stonelaw Dr. (Ruther.) G73 53 Y16
Stonelaw Rd. (Ruther.) G73 53 Y16
Stoneside Dr. G43 62 S17
Stoneside Sq. G43 62 S17
Stoney Brae, Pais. PA1 30 K13
Stoneyetts Cotts. (Chry.) 15 GG6
 G69
Stoneyetts Rd. (Chry.) G69 15 GG7
Stony Brae, Pais. PA2 46 K16
Stonyhurst St. G22 21 V10
Stonylee Rd. (Cumb.) G67 71 PP3
Storie St., Pais. PA1 46 K14
Stormyland Way (Barr.) G78 59 M19
Stornoway St. G22 22 W8
Stow Brae, Pais. PA1 46 K14
Stow St., Pais. PA1 46 K14
Strachur St. G22 21 V8
Straiton St. G32 38 AA12
Stranka Av., Pais. PA2 46 J14
Stranraer Dr. G15 7 Q7
 Moraine Av.
Stratford St. G20 21 U9
Strathallan La. G12 34 T11
 Highburgh Rd.
Strathallan Ter. G12 34 T11
 Caledon St.
Strathallon Pl. (Ruther.) G73 65 Z18
 Ranald Gdns.
Strathbran St. G31 53 Z14
Strathcarron Pl. G20 20 T9
 Glenfinnan Rd.
Strathcarron Rd., Pais. PA2 47 L16
Strathclyde Dr. (Ruther.) 53 Y16
 G73
Strathclyde Path (Udd.) G71 69 GG17
Strathclyde St. G40 53 Y15
Strathclyde Vw. (Both.) G71 69 HH19
Strathcona Dr. G13 19 R8
Strathcona Gdns. G13 20 S8
Strathcona Pl. (Ruther.) G73 65 Z18
Strathcona St. G13 19 R9
Strathdee Av., Clyde. G81 5 L5
Strathdee Rd. G44 63 U19
Strathdon Av. G44 63 U19
Strathdon Av., Pais. PA2 46 J15
Strathdon Dr. G44 63 U19
Strathendrick Dr. G44 63 U18
Strathkelvin Retail Pk. 11 Z6
 (Bishop.) G64
Strathmore Av. (Blan.) G72 68 FF19
Strathmore Av., Pais. PA1 47 M14

Strathmore Gdns. G12 35 U11
 Gibson St.
Strathmore Gdns. (Ruther.) 65 Z18
 G73
Strathmore Rd. G22 21 V8
Strathord Pl. (Chry.) G69 15 HH6
Strathord St. G32 54 BB14
Strathtay Av. G44 63 U19
Strathview Gdns. (Bears.) 7 Q6
 G61
Strathview Gro. G44 63 U19
Strathview Pk. G44 63 U19
Strathy Pl. G20 20 T9
 Glenfinnan Rd.
Strathyre Gdns. (Bears.) 8 S5
 G61
Strathyre Gdns. (Chry.) G69 15 HH7
 Heathfield Av.
Strathyre St. G41 51 U16
Stratton Dr. (Giff.) G46 62 S19
Strauss Av., Clyde. G81 6 N7
Stravaig Path, Pais. PA2 45 H16
Stravaig Wk., Pais. PA2 45 H16
Stravanan Av. G45 64 W19
Stravanan Ct. G45 64 X19
Stravanan Rd. G45 64 W19
Stravanan St. G45 64 W19
Stravanan Ter. G45 64 W19
Strenabey Av. (Ruther.) G73 65 Z18
Striven Gdns. G20 21 U10
Stroma St. G21 37 Y11
Stromness St. G5 51 V14
Strone Rd. G33 38 BB12
Stronend St. G22 21 V9
Stronsay Pl. (Bishop.) G64 11 Z7
Stronsay St. G21 37 Y11
Stronvar Dr. G14 18 P10
Stronvar La. G14 18 P10
 Larchfield Av.
Strowan Cres. G32 54 BB14
Strowan St. G32 54 BB14
Struan Av. (Giff.) G46 62 S18
Struan Gdns. G44 63 V17
Struan Rd. G44 63 V17
Struie St. G34 40 EE12
Stuart Av. (Ruther.) G73 65 Y17
Stuart Dr. (Bishop.) G64 22 X8
Succoth St. G13 19 R8
Suffolk St. G40 36 X13
 Kent St.
Sugworth Av. (Bail.) G69 40 EE13
Sumburgh St. G33 38 AA12
Summer St. G40 36 X13
Summerfield Cotts. G14 33 R11
 Smith St.
Summerfield Pl. G40 53 Y14
 Ardenlea St.
Summerfield St. G40 53 Y15
Summerhill Dr. G15 6 P6
Summerhill Gdns. G15 6 P6
Summerhill Pl. G15 6 P6
Summerhill Rd. G15 6 P6
Summerlee Rd. (Thorn.) 61 R18
 G46
Summerlee St. G33 39 CC12
Summertown Rd. G51 34 S12
Sunart Av., Renf. PA4 17 L10
Sunart Gdns. (Bishop.) G64 11 Y7
Sunart Rd. G52 33 R13
Sunart Rd. (Bishop.) G64 11 Y7
Sunningdale Rd. G23 20 T8
Sunningdale Wynd (Both.) 69 GG18
 G71
Sunnybank St. G40 53 Y14
Sunnylaw Dr., Pais. PA2 45 H15
Sunnylaw St. G22 21 V10
Sunnyside Av. (Udd.) G71 69 GG17
Sunnyside Dr. G15 6 P7
Sunnyside Dr. (Bail.) G69 41 GG13
Sunnyside Pl. G15 6 P7
Sunnyside Pl. (Barr.) G78 59 L19
Sunnyside Rd., Pais. PA2 46 J15
Surrey La. G5 51 V14
 Pollokshaws Rd.
Sussex St. G41 35 U13
Sutcliffe Ct. G13 19 R8
Sutcliffe Rd. G13 19 R8
Sutherland Av. G41 50 T14
Sutherland Av. (Giff.) G46 62 T19

Sutherland La. G12 34 T11
 University Av.
Sutherland Rd., Clyde. G81 5 L7
Sutherland St., Pais. PA1 30 J13
Swallow Gdns. G13 18 N8
Swan La. G4 36 W11
Swan Pl., John. PA5 43 C16
Swan St. G4 36 W11
Swan St., Clyde. G81 4 K6
Swanston St. G40 53 Y15
Sween Dr. G44 63 V18
Sweethope Pl. (Both.) G71 69 HH18
Swift Cres. G13 18 N8
Swift Pl., John. PA5 43 C16
Swindon St., Clyde. G81 4 K6
Swinton Av. (Bail.) G69 40 FF13
Swinton Cres. (Bail.) G69 40 FF13
Swinton Cres., Coat. ML5 57 HH14
Swinton Dr. G52 32 P13
Swinton Gdns. (Bail.) G69 40 FF13
 Swinton Av.
Swinton Path (Bail.) G69 40 FF13
 Swinton Av.
Swinton Pl. G52 32 P13
Swinton Rd. (Bail.) G69 40 EE13
Swinton Vw. (Bail.) G69 40 FF13
 Swinton Av.
Switchback Rd. (Bears.) G61 7 R7
Sword St. G31 36 X13
Swordale Path G34 40 EE12
 Swordale Pl.
Swordale Pl. G34 40 EE12
Sycamore Av. (Lenzie) G66 13 CC5
Sycamore Av., John. PA5 44 E15
Sycamore Dr., Clyde. G81 5 L6
Sydenham La. G12 20 S10
 Crown Rd. S.
Sydenham Rd. G12 20 T10
Sydney St. G2 35 V12
 Argyle St.
Sydney St. G31 36 X13
Sydney St., Clyde. G81 4 J6
Sylvania Way, Clyde. G81 5 L7
Sylvania Way S., Clyde. G81 5 L7
Symington Dr., Clyde. G81 5 L7
Syriam Pl. G21 22 X10
 Syriam St.
Syriam St. G21 22 X10

T

Tabard Pl. G13 19 Q8
Tabard Pl. N. G13 19 Q8
 Tabard Rd.
Tabard Pl. S. G13 19 Q8
 Tabard Rd.
Tabard Rd. G13 19 Q8
Tabernacle La. (Camb.) G72 66 BB17
Tabernacle St. (Camb.) G72 66 BB17
Tain Pl. G34 40 FF12
Tait Av. (Barr.) G78 59 M18
Talbot Ct. G13 18 P9
Talbot Dr. G13 18 P9
Talbot Pl. G13 18 P9
Talbot Ter. G13 18 P9
Talbot Ter. (Udd.) G71 57 GG16
Talisman Rd. G13 19 Q9
Talisman Rd., Pais. PA2 45 G16
Talla Rd. G52 32 P13
Tallant Rd. G15 6 P6
Tallant Ter. G15 7 Q6
Tallisman, Clyde. G81 5 M7
 Onslow Rd.
Tambowie St. G13 19 R8
Tamshill St. G20 21 U9
Tamworth St. G40 37 Y13
 Rimsdale St.
Tanar Av., Renf. PA4 32 N11
Tanar Way, Renf. PA4 32 N11
Tandlehill Rd. (Mill.Pk.), 42 B15
 John. PA10
Tanera Av. G44 64 W18
Tanfield Av. G32 39 CC12
Tanfield Pl. G32 39 CC12
 Tanfield Av.
Tankerland Rd. G44 63 V17
Tanna Dr. G52 49 R14
Tannadice Av. G52 49 Q14
Tannahall Rd., Pais. PA3 29 H13

Name	Page	Ref
Tannahall Ter., Pais. PA3	29	H13
Tannahill Cres., John. PA5	43	D15
Tannahill Rd. G43	63	U17
Tannoch Dr. (Cumb.) G67	71	PP4
Tannoch Pl. (Cumb.) G67	71	PP4
Tannochside Dr. (Udd.) G71	57	HH15
Tannock St. G22	21	V10
Tantallon Dr., Pais. PA2	45	H15
Tantallon Rd. G41	51	U16
Tantallon Rd. (Bail.) G69	56	EE14
Tanzieknowe Av. (Camb.) G72	66	BB18
Tanzieknowe Dr. (Camb.) G72	66	BB18
Tanzieknowe Pl. (Camb.) G72	66	BB18
Tanzieknowe Rd. (Camb.) G72	66	BB18
Taransay St. G51	34	S12
Tarbert Av. (Blan.) G72	68	FF19
Tarbolton Dr., Clyde. G81	5	M6
Tarbolton Rd. G43	62	T17
Tarbolton Rd. (Cumb.) G67	71	PP3
Tarbolton Sq., Clyde. G81	5	M6
Tarbolton Dr.		
Tarfside Av. G52	49	Q14
Tarfside Gdns. G52	49	Q14
Tarfside Oval G52	49	Q14
Tarland St. G51	33	R13
Tarras Dr., Renf. PA4	32	N11
Tarras Pl. (Camb.) G72	67	CC17
Tassie St. G41	50	T16
Tattershall Rd. G33	39	CC11
Tavistock Dr. G43	62	T17
Tay Av., Pais. PA2	45	G15
Tay Av., Renf. PA4	18	N10
Tay Cres. G33	38	AA11
Tay Cres. (Bishop.) G64	11	Y7
Tay Pl., John. PA5	43	C16
Tay Rd. (Bears.) G61	7	Q7
Tay Rd. (Bishop.) G64	11	Y7
Taylor Av. (Kilb.), John. PA10	42	A14
Taylor Pl. G4	36	W12
Taylor St. G4	36	W12
Taylor St., Clyde. G81	17	M8
Taymouth St. G32	54	BB14
Taynish Dr. G44	64	W18
Teal Dr. G13	18	N8
Tealing Av. G52	49	Q14
Tealing Cres. G52	49	Q14
Teasel Av. G53	60	P18
Teith Av., Renf. PA4	32	N11
Teith Dr. (Bears.) G61	7	Q6
Teith Pl. (Camb.) G72	67	CC17
Teith St. G33	38	AA11
Telephone La. G12	34	T11
Highburgh Rd.		
Telford Ct., Clyde. G81	5	L7
Telford Pl. (Cumb.) G67	71	PP4
Telford Rd. (Cumb.) G67	71	PP4
Templar Av. G13	7	Q7
Temple Gdns. G13	19	R8
Temple Pl. G13	19	R8
Temple Rd. G13	20	S8
Templeland Av. G53	49	Q15
Templeland Rd. G53	49	Q15
Templeton St. G40	36	X13
Tennant Rd., Pais. PA3	29	H13
Tennant St., Renf. PA4	17	M10
Tennyson Dr. G31	54	AA14
Tenters Way, Pais. PA2	45	H14
Tern Pl., John. PA5	43	C16
Terrace Pl. (Camb.) G72	67	DD17
Terregles Av. G41	50	T15
Terregles Cres. G41	50	T15
Terregles Dr. G41	50	T15
Teviot Av. (Bishop.) G64	11	Y6
Teviot Av., Pais. PA2	45	G16
Teviot Cres. (Bears.) G61	7	Q7
Teviot St. G3	34	T12
Teviot Ter. G20	21	U10
Sanda St.		
Teviot Ter., John. PA5	43	C16
Thane St. G13	19	Q9
Thanes Gate (Udd.) G71	69	GG17
Castle Gate		
Tharsis St. G21	36	X11
Third Av. (Millerston) G33	24	BB9
Third Av. G44	51	V16
Third Av. (Kirk.) G66	13	CC7
Third Av., Renf. PA4	31	M11
Third Gdns. G41	50	S14
Third St. (Udd.) G71	57	GG16
Thirdpart Cres. G13	18	N8
Thistle Bk. (Lenzie) G66	13	CC6
Thistle Cotts. G13	19	R9
Crow Rd.		
Thistle St. G5	51	V14
Thistle St., Pais. PA2	46	J15
Thomas Muir Av. (Bishop.) G64	23	Y8
Thomas St., Pais. PA1	45	H14
Thomson Av., John. PA5	43	D14
Thomson Dr. (Bears.) G61	7	R5
Thomson Gro. (Camb.) G72	54	BB16
Thomson Pl., Clyde. G81	5	M5
Thomson St. G31	37	Y13
Thomson St., John. PA5	43	D15
Thomson St., Renf. PA4	31	M11
Thorn Brae, John. PA5	44	E14
Thorn Dr. (Bears.) G61	7	Q5
Thorn Dr. (Ruther.) G73	65	Z18
Thorn Rd. (Bears.) G61	7	Q5
Thorn St. G11	34	S11
Dumbarton Rd.		
Thornbank St. G3	34	T11
Yorkhill Par.		
Thornbridge Av. G12	20	T9
Balcarres Av.		
Thornbridge Av. (Bail.) G69	40	EE13
Bannercross Dr.		
Thornbridge Gdns. (Bail.) G69	40	EE13
Thornbridge Rd. (Bail.) G69	40	EE13
Thorncliffe Gdns. G41	51	U15
Thorncliffe La. G41	51	U14
Thorncroft Dr. G44	64	W18
Thornden Cotts. G14	18	N9
Dumbarton Rd.		
Thornden La. G14	18	P10
Dumbarton Rd.		
Thorndene (Elder.), John. PA5	44	E14
Thornhill, John. PA5	44	E15
Thornhill Av. (Elder.), John. PA5	44	E15
Thornhill Dr. (Elder.), John. PA5	44	E15
Thornhill Gdns., John. PA5	44	E14
Armour St.		
Thorniewood Gdns. (Udd.) G71	57	HH16
Thorniewood Rd. (Udd.) G71	57	GG16
Thornlea Dr. (Giff.) G46	62	T18
Thornley Av. G13	18	P9
Thornliebank Rd. G43	62	S17
Thornliebank Rd. (Deaconsbank) G46	61	Q19
Thornliebank Rd. (Thorn.) G46	62	S18
Thornly Pk. Av., Pais. PA2	46	K16
Thornly Pk. Dr., Pais. PA2	46	K16
Thornly Pk. Rd., Pais. PA2	46	K16
Thornside Rd., John. PA5	44	E14
Thornton La. G20	21	U8
Thornton St. G20	21	U8
Thorntree Way (Both.) G71	69	HH18
Thornwood Av. G11	34	S11
Thornwood Av. (Kirk.) G66	12	BB5
Thornwood Cres. G11	19	R10
Thornwood Dr.		
Thornwood Dr. G11	33	R11
Thornwood Dr., Pais. PA2	45	H15
Thornwood Gdns. G11	34	S11
Thornwood Pl. G11	20	S10
Thornwood Quad. G11	19	R10
Thornwood Dr.		
Thornwood Rd. G11	33	R11
Thornwood Ter. G11	33	R11
Thornyburn Pl. (Bail.) G69	56	FF14
Thornyburn Rd. (Bail.) G69	56	FF14
Three Ell Rd. G51	34	T12
Govan Rd.		
Threestonehill Av. G32	38	BB13
Thrums Av. (Bishop.) G64	11	Z7
Thrums Gdns. (Bishop.) G64	11	Z7
Thrush Pl., John. PA5	43	C16
Thrushcraig Cres., Pais. PA2	46	K15
Thurso St. G11	34	T11
Dumbarton Rd.		
Thurston Rd. G52	32	P13
Tibbermore Rd. G11	20	S10
Tillet Oval, Pais. PA3	30	J12
Tillie St. G20	21	U10
Tillycairn Av. G33	39	CC11
Tillycairn Dr. G33	39	CC11
Tillycairn Pl. G33	25	DD10
Tillycairn Rd. G33	39	DD11
Tillycairn St. G33	39	DD11
Tilt St. G33	38	AA11
Tintagel Gdns. (Chry.) G69	15	GG6
Tinto Dr. (Bears.) G61	59	L19
Tinto Rd. G43	62	T17
Tinto Rd. (Bears.) G61	6	P5
Tinto Rd. (Bishop.) G64	11	Z7
Fintry Cres.		
Tinto Sq., Renf. PA4	31	L11
Ochil Rd.		
Tinwald Av. G52	32	N13
Tinwald Path G52	32	P13
Tiree Av., Pais. PA2	46	J16
Tiree Av., Renf. PA4	31	M11
Tiree Ct. (Cumb.) G67	70	MM4
Tiree Dr. (Cumb.) G67	70	MM4
Tiree Gdns. (Bears.) G61	6	P5
Tiree Rd. (Cumb.) G67	70	MM4
Tiree St. G22	37	Z11
Tirry Way, Renf. PA4	32	N11
Morriston Cres.		
Titwood Rd. G41	50	T15
Tiverton Av. G32	55	CC14
Tobago Pl. G40	36	X13
Tobago St. G40	36	X13
Tobermory Rd. (Ruther.) G73	65	Z18
Todburn Dr., Pais. PA2	46	K16
Todd St. G31	37	Z22
Todholm Rd., Pais. PA2	47	L15
Todholm Ter., Pais. PA2	47	L15
Tofthill Av. (Bishop.) G64	10	X7
Tofthill Gdns. (Bishop.) G64	10	X7
Toll La. G51	34	T13
Paisley Rd. W.		
Tollcross Rd. G31	37	Z13
Tollcross Rd. G32	37	Z13
Tolsta St. G23	9	U7
Tontine La. G1	36	W13
Bell St.		
Tontine Pl. (Ruther.) G73	66	AA18
Toppersfield (Mill.Pk.), John. PA10	43	C15
Torbreck St. G52	33	R13
Torbrex Rd. (Cumb.) G67	71	PP3
Torburn Av. (Giff.) G46	62	S18
Tordene Path (Cumb.) G68	70	MM2
Torgyle St. G23	8	T7
Tormore St. G51	33	Q13
Tormusk Dr. G45	65	Y18
Tormusk Gdns. G45	65	Y18
Tormusk Gro. G45	65	Y18
Tormusk Rd. G45	65	Y18
Torness St. G11	34	T11
Torogay Pl. G22	22	X8
Torogay St. G22	22	W8
Torogay Ter. G22	22	W8
Toronto Wk. G32	55	CC16
Torphin Cres. G32	38	BB13
Torphin Wk. G32	38	BB13
Torr Rd. (Bishop.) G64	11	Z7
Torr St. G22	22	W10
Torran Rd. G33	39	DD12
Torrance Rd. (Torrance) G64	11	Z5
Torrance St. G21	22	X10
Springburn Way		
Torridon Av. G41	50	S14
Torrin Rd. G23	8	T7
Torrington Av. (Giff.) G46	62	S19
Torrington Cres. G32	55	CC14
Torrisdale St. G42	51	U15
Torryburn Rd. G21	23	Z10
Torwood La. (Chry.) G69	15	HH7
Burnbrae Av.		
Toryglen Rd. (Ruther.) G73	52	X16
Toryglen St. G5	52	W15
Toward Ct. (Blan.) G72	69	GG19

Voil Dr. G44 — 63 V18
Vorlich Ct. (Barr.) G78 — 59 M19
Vulcan St. G21 — 22 X10
Ayr St.

W

Waddell Ct. G5 — 36 W13
Waddell St. G5 — 52 W14
Waldemar Rd. G13 — 19 Q8
Waldo St. G13 — 19 R8
Walker Ct. G11 — 34 S11
Walker St.
Walker Dr. (Elder.), John. PA5 — 44 E15
Walker Path (Udd.) G71 — 57 HH16
Walker Sq. G20 — 20 T8
Bantaskin St.
Walker St. G11 — 34 S11
Walker St., Pais. PA1 — 46 J14
Walkerburn Rd. G52 — 48 P14
Walkinshaw Cres., Pais. PA3 — 29 H13
Ferguslie Pk. Av.
Walkinshaw Rd., Renf. PA4 — 16 J10
Walkinshaw St. G40 — 53 Y14
Walkinshaw St., John. PA5 — 43 D14
Walkinshaw Way, Pais. PA3 — 30 J12
Broomdyke Way
Wallace Av. (Elder.), John. PA5 — 44 F14
Wallace Pl. (Blan.) G72 — 69 GG19
Wallace Rd., Renf. PA4 — 31 L11
Wallace St. G5 — 35 V13
Wallace St. (Ruther.) G73 — 53 Y16
Wallace St., Clyde. G81 — 17 L8
Wallace St., Pais. PA3 — 30 K13
Wallacewell Cres. G21 — 23 Y9
Wallacewell Pl. G21 — 23 Y9
Wallacewell Quad. G21 — 23 Z9
Wallacewell Rd. G21 — 23 Y9
Wallbrae Rd. (Cumb.) G67 — 71 PP4
Wallneuk, Pais. PA1 — 30 K13
Incle St.
Wallneuk Rd., Pais. PA3 — 30 K13
Walls St. G1 — 36 W12
Walmer Cres. G51 — 34 T13
Walmer Ter. G51 — 34 T13
Paisley Rd. W.
Walnut Cres. G22 — 22 W9
Walnut Cres., John. PA5 — 44 E15
Walnut Dr. (Kirk.) G66 — 12 BB5
Walnut Pl. G22 — 22 W9
Walnut Rd. G22 — 22 W9
Walter St. G31 — 37 Z12
Walton St. G41 — 51 U16
Walton St. (Barr.) G78 — 59 M18
Wamba Av. G13 — 19 R8
Wamba Pl. G13 — 19 R8
Wamba Av.
Wandilla Av., Clyde. G81 — 5 M7
Wanlock St. G51 — 34 S12
Warden Rd. G13 — 19 Q8
Wardhill Rd. G21 — 23 Y9
Wardhouse Rd., Pais. PA2 — 46 J16
Wardie Path G33 — 39 DD12
Wardie Pl. G33 — 40 EE12
Wardie Rd. G33 — 40 EE12
Wardie Rd. G34 — 40 EE12
Wardlaw Av. (Ruther.) G73 — 53 Y16
Wardlaw Dr. (Ruther.) G73 — 53 Y16
Wardlaw Rd. (Bears.) G61 — 7 R7
Wardpark Rd. (Cumb.) G67 — 71 QQ1
Wardrop St. G51 — 34 S12
Wardrop St., Pais. PA1 — 46 K14
Ware Path G34 — 40 EE12
Ware Rd. G34 — 39 DD12
Warilda Av., Clyde. G81 — 5 M7
Warnock St. G31 — 36 X12
Wishart St.
Warp La. G3 — 35 U12
Argyle St.
Warren St. G42 — 51 V15
Warriston Cres. G33 — 37 Z12
Warriston Pl. G32 — 38 BB12
Warriston St. G33 — 37 Z12
Warroch St. G3 — 35 U12
Washington Rd., Pais. PA3 — 30 K12
Washington St. G3 — 35 V13

Water Brae, Pais. PA1 — 46 K14
Forbes Pl.
Water Rd. (Barr.) G78 — 59 M18
Water Row G51 — 34 S12
Waterfoot Av. G53 — 49 Q16
Waterford Rd. (Giff.) G46 — 62 S18
Waterloo La. G2 — 35 V12
Waterloo St.
Waterloo St. G2 — 35 V12
Watermill Av. (Lenzie) G66 — 13 CC6
Waterside La. (Mill.Pk.), John. PA10 — 43 C15
Waterside St. G5 — 52 W14
Waterside Ter. (Mill.Pk.), John. PA10 — 43 C15
Kilbarchan Rd.
Watling St. (Udd.) G71 — 57 GG16
Watson Av. (Ruther.) G73 — 52 X16
Watson Av. (Linw.), Pais. PA3 — 28 E13
Watson St. G1 — 36 W13
Watson St. (Udd.) G71 — 69 GG17
Watt Low Av. (Ruther.) G73 — 64 X17
Watt Rd. G52 — 32 N12
Watt St. G5 — 35 U13
Waukglen Av. G53 — 60 P19
Waukglen Cres. G53 — 61 Q18
Waukglen Dr. G53 — 60 P18
Waukglen Gdns. G53 — 60 P19
Waukglen Path G53 — 60 P18
Waukglen Dr.
Waukglen Rd. G53 — 60 P18
Waulkmill Av. (Barr.) G78 — 59 M18
Waulkmill St. (Thorn.) G46 — 61 R18
Waverley, Clyde. G81 — 5 M7
Onslow Rd.
Waverley Ct. (Both.) G71 — 69 HH19
Waverley Cres. (Cumb.) G67 — 70 MM4
Waverley Dr. (Ruther.) G73 — 53 Z16
Waverley Gdns. G41 — 51 U15
Waverley Gdns. (Elder.), John. PA5 — 44 F15
Waverley Rd., Pais. PA2 — 45 G16
Waverley St. G41 — 51 U15
Waverley Ter. G31 — 37 Y13
Whitevale St.
Waverley Way, Pais. PA2 — 45 G16
Waverley Rd.
Weardale La. G33 — 39 CC12
Weardale St. G33 — 39 CC12
Weaver La. (Kilb.), John. PA10 — 42 B14
Glentyan Av.
Weaver St. G4 — 36 W12
Weaver Ter., Pais. PA2 — 47 L14
Weavers Av., Pais. PA2 — 45 H14
Weavers Gate, Pais. PA1 — 45 H14
Weavers Rd., Pais. PA2 — 45 H14
Webster St. G40 — 53 Y14
Webster St., Clyde. G81 — 18 N8
Wedderlea Dr. G52 — 32 P13
Weensmoor Pl. G53 — 60 P18
Weensmoor Rd. G53 — 60 P17
Weeple Dr. (Linw.), Pais. PA3 — 28 E13
Weighhouse Clo., Pais. PA1 — 46 K14
Weir Av. (Barr.) G78 — 59 M19
Weir St., Pais. PA3 — 30 K13
Weirwood Av. (Bail.) G69 — 55 DD14
Weirwood Gdns. (Bail.) G69 — 55 DD14
Welbeck Rd. G53 — 60 P17
Welfare Av. (Camb.) G72 — 67 CC18
Well Grn. G43 — 50 T16
Well Rd. (Kilb.), John. PA10 — 42 B14
Well St. G40 — 36 X13
Well St., Pais. PA1 — 30 J13
Wellbank Pl. (Udd.) G71 — 69 GG17
Church St.
Wellbrae Ter. (Chry.) G69 — 15 GG7
Wellcroft Pl. G5 — 51 V14
Wellfield Av. (Giff.) G46 — 62 S18
Wellfield St. G21 — 22 X10
Wellhouse Cres. G33 — 39 DD12
Wellhouse Path G34 — 39 DD12
Wellhouse Rd. G33 — 39 DD12
Wellington La. G2 — 35 V12
West Campbell St.
Wellington Pl., Clyde. G81 — 4 J6

Wellington Rd. (Bishop.) G64 — 11 Z6
Wellington St. G2 — 35 V12
Wellington St., Pais. PA3 — 30 J13
Caledonia Av.
Wellington Way, Renf. PA4 — 31 M11
Tiree Av.
Wellmeadow Rd. G43 — 62 S17
Wellmeadow St., Pais. PA1 — 46 J14
Wellpark St. G31 — 36 X12
Wells St., Clyde. G81 — 4 K6
Wellshot Dr. (Camb.) G72 — 66 AA17
Wellshot Rd. G32 — 54 AA14
Wellside Dr. (Camb.) G72 — 67 CC18
Wemyss Gdns. (Bail.) G69 — 56 EE14
Wendur Way, Pais. PA3 — 30 J12
Abbotsburn Way
Wenlock Rd., Pais. PA2 — 46 K15
Wentworth Dr. G23 — 9 U7
West Av. (Stepps) G33 — 25 CC9
West Av. (Udd.) G71 — 69 HH17
West Av., Renf. PA4 — 17 M10
West Brae, Pais. PA1 — 46 J14
West Campbell St. G2 — 35 V12
West Campbell St., Pais. PA1 — 45 H14
West Chapelton Av. (Bears.) G61 — 7 R6
West Chapelton Cres. (Bears.) G61 — 7 R6
West Chapelton Dr. (Bears.) G61 — 7 R6
West Chapelton La. (Bears.) G61 — 7 R6
West Chapelton Av.
West Coats Rd. (Camb.) G72 — 66 AA18
West Cotts. (Gart.) G69 — 26 EE10
West Ct., Clyde. G81 — 4 K6
Little Holm
West George La. G2 — 35 V12
West Campbell St.
West George St. G2 — 35 V12
West Graham St. G4 — 35 V11
West Greenhill Pl. G3 — 35 U12
West La., Pais. PA1 — 45 H14
West Lo. Rd., Renf. PA4 — 17 L10
West Nile St. G1 — 35 V12
West Princes St. G4 — 35 U11
West Regent La. G2 — 35 V12
Renfield St.
West Regent St. G2 — 35 V12
West Rd. (Kilb.), John. PA10 — 42 B14
West St. G5 — 51 V14
West St., Clyde. G81 — 18 N8
West St., Pais. PA1 — 46 J14
West Thomson St., Clyde. G81 — 5 L6
West Whitby St. G31 — 53 Z14
Westbank Ct. G12 — 35 U11
Gibson St.
Westbank La. G12 — 35 U11
Gibson St.
Westbank Quad. G12 — 35 U11
Gibson St.
Westbank Ter. G12 — 35 U11
Gibson St.
Westbourne Cres. (Bears.) G61 — 7 Q5
Westbourne Dr. (Bears.) G61 — 7 Q5
Westbourne Gdns. La. G12 — 20 T10
Lorraine Rd.
Westbourne Gdns. N. G12 — 20 T10
Westbourne Gdns. S. G12 — 20 T10
Westbourne Gdns. W. G12 — 20 T10
Westbourne Rd. G12 — 20 S10
Westbourne Ter. La. G12 — 20 S10
Westbourne Rd.
Westbrae Dr. G14 — 19 R10
Westburn Av. (Camb.) G72 — 67 CC17
Westburn Av., Pais. PA3 — 29 H13
Westburn Cres. (Ruther.) G73 — 52 X16
Westburn Dr. (Camb.) G72 — 66 BB17
Westburn Fm. Rd. (Camb.) G72 — 66 BB17
Westburn Rd. (Camb.) G72 — 68 EE17
Westburn Way, Pais. PA3 — 29 H13
Westburn Av.

Woodend Gdns. G32	55	DD15
Woodend La. G13	19	R9
Woodend Dr.		
Woodend Pl. (Elder.), John.	44	E15
PA5		
Malloch Cres.		
Woodend Rd. G32	55	CC15
Woodend Rd. (Ruther.) G73	65	Y18
Woodfield Av. (Bishop.) G64	11	Y7
Woodfoot Path G53	60	P18
Woodfoot Pl. G53	60	P18
Woodfoot Quad. G53	60	P18
Woodfoot Rd. G53	60	P18
Woodford Pl. (Linw.), Pais.	28	E13
PA3		
Woodford St. G41	51	U16
Woodgreen Av. G44	64	W17
Woodhall St. G40	53	Y15
Woodhead Av. (Both.) G71	69	HH19
Old Bothwell Rd.		
Woodhead Cres. (Udd.) G71	57	GG16
Woodhead Path G53	60	P17
Woodhead Rd. G53	60	N17
Woodhead Rd. (Chry.) G69	26	EE9
Woodhead Ter. (Chry.) G69	26	EE8
Woodhill Gro. (Bishop.) G64	23	Z8
Woodhill Rd.		
Woodhill Rd. G21	23	Y9
Woodhill Rd. (Bishop.) G64	11	Y7
Woodholm Av. G44	64	W17
Woodhouse St. G13	19	R8
Woodilee Cotts. (Kirk.) G66	13	DD5
Woodilee Rd. (Kirk.) G66	13	DD5
Woodland Av. (Gart.) G69	27	GG8
Woodland Av., Pais. PA2	46	K16
Woodland Cres. (Camb.)	66	BB18
G72		
Woodland Vw. (Cumb.) G67	71	PP2
Braehead Rd.		
Woodland Way (Cumb.)	71	PP2
G67		
Woodlands Av. (Both.) G71	69	HH18
Woodlands Ct. (Thorn.) G46	61	R19
Woodlands Rd.		
Woodlands Cres. (Thorn.)	61	R18
G46		
Woodlands Cres. (Both.)	69	HH18
G71		
Woodlands Dr. G4	35	U11
Woodlands Gdns. (Both.)	69	GG18
G71		
Woodlands Gate G3	35	U11
Woodlands Gate (Thorn.)	61	R18
G46		

Woodlands Pk. (Thorn.) G46	61	R19
Woodlands Rd. G3	35	U11
Woodlands Rd. (Thorn.) G46	61	R19
Woodlands Ter. G3	35	U11
Woodlands Ter. (Both.) G71	69	HH18
Woodlea Dr. (Giff.) G46	62	T18
Woodlinn Av. G44	63	V17
Woodneuk Rd. G53	60	P17
Woodneuk Rd. (Gart.) G69	27	GG9
Woodneuk Ter. (Gart.) G69	27	GG9
Woodrow Circ. G41	50	T14
Woodrow Pl. G41	50	T14
Maxwell Dr.		
Woodrow Rd. G41	50	T14
Woods La., Renf. PA4	17	M10
Woodside Av. (Thorn.) G46	62	S18
Woodside Av. (Lenzie) G66	13	CC5
Woodside Av. (Ruther.) G73	53	Z16
Woodside Cres. G3	35	U11
Woodside Cres. (Barr.) G78	59	M19
Woodside Cres., Pais. PA1	46	J14
William St.		
Woodside Pl. G3	35	U11
Woodside Pl. La. G3	35	U11
Elderslie St.		
Woodside Rd. G20	21	U10
Woodside Ter. G3	35	U11
Woodside Ter. (Bishop.)	10	W6
G64		
Woodside Ter. La. G3	35	U11
Woodlands Rd.		
Woodstock Av. G41	50	T15
Woodstock Av., Pais. PA2	45	G16
Woodvale Av. (Bears.) G61	8	S7
Woodvale Dr., Pais. PA3	29	H13
Woodville Pk. G51	34	S13
Woodville St.		
Woodville St. G51	34	S13
Wordsworth Way (Both.)	69	HH18
G71		
Works Av. (Camb.) G72	67	DD17
Wraes Av. (Barr.) G78	59	M18
Wraes Vw. (Barr.) G78	58	K19
Wren Pl., John. PA5	43	C16
Wright Av. (Barr.) G78	59	L19
Wright St., Renf. PA4	31	L11
Wrightlands Cres., Ersk.	16	K8
PA8		
Wykeham Pl. G13	19	Q9
Wykeham Rd. G13	19	Q9
Wynd, The (Cumb.) G67	71	PP1
Wyndford Dr. G20	20	T9
Wyndford Pl. G20	20	T9
Wyndford Rd.		

Wyndford Rd. G20	20	T9
Wyndham Ct. G12	20	T10
Wyndham St.		
Wyndham St. G12	20	T10
Wynford Ter. (Udd.) G71	57	HH16
Myrtle Rd.		
Wyper Pl. G40	37	Y13
Gallowgate		
Wyvil Av. G13	7	R7
Wyvis Av. G13	18	N8
Wyvis Pl. G13	18	N8
Wyvis Quad. G13	18	N8

Y

Yair Dr. G52	32	P13
Yarrow Ct. (Camb.) G72	67	DD17
Yarrow Gdns. G20	21	U10
Yarrow Gdns. La. G20	21	U10
Yarrow Gdns.		
Yarrow Rd. (Bishop.) G64	11	Y6
Yate St. G31	37	Y13
Yetholm St. G14	18	N9
Yew Dr. G21	23	Y10
Foresthall Dr.		
Yew Pl., John. PA5	44	E15
Yoker Ferry Rd. G14	18	N9
Yoker Mill Gdns. G13	18	N8
Yoker Mill Rd. G13	18	N8
Yokerburn Pl. G13	18	N8
Yoker Mill Rd.		
Yokerburn Ter., Clyde. G81	17	M8
York Dr. (Ruther.) G73	65	Z17
York La. G2	35	V12
York St.		
York St. G2	35	V13
York St., Clyde. G81	5	M7
York Way, Renf. PA4	31	M11
Yorkhill La. G3	34	T12
Yorkhill St.		
Yorkhill Par. G3	34	T11
Yorkhill Quay G3	34	S12
Yorkhill St. G3	34	T12
Young Pl. (Udd.) G71	57	HH16
Young St., Clyde. G81	5	L6
Young Ter. G21	23	Y10

Z

Zambesi Dr. (Blan.) G72	68	FF19
Zena Cres. G33	23	Z10
Zena Pl. G33	23	Z10
Zena St. G33	23	Z10
Zetland Rd. G52	32	N12